THE JEWS-HARP IN BRITAIN AND IRELAND

Dedicated to John Wright, 1939–2013

John Wright by Denis Cantiteau.

The Jews-Harp in Britain and Ireland

MICHAEL WRIGHT

ASHGATE

© Michael Wright 2015

All rights reserved. No part of this publication may be reproduced, stored in a retrieval system or transmitted in any form or by any means, electronic, mechanical, photocopying, recording or otherwise without the prior permission of the publisher.

Michael Wright has asserted his right under the Copyright, Designs and Patents Act, 1988, to be identified as the author of this work.

Published by
Ashgate Publishing Limited
Wey Court East
Union Road
Farnham
Surrey, GU9 7PT
England

Ashgate Publishing Company
110 Cherry Street
Suite 3-1
Burlington, VT 05401-3818
USA

www.ashgate.com

British Library Cataloguing in Publication Data
A catalogue record for this book is available from the British Library.

The Library of Congress has cataloged the printed edition as follows:
Wright, Michael (Jew's harp player)
  The Jews-harp in Britain and Ireland / by Michael Wright.
    pages cm. -- (SOAS musicology series)
  Includes bibliographical references and index.
  ISBN 978-1-4724-1413-7 (hardcover) 1. Jew's harp--Great Britain. 2. Jew's harp--Ireland. I. Title.
  ML1087.W75 2015
  786.8'87--dc23
                                                                           2015014778

ISBN 9781472414137 (hbk)

Printed in the United Kingdom by Henry Ling Limited,
at the Dorset Press, Dorchester, DT1 1HD

Contents

List of Figures   *vii*
List of Maps   *xi*
Preface   *xiii*
Acknowledgements   *xvii*

PART I THEORIES

1 Theorists   3

2 Origins   23

3 The Name   37

PART II COMMERCIAL EXPLOITATION

4 Imports and Distribution   57

5 Makers   77

6 Exports   105

PART III CULTURAL ASPECTS

7 Art, Architecture and Mass Media   123

8 The Jews-Harp in Popular Culture   137

9 Players   155

   Conclusion   183

Appendix: Accompanying CD Track Notes   *185*
Bibliography   *191*
Index   *203*

List of Figures

1.1	Idioglot/outward-orientated string-pull jews-harp	5
1.2	Heteroglot/inward-orientated jews-harp	6
1.3	Lamella alignment, the right being poorly aligned	7
1.4	The slightly rounded edge of the lamella of a melodic Norwegian *munnharpe*	8
1.5	Five connected jews-harps, left to right: 'A', 'D', 'G', 'C' and 'F'	8
1.6	Embouchure of a jews-harp and cross-section of jews-harp and mouth sound-box	9
1.7	*Always keep your teeth out of the way of the vibrating lamella*, by John Wright	10
1.8	John Wright, using his second playing technique	11
1.9	John Wright in Montreal, Canada, 1975	18
1.10	Gjermund Kolltveit	20
1.11	Frederick Crane with his favourite F.A. Schlütter 'trumps'	21
2.1	Examples of world jews-harps	29
2.2	European types with British Isles types circled	34
2.3	Customs House, London find	35
3.1	*Punch* cartoon, 18 July 1857	43
3.2	Jews-harp staple	47
3.3	Jews-harp shackle	48
3.4	Jews Harp House locations from 1741 to 1814, with possible location of site in Regent's Park, and conjectural sketch of a sign for the Jew's Harp Inn	50
4.1	Typical finds from around the British Isles	59
4.2	'Stafford' and 'Rochester' types	61
4.3	John Barnsley price list	70
4.4	Barnsley jews-harps from promotional material	71
4.5	West Midland jews-harps from the nineteenth and twentieth centuries	74
5.1	Sidaway 'Stafford' type	81
5.2	Isometric drawing of a segment of Worcestershire indicating the location of the Barnsley jews-harp works	82

5.3	Named makers in the Netherton, Rowley Regis area from an 1822 price list (detail)	83
5.4	Barnsley jews-harps	84
5.5	Family tree of eighteenth-century Troman makers	85
5.6	Derek Troman, *c*.1950	86
5.7	David Troman's workshop from late 1940s	87
5.8	Troman jews-harps	88
5.9	Typical workshop in the West Midlands of the nineteenth century	89
5.10	Left: Sharkey dispatch stamps and jews-harp. Right: 'Sharkey' and 'Belfast' stamped on arms of jews-harp	92
5.11	James Sharkey in 1892, aged 21	93
5.12	Smith harps	95
5.13	Nickel-plated jews-harps from the last period of makers in the British Isles	98
5.14	Sid Philip, the last British maker, working on a lamella (tongue) at his workshop in his house, *c*.1968	99
5.15	Stump, stool and stake	100
5.16	Notching on jews-harps indicating makers	102
6.1	Elijah Williams invoice from 1750	111
6.2	'Gloucester' and 'Stafford' types found at Sutler's Store, Fort Edward, NY	112
6.3	Mampolwane Ngomonde, Usuthu Gorge, South Africa	118
6.4	Top: Letterhead. Bottom: D & B Troman business card	119
7.1	Thirteenth-century carving in the Chapter House, York Minster	123
7.2	Left: 'Jew's Harp Pattern' in situ at Stow Minster, Lincolnshire. Right: Schematic sketch	125
7.3	Left: Conjectural drawing of Scopham stained glass window in St Oswald's Church, East Stoke Church. Right: The Scopham crest	126
7.4	*The Jew's Harp*, engraving by David Wilkie, with detail	127
7.5	*Girl with Jews Harp*, by F.W. Jopham	129
7.6	*Lindsay Porteous*, by Nora Porteous	131
7.7	*Jews-harp in the forge*, by Jonathon Cope	132
7.8	CD cover concept, by Mark Ware	133
7.9	*Self-portrait with harps*, by Paul Gardner	134
7.10	Caricature of Michael Wright, by Jonty Clark	135
8.1	*World's largest mouth harp*, by Nigel Porteous	139
8.2	*The Giant of Towadnack*, by Michael Wright	145
8.3	*The Performer*, by Nigel Porteous	147
8.4	*Scots Trump Player*, by Nigel Porteous	149

9.1	Plough Sunday, Bolton Percy, Yorkshire, 1990s	155
9.2	Entrance port of the ruined North Berwick Kirk	158
9.3	'Diddlers who competed at the Forfar Ploughing Association's diddling competition. A prizewinning trio of two Jew's harps and an accordion'	165
9.4	Thomas McManus, *c.*1968	167
9.5	John Campbell	169
9.6	Recording of *The Lark in the Clear Air*, Topic Suite, 1974	172
9.7	Allan MacDonald, by Sean Purser	173
9.8	Miss Flo Hastings, from a music sheet cover (detail)	176
9.9	Author and Dogan Mehmet at the Traditional Music Day, Stowmarket, Sussex, UK	180
9.10	'Desoeuvrement-breath mask'	180
9.11	Jonathan Cope playing jews-harp at the MBS Festival 2013	181
A.1	The Wright Family recording at the SOAS studio, 2008	186

List of Maps

2.1	Archaeological finds in Asia and Europe	25
2.2	Spread of jews-harps throughout Asia and Europe	27
2.3	Archaeological finds in Europe	31
2.4	Greifswald type spread	36
4.1	British and Irish find locations	58
4.2	British and Irish find locations – thirteenth to eighteenth centuries	60
4.3	Cast types found in northern Europe	65
4.4	British and Irish traders up to 1800	66
5.1	Location of British and Irish makers	79
6.1	Seventeenth- and eighteenth-century North American find locations	108
6.2	Eighteenth-century North American trader locations	110

Preface

It was this time I was talking to Dave Itkin, whom I knew to be a Jew, in his store in Haverstraw. He held up a small musical instrument and said, "What would you call this, Jack?" "A Jew's harp", I said promptly, then caught myself up, and began to think how to apologise. "So would I", Dave said. "Do you know what they're trying to call it now? A Bruce harp. This damned discrimination's driving me nuts."[1]

The English writer John Masters's conversation with a New York State retailer touches on a number of themes that will be explored in this book. The name is the most obvious, but how was it that a manufactured musical instrument, with a racially sensitive name, came to be sold in a small outlet 40 miles from New York City? It must have been made somewhere, given a financial value, distributed, and considered a sellable product for an interested purchaser who, presumably, either saw it as a novelty or as a viable musical instrument. What is extraordinary is the role that two islands off the coast of Europe played in this story.

A book on the jews-harp in Britain and Ireland could have been on the *munnharpe* of Norway, the *maultrommel* of Austria, the *khomus* of Sakha-Yakutia or any of the many countries worldwide where this particular musical instrument has either been incorporated into the musical culture or been part of a commercial enterprise. The story of the jews-harp can be told from many points of view – players, makers, seller – and this book could also have been about whistling, diddling or lilting, or any of the many other ways in which music can be produced at minimal expense. That it is about the jews-harp in Britain and Ireland is because these islands have played a significant part in the world history of the instrument, particularly in its manufacture and distribution. Its use musically has a more mixed picture. In Scotland and Ireland there is evidence that it is recognised as having musical value, whereas in England it is more often dismissed as toy or plaything, though commercially exploitable.

What this publication seeks to show is how a musical instrument considered by many to be of little value has a history that runs parallel with more established musical instruments, and has a story just as eventful and interesting as any. The fact that throughout its history on these islands it has been marginalised and thought of as having little worth, does not make it so. Thomas Busby in his *A Complete Dictionary of Music* published in 1801 described it as '[t]his insignificant instrument'.[2] While its role in the musical culture of Britain cannot be described as

---

[1] John Masters, *Pilgrim Son: A Personal Odyssey* (London: Corgi Books, 1973), p. 137.
[2] Thomas Busby, *A Complete Dictionary of Music* (London, 1801), p. JH.

'significant', there are many small noteworthy moments that when drawn together make an amazing story of resilience, if nothing else; this in the face of some fairly negative attitudes to the sound it makes and particularly to its name in English.

The musical instrument referred to as a 'jews-harp' in this publication is an ancient, international instrument played around the world and an integral part of many musical cultures. It can be found in many forms and shapes and has at least 1,000 different names, such as Norwegian *munnharpe*, Austrian and German *maultrommel*, Hungarian *doromb*, Sakha-Yakutia *khomus* and Japanese *koukin*. The name jews-harp, however, is only applied in the English language, where it is also called a jews-trump, jaws harp, juice harp, trump, mouth harp and gewgaw, along with commercial names such as New Ducie Harp, Bruce Harp and Snoopy's Harp. To complicate matters there is the belief in some quarters that calling it a jews-harp is anti-Semitic, with a further problem, particularly in England, in that it is thought of, if at all, as a child's toy undeserving of the description of musical instrument.

* * *

Why, then, write a book called *The Jews-Harp in Britain and Ireland* with so many negative associations attached to it? The name is objected to and there are places in the world where it is considered as far more musically relevant.

The first issue it is necessary to tackle is the name and how it will be used throughout this publication. It is important to note that the instrument is not part of Jewish musical culture, nor does it come from the Middle East, but from China and Asia. The simple answer as to why it is called a jews-harp is that we do not know. The name appears to be thought of as anti-Semitic because as a musical instrument it is perceived to be 'simple', incapable of achieving anything more than a crude 'twang' and unworthy of being taken seriously. The term is, therefore, considered to be derogatory and, therefore, anti-Semitic. As will be discussed in Chapter 3, it has certainly been used as such, particularly during political debates of the nineteenth century, and there are many comments concerning its lack of musicality throughout its known history. The truth, however, is that what we have is a subtle, expressive musical instrument with a distinctive sound and capable of being played melodically, atmospherically and rhythmically. Like any other musical instrument, to play it requires musical skill that goes far beyond treating it as a novelty. However, generally it has been so badly played and misused over the years that the playing of the instrument has done little to rectify that opinion.

Historically the vast majority of the 6,000 references sourced use the term jews-harp. Of the 4,000 British newspaper references from 1730 to 1950, for instance, there are only just over 100 that use other names such as jaws harp, juice harp, jews-trump or trump. You will also find throughout the world that, when not using the local name, the default name is jews-harp, a name given no significance. Today players in Britain refer to it as anything from 'jaw-harp' to the Scottish and Irish 'trump', and there is a growing use by younger players of 'mouth harp', a name derived from European names such as the Norwegian *munnharpe*. Providing the instrument is played and the audience recognise its musicality, it should not matter what it is called. However, faced with needing to call the instrument something, I have decided to give it its most common name, both historically and internationally. Throughout this book, therefore, it will be referred to as a jews-harp. There are many ways in which the name is written, including Jew's harp, Jews' harp and jews-harp, and where used in quotes the original spelling remains. In order to differentiate between the instrument and the people, this book uses the nomenclature jews-harp.

Next there is the issue of its importance in Britain and Ireland. Today there is little or no interest in the instrument on these isles, yet for centuries Britain was a major shipping point for jews-harps around the world and from at least the eighteenth century to the mid-twentieth century the West Midlands of England in particular was a leading manufacturing area for their production and export. The British experience, however, is an example not only of the way a cheaply produced musical instrument can become a part of popular culture, but also of the way objects that are perceived as common and historically irrelevant are touched by historical events, whether wars, trade, the commercial and industrial revolutions, social movements such as workers' rights, and everyday interests, like sport and all forms of entertainment. Thomas Busby may well have described it as '[t]his insignificant instrument', yet what is fascinating is just how much historical events impact upon its story.

* * *

The main focus of the story is the social history of a musical instrument almost completely ignored by academia and music historians that has nevertheless been a section of the fabric of popular musical culture for nearly 700 years. This story is divided into three parts: first, an overview explaining various theories, including a description of what a jews-harp is and how researchers, organologists and historians have viewed the instrument; then where the jews-harp came from; and what we know about the name. The second part explores its commercial exploitation, including its importation from mainland Europe, what archaeology tells us about its spread, what we know about its distribution, followed by where manufactories were established, and the importance of the export market, particularly to North America, Southern Africa and Australia. Finally, the third part looks at the instrument's cultural impact, including the arts and architecture; its use in literature and its role in popular culture; concluding with the players, their recordings and its use in films, television and the worldwide web.

Although for convenience the chapters are divided into topics, these topics interconnect and influence each other. We cannot understand distribution and export without some knowledge of manufacturing. Similarly, manufacturing requires players, and there has to be a common name that all use, one that is understood and noted by compilers of dictionaries and other compendiums.

While the trend of the book is from ancient to contemporary, each chapter includes an historical overview. Each of the regions is featured too, though in no particular order and only when relevant to a particular topic.

Much of the material referenced comes from previously unidentified written sources taken from original manuscripts and newspaper clippings, along with material from journals, general historical works and responses to personal communications, some providing remarkable new information or photographs. The transcript of a recording of John Wright was made two months before his death, and provided an insight into the reminiscences of an internationally admired player and student of the instrument – views, knowledge and opinions that would otherwise have been lost.

In the end, however, the instrument will survive because it is seen as relevant in some way to a particular musical culture. In Britain and Ireland its future may well still be as a novelty and a toy, but at least there is no doubt about its historical past.

Acknowledgements

My thanks go to the many people who have given inspiration and support. My wife, Debbie, has consistently encouraged me, particularly to source original material to justify any statements. Thanks go to my sister-in-law, Catherine, for providing essential material and invaluable information, to my brother, David, for finding some amazing imagery, and to all my family and friends for unstinting encouragement: to Alice, Jason, Gill, Lucy, Tim, Paul, Emily, Stephen, Philippa, Sue, Lorna, Jay, Deirdre, Peta, Ken – there are too many to mention everyone, but all have provided the right words at the right time. Thanks to Keith Howard of SOAS (the School of Oriental and African Studies) for insisting I take this project on; to Natalie Uomini and Chris Shorten for timely advice; to Andy Lamb of the Bate Collection of Musical Instruments, Jeremy Montagu and Ian Russell for invaluable support over the years. A special thanks goes to the descendants of the jews-harp-maker families, to Louise Troman, Bob Adams, Kate Watson, David Barnsley, Paul Sharkey, Dave Miller and Frank Southall. Thanks also to the many archaeologists, newspaper publishers and museum curators who have supplied information and granted permission to use their imagery. Additionally I am grateful to Gjermund Kolltveit, Ann-Turi Ford, Lois Crane, Angela Impey, Justin Reay, Harm Linsen, Aksenty Beskrovny, Grace Toland, Deirdre Ní Chonghaile, Keith Chandler, Jonny Handle, Kevin McBride, Dave Starbuck, Lindsay Porteous, Jim Spriggs, Ward Cooper, John David, Denis Cantiteau, Max Tyler, Mark Ware, Peter Hope-Evans, Jonathon Cope, Paul Gardner, Franz Kumpl, Sean Breadin and Dianna Boullier, all of whom provided references, images or comments. The late Roy Palmer provided useful references – and I admired his approach to folklore. A special thanks to Jerry Glasgow and Dogan Mehmet for all their support in the recording and editing of the accompanying CD. Finally, and most importantly, I need to acknowledge two people who inspired me to start researching, Frederick Crane (1927–2011) and John Wright (1939–2013). Frederick was the first researcher to look at the social history of the jews-harp in depth. He was always interested in hearing about new discoveries and became very excited by new finds anyone came across. John introduced me to the jews-harp in 1968 and provided many insights into the instrument, particularly its organology. He was perhaps the single most important influence on what has become a life's work.

PART I
Theories

The two most common questions asked about this musical instrument are why is it called a jews-harp and where does it come from? To these may be added, how does it work and is it a musical instrument anyway? The answer to the first two questions in particular is that we do not know, though recent research is providing some light on what is a complicated story. Writers, researchers and academics have touched on all these questions over the years, if sometimes only in a cursory fashion. However, especially from the nineteenth century, there has been intensive study of the instrument's mechanics and acoustics.

Chapter 1
Theorists

... and besides hath the vantage of penning the Air in the Mouth.
Sir Francis Bacon, 1626[1]

Leonard Fox, in his introduction to *Jew's Harp: A Comprehensive Anthology*, published in 1968, opens by making the point that:

> Despite the great intrinsic interest presented by many of its aspects – typographical, historical and acoustic, especially – the Jew's harp has attracted relatively little scholarly attention amongst musicologists, social historians, ethnologists and acousticians ... [being] more or less consigned to oblivion as far as scholarship in concerned.[2]

Twenty-five years on, we can make a similar statement. The jews-harp appears to be a readily available musical instrument, but, as Andrew Lamb of the Bate Collection of Musical Instruments notes,

> In common with a number of other instruments such as the theremin and the accordion, [it] does not feature as part of the Ark of Civilization. It does not sit within the boundaries of the recognized Western art movement of the medieval period or the modern period since the Renaissance. Instead, it transcends established cultural boundaries.[3]

What is a Jews-Harp?

Understanding what a jews-harp is, is not as easy as it might appear because it seems to defy standard categorisation. The Hornbostel–Sachs system of musical instrument classification describes jews-harps as lamellophones or plucked idiophones 'equipped with one or more tongues or lammelae that produce sound by being plucked by the performer', and links them with the thumb piano: '121.2 Guimbardes and Jew's harps – The lamella is mounted in

---

[1] Francis Bacon, *Sylva Sylvarum: or A Natural History, in Ten Centuries*, tenth edition (London, 1670), p. 33.
[2] Leonard Fox (ed.), *The Jew's Harp: A Comprehensive Anthology* (Lewisburg, PA: Bucknell University Press; London: Associated University Presses, Inc., 1988), p. 15.
[3] Andrew Lamb, personal correspondence, 2009.

a rod- or plaque-shaped frame and depends on the player's mouth cavity for resonance'.[4]

Frederick Crane argues that jews-harps are in fact aerophones and not lamellophones, because the main musical dynamic is the use of air rather than the lamella itself and the sound is primarily produced by vibrating air,[5] a theory developed by Ola Kai Legand, who, using sonographs, points out, 'the sound spectrum is primarily created, not by the elastic lamella, but by the surrounding turbulent air'.[6]

The Hornbostel–Sach system goes on to define the instrument further:

> 121.21 Idioglot guimbardes – The lamella is of one substance with the frame of the instrument.
>
> 121.22 Heteroglot guimbardes – The lamella is attached to the frame.[7]

John Wright disputes the idioglot/heteroglot classification as too narrow. He looks at the jews-harp from the point of view of applying the action to 'correspond to two basic ways of holding the instrument':

> Outward orientated: in which the instrument is held by the base in order to render accessible the tip of the lamella for plucking.
>
> Inward orientated: in which the frame extends beyond the tip to the lamella to form a handhold and the lamella points inwards towards the mouth, thus allowing the action to be applied to the base.[8]

Francis W. Galpin in *A Textbook of European Musical Instruments: Their Origin, History and Character* notes, 'The representative instrument in the plucked type of Autophones is the Crembalum or Jew's-harp'.[9]

Andrew Lamb suggests,

> [the] Jew's Harp is a lamellophone that works as a free reed instrument. The fundamental is predicated on the playing length of the tine and moderated by the

---

[4] Eric M. Von Hornbostel and Curt Sachs, 'Classification of Musical Instruments: Translated from the Original German by Anthony Baines and Klaus P. Wachsmann', *The Galpin Society Journal*, XIV (March 1961), p. 16.

[5] Frederick Crane, 'The Jew's Harp as Aerophone', *The Galpin Society Journal*, XXI (March 1968), pp. 66–9.

[6] Ola Kai Legand, 'On the Acoustics and the Systematic Classification of the Jaw's Harp', *Yearbook of the International Folk Music Council*, 4, 25th Anniversary Issue (1972), p. 102.

[7] Von Hornbostel and Sachs, 'Classification of Musical Instruments', p. 16.

[8] John Wright, 'Another Look into the Organology of the Jew's Harp', *Bulletin du Musée Instrumental de Bruxelles*, II (1972), pp. 55.

[9] Francis W. Galpin, *A Textbook of European Musical Instruments: Their Origin, History and Character* (London: Williams & Norgate, Ltd., 1937).

player's mouth which acts as the acoustical chamber. If you were to apply this principal to a concertina-type instrument you could get a similar effect if all the reeds were the same length but were placed in different sized chambers. You are now adding the concept of there being jews-harps with multiple tines, each with a different sized chamber (thus making it more sophisticated than a concertina). Yet it retains the fundamental characteristics of a free reed instrument with changing acoustical chambers.[10]

Disagreement and confusion seem to comprise a part of the instrument, whether in describing its classification, function, origin or, in English, its name. Perhaps the most intriguing aspect of a jews-harp is the variety of shapes, types and materials we find, particularly in Asia. Jews-harps there are made of wood, palm wood, bamboo, bone and brass, and in some cases combinations of these. The lamella is either cut into the material, such as in the bamboo *kubing* from the Philippines or the brass *dan moi* from the Hmong people in northern Vietnam and Cambodia, or on rare occasions the lamella is separate and tied to the frame. To play all of these, the instrument is held against the lips to connect it to the sound-box (the mouth cavity) and the action of the lamella is triggered either by plucking or in many cases from the Japanese *mukkuri* to the Nepalese *morchanga* and the Bashkir *agach-kumyz*, by the use of a string-pull system. The more common type, and the one found in Europe with a frame made of iron or copper-alloy (cu-alloy, often described in adverts as 'brass'), has a separate steel or flexible metal lamella attached to a rigid frame. To play this type, the instrument has to be placed firmly on the teeth both to stop the reciprocal action of the frame and to act as a bridge between the sound producer (the jews-harp) and the sound-box (the mouth cavity).

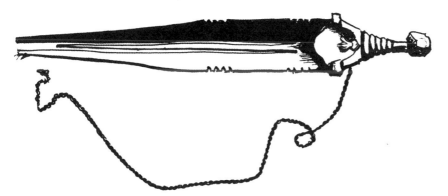

Figure 1.1   Idioglot/outward-orientated string-pull jews-harp
Source: Drawing by John Wright, by kind permission of Catherine Wright-Perrier.

---

[10]   Andrew Lamb, personal correspondence, 2009.

The musical instrument we call a 'jews-harp' is in fact the jews-harp itself and the player's mouth and is a 'fine example of an instrument that acts together with the musician to produce the required sound'.[11] By manipulating their tongue inside the mouth cavity, different notes and sounds can be achieved by the player, and while making a sound is relatively easy to achieve, turning it into a musical instrument, like any other, takes time and practice. One interesting side effect of the mouth as a sound-box was noted by Hélène La Rue, late of the Pitt Rivers Museum. When the author played for her she remarked that she could hear the player's voice, the implication being that the same instrument played by a different player will have a subtly different sound.

Figure 1.2   Heteroglot/inward-orientated jews-harp
Source: Photograph by Jason Ashton, from author's collection.

[11]   Andrew Lamb, personal correspondence, 2014.

Playing Techniques

Jews-harps are capable of producing melodic, atmospheric and rhythmic sounds. There are, however, a number of misconceptions or preconceptions relating to the sound produced, which, given its main function is to be a musical instrument, is critical to its usefulness. The first of these is, that it is so quiet as to be heard only by the player or where there is complete silence; second, that if it is to be heard, it is a percussive instrument; third, that it cannot be played with other musical instruments or to accompany the voice. All of these can relate directly to the quality of the instrument. If the lamella is poorly fixed to the frame or, in particular, badly aligned with the side of the frame arms, the sound production is severely affected. Unfortunately, with many of the instruments purchasable both today and, it would seem, in the past, this particular fault is and was thought to be acceptable. In order, therefore, to project any sound, the player needs to blow harder, the effect being to reduce the subtle harmonic nuances, sometimes completely, and to emphasise the percussive quality of the instrument. Forcing air through the instrument will make it louder and while the instrument cannot compete with melodeons and the like without microphones, yet even in a noisy environment it is remarkable how clearly a craftsman-made instrument can be heard, seemingly cutting through a mass of sound.

Atmospheric and melodic qualities can only be achieved with a good-quality instrument. It would appear that these are enhanced by the feathering of the edge of the lamella and the frame, the relationship between the edge of the lamella and the frame having a significant impact. That is, the sharper the edges, the louder the sound, while the very subtle rounding of those edges enables the delicate harmonics to come to the fore. The best melodic instruments achieve a compromise between percussive sharpness and melodic roundness. These instruments, therefore, are quite capable of effectively accompanying other musical instruments and the voice – with two provisos. First, and these instruments are easily purchased today, the instrument needs to be in the key of the particular tune – that is, the fundamental of the instrument tuned to a specific key: A, D and G, for instance, being the most popular when playing British or Irish traditional tunes. Second, because the jews-harp works with harmonics, certain notes in a scale are not achievable with a particular instrument. This can be overcome by switching instruments to one where the particular note required can be

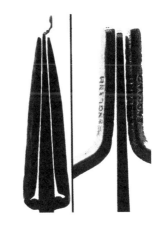

Figure 1.3   Lamella alignment, the right being poorly aligned

Source: Photograph by author.

achieved, say from a D harp to a C harp, a technique that is especially popular with Austrian players. As an alternative, by bending or pushing the notes possible by a particular instrument, hitting an approximate note, the continuity of a tune is possible. Having more than one instrument, held in either hand or fixed together, also allows the player to switch keys if demanded by the tune.

Figure 1.4   The slightly rounded edge of the lamella of a melodic Norwegian *munnharpe*
Source: Photograph by author.

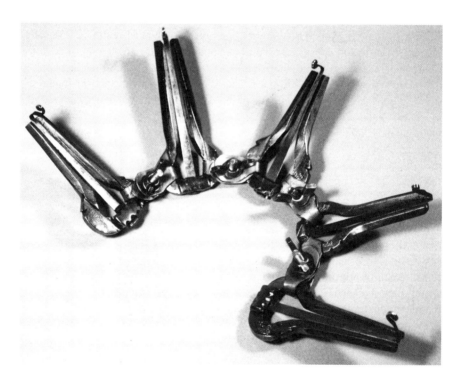

Figure 1.5   Five connected jews-harps, left to right: 'A', 'D', 'G', 'C' and 'F'
Source: Photograph by author.

The Basics of Playing a Jews-Harp

Playing the jews-harp is considered to be easy. Certainly, making a sound can be taught in a few minutes, though getting a sound from a piano is even quicker. Turning the sounds the jews-harp is capable of into music takes time and effort, like any musical instrument. To make a sound at all requires three elements: the jews-harp as the sound instigator, the mouth cavity as the sound-box and a finger or hand as a stimulator. To make the musical instrument the player presses the jews-harp against the teeth with one hand firmly holding the frame. With the player using the other hand or a finger, the instrument's tongue or lamella is pulled back (or pushed forward, a technique discouraged at first for reasons that will become obvious) and let go, allowing the lamella to spring backwards and forwards, passing freely between the teeth. That the lamella runs freely is essential, the most common mistake being the catching of the teeth as the lamella attempts to pass through.[12] The teeth act like the bridge of a violin or guitar – they not only connect the jews-harp to the sound-box, but when the player presses it firmly with one hand to the teeth this stops the reciprocal action of the frame, preventing the other common mistake of the novice jews-harp player, that of rattling on the teeth.

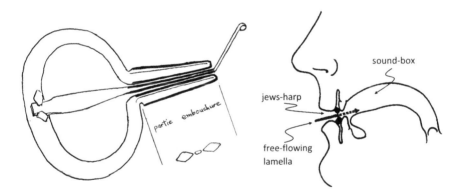

Figure 1.6   Embouchure of a jews-harp and cross-section of jews-harp and mouth sound-box
Source: Left: Preliminary sketch by John Wright, by kind permission of Catherine Wright-Perrier. Right: Drawing by Gary Scarborough, author's collection.

---

[12]   If a new player has not allowed enough of a gap in the teeth for the lamella to pass through, pushing the lamella forward will inevitably snap against the teeth. By pulling backwards a novice player can immediately, and without harm, feel that the teeth are in the way.

Figure 1.7　*Always keep your teeth out of the way of the vibrating lamella,* by John Wright
Source: Sketch by kind permission of Catherine Wright-Perrier.

Sound Control

All this does is to create the musical instrument. To explore its rhythmic, melodic and atmospheric possibilities requires control of the plucking hand, the player's breath, and the subtle manipulation of their mouth, lips and tongue. The word 'subtle' might appear to be overstating the point, but is a valid one. All the sounds that are projected come from the sound-box – the mouth cavity. By the player manipulating their tongue, various sounds and notes can be achieved; by using or blocking the breath, other dynamics are possible; by opening the side of the mouth, the back of the throat or using the lips against frame, achieves more possibilities. The total being the 'musical palette of sounds available to the musician'.[13]

It can be very difficult to understand how the various sounds are achieved because they all happen out of sight, inside the mouth. A guitarist can see where they put their fingers and to change a note requires distinctive movements. The action used to achieve different notes using a jews-harp is hidden and a player's movement of their tongue in the smallest way can profoundly change what sound is produced. Fundamentally, the smaller the sound-box volume (achieved by the player's tongue raised high in the mouth cavity), the higher the note produced. To find a lower note requires an almost infinitesimal movement of the tongue, thereby making the sound-box slightly larger. Add to this that the player is using harmonics that require breath control to emphasise some notes while holding

---

[13] Alistair Anderson describing the harmonica playing of Will Atkinson, equally relevant to the jews-harp, at a talk during Whitby Folk Week, 2003.

the breath for others, controlling the plucking hand to provide rhythm, whether 4/4 or 3/4, or any other time signature, and it is clear that subtlety and skill are essential requirements.

Keys

As noted above, it should also be understood that jews-harps come in a range of sizes, the length, weight and shape of the lamella creating a different fundamental key note. Jews-harps made with fundamentals such as 'G' or 'D' are common today and there is no reason to believe that requirement was not needed in the past.

Figure 1.8 John Wright, using his second playing technique
Source: Photograph by Bertrand Cormier, by kind permission of Catherine Wright-Perrier.

A player in Ireland in a 'Wanted' advert in 1882, for instance, was prepared to pay 'Five Shillings ... for two Jew's Harps to match, in tune'.[14]

Life-Long Learning

Beyond the basics, the subtleties can be exploited to enhance the sound and musicality of the instrument. For experienced players it can be a case of life-long learning:

> In '84 when I was at the first international Jew's harp conference I played a whole sequence just using closed throat. I had stumbled upon that technique just before leaving for the festival. I had long known that if you hold your breath you get a bell-like sound but it was only when I was preparing my talk and my concert that I suddenly realised that I was only getting odd-number harmonics by holding my breath. I was fascinated by that and the fact you never could be in tune with the drone; I called it the "parallel series" and you felt you were in a parallel world. What I didn't realise was that you could alternate the breath/no-breath techniques, to produce the whole series of harmonics, odd and even – a thing that the Norwegian revivalists had identified long since. When I finally realised that around 10 years ago I had to put it all together and that took time as I had rethink all my technique, relearn all my repertoire – and it's not finished yet.[15]

Early References

While the jews-harp has not attracted much attention from British collators of dictionaries and encyclopaedias, scholars, and general musical works, it has not been completely ignored. Eminent scholars have noted its attributes since the seventeenth century, though often as an interesting addition to another theme, such as acoustics. Their references can be divided into three types: the name is noted with minimal information, the name is noted with a description, and the name is noted with a more detailed analysis, usually focused on the instrument's acoustic qualities.

Additional to these published works are museums with collections of international significance and private collectors providing possibilities to study world instruments at close quarters.

Noted References

Brief descriptions are usually found in dictionaries, the main names being variations in spelling of jews-harp, jews-trump and trump. John Minsheu's

---

[14] *Freeman's Journal*, 20 September 1882, p. 1.
[15] Interview with John Wright by Michael Wright, Angers, France, 20 July 2013.

A Dictionary in Spanish and English of 1599 gives 'Trompe de Paris, a Iewes harpe', while *Vocabbulario Italiano & Inglese, A Dictionary Italian & English* compiled by Giovanni Torriano in 1659 is slightly more expansive – 'Zampogno, a jews-harp. Scaccia pensiere, a kind of country croud or bagpipe, a jew's-harp or trump'. Henry Hexham in *A copious Englisg* [*sic*] *and Nederduytch dictionarie* of 1660 has 'Jeught, Youth or Adolescence Tromp, A rattle for little children Trompet, Trump or Trumpet', which may refer to the instrument. The name is more explicitly used by Guy Miège in *A New DICTIONARY French and English With Another English and French* of 1677, with 'Trompe, a Trump, or Trumpet / Trump, or Jewes Trump, a Musical Instrument, Trompe, trompette', though his 1688 edition gives the alternative name 'Trompe (f.) ... a Jew's Harp, for Boys to play upon. Jouet de la Trompe, to play upon the Jews harp'. By the eighteenth century, in *Dictionarium Britanicum*, revised by N. Bailey in 1730, it is described as 'Jews Trump, a musical instrument; Trump [trompe, Du] a trumpet'. *The English Irish National Dictionary* of 1732 gives an early reference to the Irish name, 'Jews-trump – Trompadh', and the *Universal Etymological English Dictionary* of Nathan Bailey has 'Jews-trump, an instrument of Musick'.

From the eighteenth century onwards, and particularly from the nineteenth century, dictionaries recognise the instrument's existence usually under the appellation of jews-harp in various spellings, referring to trump and jews-trump as derivatives, though sometimes acknowledging its other well-known names, such as jaw harp.

More Detailed Descriptions

Samuel Johnson's *Dictionary* of 1755 gives a short description of the instrument – 'Jews-harp. N. f. A kind of musical instrument held between the teeth, which gives a sound by the motion of a broad spring of iron, which, being struck by the hand, plays against the breath'.[16] Johnson, however, is not the first. *The Nomenclator, or Rememberbrancer of Adrianus Iunius* of 1585 gives the Latin name and goes on to describe the motion:

> Cymbalum ... others think the word crembalon refers to that instrument made of steel, commonly used by boys, which, held by the lips, gives a musical sound when the bent tongue that passes through the middle, put in motion by the finger, makes a sound. A Jewes trumpe ... or harpe.[17]

In 1778 Samuel Pegge provided more information, including the name and its possible origins:

---

[16] Samuel Johnson, *A Dictionary of the English Language* (1755), p. JEW-ING.
[17] Ralph Newberie and Henrie Denham, *The Nomenclator, or Rememberbrancer of Adrianus Iunius* (1585), p. 350.

The Jews-trump, or, as it is more generally pronounced, the Jew-trump, seems to take its name from the nation of the Jews, and is vulgarly believed to be one of their instruments of music. Dr. Littleton renders Jews-trump, by Sistrum Judaicum. But, upon enquiry, you will not find any such musical instrument as this described by the authors that treat of the Jewish musick. In short, this instrument is a mere boy's play-thing, and incapable in itself of being joined either with a voice or any other instrument, and I conceive the present orthography to be a corruption of the French Jeu-trump, a trump to play with that in the Belgick, or Low-Dutch, from whence come many of our toys, a tromp is a rattle for children. Sometimes they will call it Jews-harp; and another etymon given of it is Jaws-harp, because the place where it is played is between the jaws. It is an instrument used in St Kilda.[18]

Thomas Busby gives one of the most dismissive, and erroneous, descriptions in his *Complete Dictionary of Music* of 1801:

The form, size and character of this insignificant instrument are so well known, that it would not have been introduced into this dictionary, but for the opportunity of observing that, contemptible as it may seem to those who are acquainted with more superior instruments, it is the only one practised by the ingenious and simple inhabitants of St. Kilda, and forms the constant accompaniment to the performance of their lyric poetry.[19]

The St Kilda reference is a misinterpretation of Martin Martin's casual mention that on the island, 'The Trump or Jewish Harp is all the Musical Instruments they have, which disposes them to dance mightily'.[20] This has often been quoted over the years, but it is the sole source for the jews-harp's being played on St Kilda, a 'fact' that has become almost mythical in its use.[21] The 'insignificant instrument' remark is indicative of a general attitude towards the instrument, one that will be noticeable throughout this book.

The St Kilda reference is mentioned by William Dauney in *Ancient Scottish Melodies*, published in 1838, though with a more positive slant on the jews-harp's musical possibilities:

One word as to the "trump", i.e. the Jew's harp. This is said to have been the only musical instrument of the inhabitants of St. Kilda, and to be still used by the peasantry in some parts of Scotland, though, we fear, with a success very

---

[18] Samuel Pegge, *Anonymiana or, Ten Centuries of Observations on Various Authors and Subjects* (London, 1809), pp. 48–9.
[19] Busby, *Complete Dictionary of Music*, n.p.
[20] Martin Martin, *A Late Voyage to St. Kilda, the Remotest of All the Hebrides or Western Isles of Scotland &c* (London, 1698).
[21] See Michael Wright, 'The Mystery of St Kilda and the Jew's Harp', *Journal of the International Jew's Harp Society* (hereafter *JIJHS*), 2 (2004), pp. 53–5.

inferior to that of the celebrated "Eulenstein"[22] ... Genius, and particularly that of music, as has been proven in a variety of instances, is ever ready to burst the fetters that bind it. Let the instrument, therefore, be what it may, where a soul for music exists, there will always be a way of producing pleasing effects ...[23]

Sir John Graham Dalyell in *Musical Memoirs of Scotland* also has a positive perspective:

In our latest era we have beheld the beautiful combination of musical mechanics in the systematic arrangement of a definite number of springs.

Trump. But this is a great, an ingenious, and an admirable advance from its elements exhibited in an instrument of the simplest form and humblest character, familiar to us from earliest youth as the Trump or Jews' Harp, composed of two members only. A single spring set in a frame constitutes the whole appearance, which, secured in the teeth, emits such musical tones as are modulated by the breath while the spring vibrates.[24]

Murray's *A New English Dictionary on Historic Principles*, compiled between 1879 and 1928, has a passage that succinctly describes the instrument:

A musical instrument of simple construction, consisting of an elastic steel tongue fixed at one end to a small lyre-shaped frame of brass or iron, and bent at the other end at right angles; it is played by holding the frame between the teeth and striking the free end of the metal tongue with the finger, variations of tone being produced by altering the size and shape of the cavity of the mouth.[25]

Dictionaries of music and encyclopaedias published throughout the twentieth century mainly offer adequate descriptions, though the two most important, *The Oxford Companion to Musical Instruments*[26] and *The New Grove Dictionary of Musical Instruments*, give very extensive details.[27]

The *Companion* provides a nominal selection of names and has a section describing the instrument and how it is played, looking briefly at the harmonic

---

[22] See Chapter 9.
[23] William Dauney, *Ancient Scottish Melodies* (Edinburgh, 1838), pp. 131–2.
[24] Sir John Graham Dalyell, *Musical Memoirs of Scotland: With Historical Annotations and Numerous Illustrative Plates* (Edinburgh: T.G. Stevenson, 1849), p. 181.
[25] James A.H. Murray (ed.), *A New English Dictionary on Historic Principles* vol. V. E–K (Oxford: Clarendon Press, 1901), p. 579.
[26] Anthony Baines, *The Oxford Companion to Musical Instruments* (Oxford: Oxford University Press, 1992).
[27] Laurence Libin (ed.), *The Grove Dictionary of Musical Instruments*, second edition (New York and Oxford: Oxford University Press, 2014).

sequence, acoustics and classification. The second section considers its history in the West, including references to 'Anglo-Saxon' finds, St Kilda players, makers in Austria, virtuoso player Karl Eulenstein and the compositions of Albrechtsberger. The final section looks at the jews-harp in Asia, including New Guinea and Siberia.

New editions of *Grove*, first published between 1878 and 1889, continue to draw on the expertise and knowledge of researchers and authors. In the most recent online edition, the jews-harp entry is written by John and Michael Wright. The entry includes brief explanations of the instrument's international importance, including the name, methods and principles of playing, morphological types, overtones, the plucked idiophone versus aerophone discussion and melodic possibilities.

Analytical Works

Many of the works that are analytical focus on the acoustics of the instrument. The jews-harp is briefly mentioned by Francis Bacon in *Sylva Sylvarum*, first published in 1626, under the section 'Natural History, Experiments in Consort touching Sounds; and first touching the Nullity and Entity of Sounds'. The section is worth quoting in full:

> But in *Open Aire*, if you throw a Stone or a Dart, they give no sound. No more do Bullets, except they happen to be a little hollowed in the casting; which hollowness penneth the Air: Nor yet Arrows, except they be ruffled in their Feathers, which likewise penneth the Air. As for small Whissles, or Shepherds Oaten Pipes, they give sound, because of the extream slendernesse whereby the Air is more pent than in a wider Pipe. Again, the voices of Men and Living Creatures, pass through the Throat, which penneth the breath. As for the Jews- Harp, it is a sharp percussion, and besides hath the vantage of penning the Air in the Mouth.[28]

Charles Wheatstone

Charles Wheatstone, the inventor of the English concertina, went to some lengths during the early nineteenth century in creating experiments to demonstrate resonance, using the jews-harp as an interesting example:

> when the number of vibrations of a column of air are any sub-multiple of those of the original sounding body, there is no resonance. To prove this with regard to the octave, let the length of the column of air unison to the sound of a (tuning) fork be doubled, and not the slightest trace of the octave below (i.e. the real

---

[28] Bacon, *Sylva Sylvarum*, p. 33.

sound of the column) will be perceptible: this negative experiment must be tried with a closed tube which is incapable of producing a harmonic octave; an open tube would resound unisonantly to the fork by its subdivision.

On the law experimentally established in the preceding paragraph depends the explanation of the production of sounds by the guimbarde or Jew's harp. This simple instrument consists of an elastic steel tongue riveted at one end to a frame of brass or iron ... the free extremity of the tongue is bent outwards to a right angle, so as to allow the finger easily to strike it when the instrument is placed to the mouth, and firmly supported by the pressure of the parallel extremities of the frame against the teeth.[29]

Wheatstone goes on to discuss the harmonic sequence in some detail and describes an experiment resembling a large swanee whistle of a tube with a jews-harp at one end and a moveable piston at the other, presumably used in the talk at the Royal Institution given on 15 February 1828 on 'Resonance'. This was actually delivered by James Faraday, due to Wheatstone's intense shyness. This talk apparently included Javanese musical instruments, the jews-harp, the khon or khone, and a free-reed bamboo mouth organ having resonant tubes associated with metal free reeds.[30]

Similar experiments were used in lectures on acoustics that appear to have been a regular feature at Musical Association and Society of Arts groups throughout Britain, evidenced by the number of nineteenth-century newspaper articles referring to or advertising lectures and talks on acoustics and the study of vibration where jews-harps featured. A Mr Addams gave a series of lectures in the 1830s and 1840s in various venues from Chester to Norwich, some of the articles being quite descriptive. Professor Tyddall gave at least two lectures on sound at the Royal Institute in 1866 and 1871, and there are a number of local speakers who found the jews-harp a useful prop. The Pitt Rivers Museum in Oxford held a Folk-Lore Congress in 1891, where the 'Jew's harp in many forms and development – none dating beyond the 16th century, however – finds place, together with an interesting collection of primitive reed-instruments'.[31]

John Wright

The Pitt Rivers was also very influential in the work of a further researcher into acoustics, John Wright. In 1966 Wright began to analyse their collection in some

---

[29] 'Mr. Wheatstone on Resonance', reproduced in Derek H. Troman, *Scattia Pensieri: A History of the Jews Harp and its Manufacture* (unpublished thesis, Birmingham and Midland Institute, 1953), n.p.
[30] *Charles Wheatstone and the Concertina*, at http://www.free-reed.co.uk/galpin/g2.htm (accessed 15 June 2015).
[31] *The Times*, 5 October 1891, p. 8.

detail and was asked by the then curator, Bernard Fagg, to make a recording of their pieces. In 1966–67 Emile Leipp, head of the Acoustics Lab of the Faculté des Sciences de Jussieu in Paris, made sonograms of Wright's playing, and later Wright carried on working with Michèle Castellengo, Leipp's successor. This led to his co-authorship with Genevieve Dournon-Taurelle of the seminal work *Les Guimbardes du Musée de l'Homme* in 1978.[32] This work describes what a jews-harp is, considers acoustical and mechanical issues, and also notes its morphology, thereby allowing the reader to use these first chapters to set the scene and construct a terminology that is fully described in the catalogue itself.[33] The work also recognises the need to revise the way the instrument is classified. To this day scholars use the Hornbostel–Sachs classification system, which, as discussed above, when looking at the finer details of the instrument, Wright found inadequate.

Figure 1.9   John Wright in Montreal, Canada, 1975
Source: Photograph by Louise de Grosbois, by kind permission of Catherine Wright-Perrier.

---

[32] Geneviève Dournon-Taurelle and John Wright, *Les Guimbardes du Musée de l'Homme* (Paris: Institut d'Ethnologie, Musée de l'Homme, 1978).
[33] John Wright interview, Angers, 2013.

His views were first proposed in an article in 1972, where he suggests that the instruments should be described as either being inward orientated or outward orientated towards the mouth.[34] While this may seem a rather simple form of classification, it did serve to overcome many of the descriptive difficulties Wright faced and was a fundamental influence in the way the final catalogue was formatted. The year 1972 is interesting as, along with Wright's article 'Another Look at the Organology of the Jew's Harp', two other papers were published by Legand and Adkins on the acoustic and sound-producing mechanism of the jews-harp,[35] all using sonography to develop their points.

Other Researchers

Archaeologists have written papers on specific regional or site finds, providing valuable insights into the instrument. Anne Buckley has studied Irish finds, publishing her conclusions in various periodicals from 1986 to 1991, the most significant being 'Jew's Harps in Irish Archaeology' in *Second Conference of the ICTM Study Group on Music Archaeology*.[36] Graham Lawson has also identified jews-harps at a number of sites, one of the most interesting being at Fast Castle, Berwickshire.[37] A number of non-British academics and researchers have also influenced research into the British jews-harp, including Fox, Plate and Ypey,[38] along with numerous enthusiastic researchers who contribute to the *Journal of the International Jew's Harp Society*.

Gjermund Kolltveit and Frederick Crane

There are two researchers, however, whose work has been particularly significant.

Gjermund Kolltveit of Oslo University, Norway, has created a type classification for archaeological finds and has considered many of the issues of origin.[39] His work will be referred to in many parts of this publication.

---

[34] Wright, 'Another Look', p. 55.

[35] Legand, 'On the Acoustics'; C.J. Adkins, 'Investigations of the Sound-Producing Mechanism of the Jew's Harp', *The Journal of the Acoustical Society of America*, 55(3) (1974), pp. 667–70.

[36] Anne Buckley, 'Jew's Harps in Irish Archaeology', in *Second Conference of the ICTM Study Group on Music Archaeology* (Stockholm: Royal Swedish Academy of Music, 1986), pp. 49–71.

[37] G. Lawson, 'Musical Relics', in K.L. Mitchel, K.R. Murdock and J.R. Ward (eds), *Fast Castle Excavations 1971–86* (Edinburgh: Edinburgh Archaeological Field Society, 2001), p. 114.

[38] Fox (ed.), *Jew's Harp*; Regina Plate, *Kulturgeschichte der Maultrommel* (Bonn: Verlag für systematische Musikwissenschaft, 1992); and J. Ypey, 'Mondharpen', *Antick*, 11(3) (1976), pp. 209–31, translated for author by Harm Linsen.

[39] Gjermund Kolltveit, *Jew's Harps in European Archaeology*, BAR International Series 1500 (Oxford: BAR, 2006); Gjermund Kolltveit, 'The Jew's Harp in Western Europe:

Figure 1.10   Gjermund Kolltveit
Source: Photograph by Ann-Turi Ford, by kind permission of Gjermund Kolltveit and Ann-Turi Ford.

Trade, Communication, and Innovation, 1150–1500', *2009 Yearbook for Traditional Music*, 41 (2009), pp. 42–61.

Figure 1.11 Frederick Crane with his favourite F.A. Schlütter 'trumps'
Source: Photograph by author.

Frederick Crane of Iowa State, USA, was the first academic to truly recognise the international and social impact of the jews-harp, for which he preferred the name of trump. The journal entitled *Vierundzwanzigsteljahrschrift der Internationalen Maultrommelvirtuosengenossenschaft* (the name is an academic joke and it is affectionately known as *VIM* for short) was first published in 1982 and ran until 2003, becoming the *Journal of the International Jew's Harp Society* in 2004. These are the most significant journals 'devoted exclusively to all aspects of the Jew's harp',[40] though there are a number of others that focus on regional activities. These two publications have given a voice to the many musicians, researchers and enthusiasts worldwide, and Crane's importance in the development of our understanding of the jews-harp cannot be understated.

Collections

While there is the odd instrument displayed in museums in Britain, the Pitt Rivers Museum, Oxford, is one of only two with major collections of jews-harps, the other being in the Horniman Museum in South London. These collections mainly focus on world instruments, with special emphasis on Asia and Polynesia. The Pitt Rivers Museum catalogue indicates they have 191 instruments, of which 56 are on display. The collection includes four early English types, two of which are on public view. The Horniman's catalogues have 44 instruments, though there are no British examples. The Bate Collection of Musical Instruments, also in Oxford, has a small collection displaying eight very interesting finds. These were donated by the then curator, Jeremy Montagu, a collector of international jews-harps. There are in fact numerous private collections as a new generation begins to recognise the value of an instrument that, with the ever-increasing use of metal detectors, is beginning to provide an overall picture of different types and their spread, even though accurate locations and/or find circumstances are often not recorded.

Revival

In recent times there has been an increasing interest in analysing the jews-harp, with a particular focus on its musical qualities. While it is unlikely that the jews-harp will ever be recognised as a valid and valuable musical instrument worthy of serious consideration other than by a few enthusiasts, the work of Frederick Crane, Gjermund Kolltveit, John Wright and others enables the continued uncovering of new material on a history worthy of any musical instrument.

---

[40] Fox (ed.), *Jew's Harp*, p. 9.

Chapter 2
Origins

The most ancient of musical instruments with the most modern sound.

Anton Bruhin

Overview

The jews-harp's origins are obscure. There is an argument that, because of its perceived simplicity, the instrument could have evolved in many places in the world at any time. Kolltveit points out, however: 'archaeology unambiguously confirms that Asian jew's harps made of various materials and with varying construction principles by far pre-date the finds of Europe'.[1] Indeed, it certainly arrived in Europe fully developed and was exported from there to the Americas and Africa. As for its simplicity, it can unquestionably be mass produced and requires relatively unskilled workers for some aspects of manufacture, but close examination of the jews-harp shows that creating an instrument capable of nuance and true musicality requires much higher degrees of skill. As we shall see, in some parts of the world makers are highly esteemed.

A number of writers over the years have given their opinions as to the jews-harp's origins – some are quite considered, while others are plainly ridiculous. A newspaper in 1939, in response to the question, 'Who invented the Jew's harp?', sensibly answered, 'Archeologists have traced the original home of this instrument to the border-line between Burma and Yunnan province, China, and it is widely distributed in India, Tibet, Assam, Burma, Siam, Japan, the Philippines, Fiji and Samoa. It is one of the most ancient musical instruments'.[2] Two others are somewhat wide of the mark:

> The origin of music and musical instruments was the subject of an address to Rotarians by Max Horwinski, past president of the Oakland Rotary club ... The jew's harp, he explained, was one of the world's oldest instruments. He stated that when Moses was sent down to Egypt to lead the Israelites out of bondage they tried to organize a brass band to lead the procession. "They wanted a band of 80 pieces but had to fall back on the jew's harp", he said. "The beauty of the jew's harp is that both Catholics and Protestants can and do play it".[3]

---

[1] Kolltveit, 'The Jew's Harp in Western Europe', p. 43.
[2] *Greensboro Record*, 13 June 1939, p. 6.
[3] *Riverside Daily Press*, 29 October 1930, p. 6.

HOW IT BEGAN by Russ Murphy and Ray Serusky

THE JEW'S HARP

ANCIENT PHOENICIAN FISHERMEN DEVISED THE JEW'S HARP, USING A SEA SHELL AND TAUT STRINGS. IT WAS FIRST CALLED A JAW'S HARP AND LATER CORRUPTED TO JEW'S HARP.[4]

Given that, as with many aspects of this instrument, whether name or origin, evidence is hard to come by, particularly for its early history, it is necessary to sift through what evidence we have, mainly taken from archaeological finds and the regions where the instrument has a social status.

Typology

There is so little written evidence on the instrument that our main source for understanding its origins relies heavily on archaeology. Gjermund Kolltveit has extensively researched European finds and considered how instruments could have travelled to Europe, while Tadagawa Leo has written on early finds from Mongolia and other parts of Asia dating back some 2,500 years,[5] and more recently Aksenty Beskrovny has been collating information on finds in the region of the Urals.[6] If we then overlay where the jews-harp has become an integral part of the culture of societies, particularly throughout Asia and East Europe, information taken from Vertkov, Blagodatov and Yazovitskaya's article 'The Jew's Harp among the Peoples of the Soviet Union',[7] an interesting pattern arises, one that helps explain how the instrument could well have moved from Asia to Europe and beyond.

Archaeology

The earliest jews-harps found to date come from grave sites in Inner Mongolian at Xiajiadian, believed to be 2,500 to 2,800 years old, and Mongolia at Xiongnu, 2,100 to 2,300 years old. Both finds are bone and classified as idioglot, with at least one with a hole thought to be for a cord – that is, it is a string-pull type.[8] Thirty-six almost identical bronze, copper, bone and horn finds have been identified in the region of the Ural Mountains dating from 1,000 to 1,700 years old.

---

[4] *Greensboro Daily News*, 16 November 1931, p. 11.
[5] Tadagawa Leo, 'Asian Excavated Jew's Harps: A Checklist', *JIJHS*, 4 (2007), pp. 5–11.
[6] Aksenty Beskrovny, 'Jew's Harps in Russian Archaeology (II BC–XIII AD)', unpublished research (2013).
[7] Konstantin Vertkov, Georgiy Blagodatov and El'va Yazovitskaya, 'The Jew's Harp in the Soviet Union', *Vierundzwanzigsteljahrschrift der Internationalen Maultrommelvirtuosengenossenschaft* (hereafter *VIM*), 3 (1987), pp. 39–59.
[8] Tadagawa Leo, 'Asian Excavated Jew's Harps', pp. 5–11.

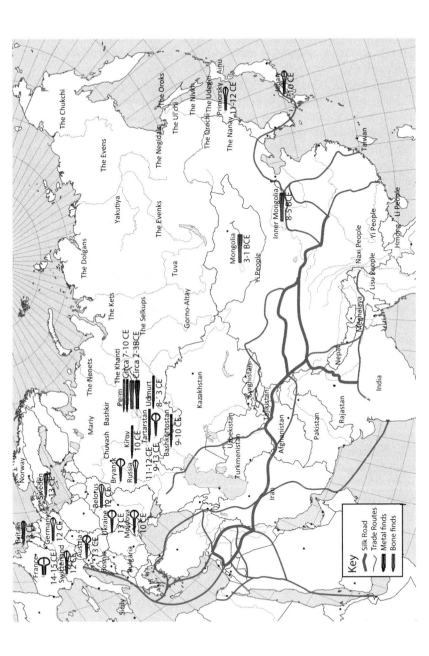

Map 2.1　Archaeological finds in Asia and Europe

The earliest from Perm Krai is a horn specimen dated second century BCE to third century CE, which gives us a 500-year bracket, though still making it the earliest in the region. Another copper find from the Republic of Tatarstan is dated third to fifth century, while the majority of the other idioglot finds from Kirov Oblast, Udmurtia, Perm Krai and Bashkortostan are all from the period ranging from the eighth to thirteenth century.[9]

Heteroglot types found in Omiya, Japan and Moldova are dated at around 1,000 years, raising a most intriguing question as to why the change was made at all. Turning the lamella and bending its end at right angles for activation does give the player more musical control, but it is quite a fundamental conceptual change of thinking and significant in the development of the instrument, not to be underestimated. Looking at the two types, you can see that the basic technology of reed passing through frame is the same, but the mechanics of each are quite different – to almost make one wonder if they are the same instrument (see figures 2.1 and 2.2). Other early finds include eleventh-century pieces from Primorsky Krai, north of Japan and, 5,000 miles west, Volga Bulgaria. There are also twelfth-century heteroglot finds in Bryansk Oblast, Eastern Russia and Belarus, plus thirteenth-century finds in the Ukraine and Russia.

The vast majority of European finds date from 800 years ago and it is from this point that there are signs of mass production, coinciding with what has been described as the European Commercial Revolution.[10] While some finds in Britain have been dated as Saxon period (fifth to eleventh century), the earliest verifiable find retrieved from the mudflats of the River Thames dates from the late thirteenth century, early fourteenth century or some 700 years ago.[11] There is no evidence of an instrument that might be designated a jews-harp in the Americas before European intervention in the sixteenth century – and the same applies to Africa before the eighteenth century. It was these two markets that were exploited particularly by British traders and had a significant impact on the mass production of jews-harps in these islands made especially for export.[12]

Worldwide Dispersal

The spread of instruments from Asia to the rest of the world can be divided into two distinctive phases. The first phase of social interaction centres on the area mainly covered by Inner Mongolia, Mongolia and North and Central Asia from Eastern Siberia to the Ural Mountains. The second phase of commercial expansion focuses on Europe, the Americas and Africa.

---

[9] Beskrovny, unpublished research.
[10] Peter Spufford, *Power and Profit: The Merchant in Medieval Europe* (London: Thames & Hudson, 2002), p. 16.
[11] Geoff Egan, *The Medieval Household: Daily Living c.1150–c.1450* (London: The Stationery Office, 1998), pp. 284–5.
[12] Beskrovny, unpublished research.

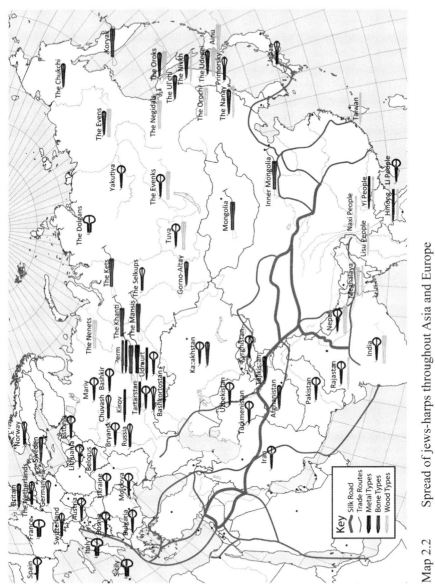

Map 2.2 Spread of jews-harps throughout Asia and Europe

Phase One: Social Interaction

The jews-harp can hold a very important place in many Asian societies. Today the *khomus* (the Sakha-Yakut Russian Republic jews-harp) plays a very significant part in Yakut society, to a point where it is recognised by the United Nations as significant to cultural heritage. Some Yakuts believe that the large elaborate silver ornaments that women traditionally wear at festivals and ethnic celebrations function as protection from evil spirits. For this reason, the blacksmith/metalworker is believed by many Yakuts to wield enormous spiritual power – there is a Yakut proverb stating that the 'blacksmiths and shamans are from the same nest'. This spiritual power extends to the making of the *khomus*, and the relationship between the maker and the player is highly significant. Yakut players believe that the *khomus* finds its owner, not the other way around. There is also a connection with shamanism, the *khomus* being part of spiritual ritual.[13] According to Vyacheslov Shurov, 'In shamanistic practice the onomatopoeia of the instrument [*khomus*] was especially significant, as it drew the shaman closer to the powers of the other world'.[14] This means that the maker has a particular importance, as shaman instruments were 'made by smiths who trace their origin to the divine smith; a well-made *khur* [*khomus*] always tells the truth in divination and, for that reason, careful attention is devoted to its forging'.[15] Professor Ivan Alexeyev, *President of the International Centre for Khomus Music in Yakutsk*, notes,

> a good instrument can be made in five to six days. Instrument makers attach great importance to the material – the khomus is hammered by metal fusion – and the way of chilling: salt, butter, and other mixtures – always containing powder of ground bull's horns – are mixed with distilled water. The process of chilling and attaching the lamella with a small hammer is done at dawn and is accompanied by ritual invocations.[16]

This relationship of the spiritual, the maker and the player appears in a similar or lesser extent throughout the North Asian region, which brings us to the question of how the instrument spread. One theory suggests that it was part of the goods traded along the Silk Road. The problem with this is that, while there are variants of the *khomus* along the route, the spread is far more general and extends well beyond the Silk Road and throughout the region. Also we have to accept that the *khomus* has no real value when compared with other goods we know were traded along the route and, therefore, other than as incidental trade, was not particularly commercial.

---

[13] Franz Kumpl, personal correspondence, 2014.
[14] Vyscheslav Shurov, *Khomus: Jew's Harp Music of Turkic Peoples in the Urals, Siberia, and Central Asia* (Paradox PAN 2032CD, 1995), p. 4.
[15] Vertkov, Blagodatov and Yazovitskaya, 'The Jew's Harp in the Soviet Union', p. 31.
[16] Shurov, *Khomus*, p. 4.

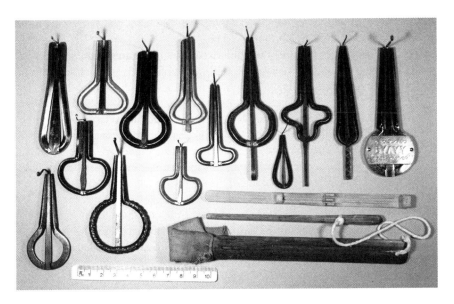

Figure 2.1 Examples of world jews-harps
Source: Photograph by author, from author's collection.

The most likely reason is social interaction. Erich Stockmann's Cybernetic Model system suggests that, in order for a musical instrument to spread, it needs:

1. a maker of the instrument with his special knowledge of the material;
2. the technology and skill to build the instrument;
3. a player of the instrument with his special knowledge of the instrument's function and his ability to play the instrument as well as to reproduce the traditional music;
4. the musical instrument itself with its characteristic features and peculiarities;
5. the music produced by the player and his instrument.[17]

All of these can be applied to the *khomus*. Without drawing too many conclusions given the region was under Russian influence, even the name can be found in various forms from the Chukotka region (*Komys*) in the northeast to Kirghizstan (*Chang-Kobuz*) in the south and Chuvash (*Kúpas*) in the west.[18] The most likely reasons for the spread, apart from inter-community trade, are the migrations and invasions that took place from the first century, and it is my contention that it

---

[17] See Erich Stockman, 'The Diffusion of Musical Instruments as an Internal Process of Communication', *Yearbook of the International Folk Music Council*, 3 (1971), pp. 128–37.

[18] Another Chuvash name is Varkhán, obviously closely associated to the Russian *Vargan*.

was the later migrations of the sixth and seventh centuries that first brought the jews-harp into Eastern and Northern Europe.

Possible ways the instrument might have moved into Europe could have been the trade routes to the East we know were well established by the twelfth century. As Kolltveit points out,

> Some trade routes were of particular importance and connected larger regions, including the Mediterranean Sea, the Baltic, and the Rhine River. With the exception of the Mediterranean, excavations along the major trade routes have revealed several jew's harps, suggesting, perhaps, that they were objects of trade.
>
> ...
>
> The seafaring merchants in the Hanseatic League controlled trade in the Baltic from the twelfth century. The important cities in their network, such as London, Hamburg, Lübeck, Greifswald, Danzig, Riga, Visby, and Novgorod, have all yielded jew's harps from excavations.[19]

Phase Two: Jews-Harp as Commodity

While early finds in Europe are dated to the twelfth century, and in some cases believed to be considerably earlier, there is no evidence of jews-harps gaining a similar social standing here to that in Asia. There is no reason to believe that jews-harps were not traded in a comparable fashion as above on a small scale and possibly adopted by individuals, which might account for four alleged Gallo-Roman finds of Rouen, for instance, that were discovered in the hypocaust of a large Roman house by the amateur archaeologist J.M. Thaurin in 1861.[20] These appear to be the earliest finds in Western Europe, though there is some doubt as to the dating.[21]

This does not, however, account for the explosion of dateable finds from the thirteenth century onwards. Even with the relatively small number of finds we know of – just over a thousand – there is a significant upsurge of dateable finds that coincides with the economic period that goes under the general title of the 'Commercial Revolution' that took place from the tenth century and was well established by the thirteenth century.

---

[19] Kolltveit, 'The Jew's Harp in Western Europe', pp. 45, 46.
[20] Sylvie R. Roussignol, *J.M. Thaurin et Rouen Gallo-Romain, vol. 1* (thesis, U.F.R. Lettres et Sciences Humaines, Institut d'Histoire, University de Rouen, 1991–1992).
[21] According to Laurence Lyncée, Musée départemental des Antiquités – Rouen, 'Thaurin has found one of them with roman terracotta. But he did without modern archaeological methods (no stratigraphic method) ... Thaurin has sincerely watched the context of the discovery, but with eyes of a person of nineteenth century'. Personal correspondence.

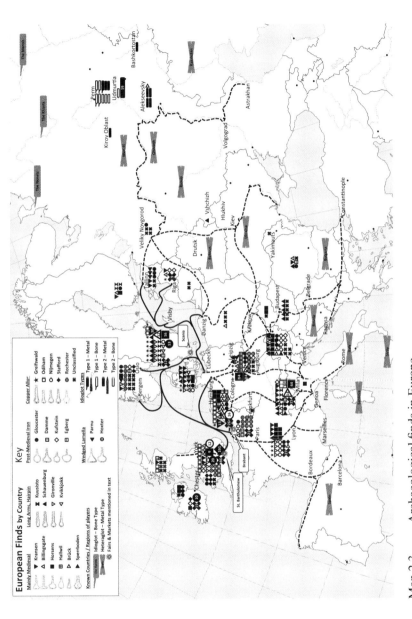

Map 2.3　Archaeological finds in Europe
Source: From the research of Gjermund Kolltveit.

To explain this, there is Schumpeter's view of economic development, as noted by S. Shane:

> [It must] be seen as a process of qualitative change driven by innovation taking place in historical time. As examples of innovation, Schumpeter mentioned new products, new methods of production, new sources of supply, exploitation of new markets, and new ways to organize business. He defined innovation as a new combination of existing resources. Through these combinations he labelled the entrepreneurial function.[22]

The jews-harp was not only affected by this innovative and economic pressure, but appears to have become a popular item because of it. The question we need to address is, why did the jews-harp gain such popularity from the thirteenth century? There is no evidence of its attaining any ritual or social status and it has never achieved much in the way of monetary value, yet we know that from the thirteenth century onwards considerable numbers were shipped from country to country. While it is possible that a blacksmith might make jews-harps for local consumption, all the evidence points to manufacturing centres in both Northern and Central Europe set up to exploit a known market, though we have no idea where they were they were situated before the sixteenth and seventeenth centuries. Jews-harps were new products to the merchants and buyers exploiting new methods of production, utilising rapidly developing supply routes and markets. Proof of this are the finds throughout the Northern European coastlines that have cast frames that are similar if not identical and date from 1200 to 1400. This is important because a cast frame assumes a mould, which in turn is taken from a pattern master. As Kolltveit points out, casting 'is a rather advanced technology requiring a high degree of skill of the craftsmen working with it'.[23] The chances of the same pattern being in as diverse locations as Sweden, Germany and France has to be seen as extremely unlikely, the most probable reason being a specific manufactory exporting their wares. There are also 51 wrought iron frames, mainly from Switzerland and the Netherlands, that have maker's punch marks.[24]

In order for it to be worthwhile to manufacture a product in any quantity, there had to be traders willing to transport the goods and a purchaser willing to buy them either for personal use or in bulk for further distribution. A 1481 customs record shows that William Codde, an alien merchant based in London, imported 864 jews-harps in two shipments from Arnemuiden near Antwerp. The Coddes were a well-known family of traders with links to the Hanseatic League. Other goods in William's shipment were small pedlar-type items – some 7,000 individual items

---

[22] S. Shane, *A General Theory of Entrepreneurship: The Individual Opportunity* (London: Springer, 2003).
[23] Kolltveit, *European Archaeology*, p. 26.
[24] See Kolltveit, *European Archaeology*, pp. 85–9.

all told with an average value of 2d each.²⁵ It should also be noted that jews-harps, officially known as 'Jews trumps', are in the Petty Customs *Rates of Merchandizes* books until the middle of the eighteenth century, the implication being that officially they were seen as having a small value to the Exchequer and were imported in such quantities as to be considered worthy of being on the list. While the Codde document is 200 years later than the earliest finds, it is nevertheless evidence of an established trade. There must have been a market and, if we recognise that there is no ritual or social status in owning one, it has to be because jews-harps were cheap enough to be purchased by people with spare cash. In other words, they were part of the growing economy that developed as a consequence of the Commercial Revolution.

The jews-harp was a recognisable musical instrument in Britain certainly by the fourteenth century. Archaeological finds from that period have been discovered all over Britain and Ireland, the overwhelming majority being the frame only, the lamella being the first part of the instrument to rot away. This is unfortunate, but it does not impact on their study, as close examination of the frame shows that there are identifiable frame types. These can be sub-divided into forged iron (fe) and cast copper alloy (cu-alloy), while a system of identifying European types devised by Gjermund Kolltveit of Norway not only provides a means of categorising finds, but helps in our understanding of the evolution and spread of the instrument throughout Europe.²⁶ Kolltveit identified 22 European types, of which 15 can be found in the British Isles and Ireland. To make type identification easier, Kolltveit devised names for designated types based on where finds were either most common or first found, and five have been given English site names – types 'Billingsgate', 'Odiham', 'Gloucester', 'Rochester' and 'Stafford'. These names are arbitrary and, therefore, no implication should be made that the names have any bearing on places of manufacture or commercial distribution. Kolltveit's criteria were firstly geographical; secondly, that the find from a potential site/type name should have good dating from the find circumstances; and thirdly, to include as many countries and regions as possible. It is, therefore, coincidental that there are five English names. One of the key conclusions of Kolltveit's research, however, is that the vast majority of jews-harps were mass produced and not made by local blacksmiths.

The earliest find from Britain has been designated a 'Kuusisto' type, recovered from a Customs House by the River Thames, London, dated 1270–1350.²⁷ Only 15 examples of this type have been uncovered in Europe so far, the majority being situated in Sweden and Finland with another small group in Switzerland, and just the single find in London. Other early types specifically found in Britain are classified 'Odiham' (dated 1250–1400), 'Billingsgate' (dated 1350–1400) and 'Greifswald' (dated 1350–1500, although the earliest verified is from Greifswald, Germany, dated 1270).

---

²⁵ The National Archive, P.R.O.E.122/194/25 and H.S. Cobb (ed.), *The Overseas Trade of London Exchequer Customs Accounts* (London: London Record Society, 1990), pp. 43–4, 64.
²⁶ Kolltveit, *European Archaeology*.
²⁷ Kolltveit, *European Archaeology*, p. 155.

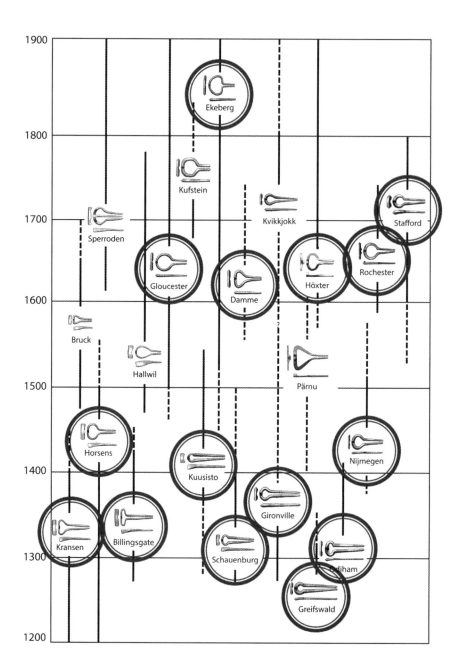

Figure 2.2   European types with British Isles types circled
Source: Drawing by Ann-Turi Ford, by kind permission of Gjermund Kolltveit and Ann-Turi Ford.

Figure 2.3   Customs House, London find
Source: From the Museum of London collection. Photograph by author.

An example of the early spread throughout Europe, the 'Greifswald' type with a cast frame has been found from Latvia to Southern France, mainly concentrated around Southern Sweden and North Germany. Nineteen have been identified, the majority dated thirteenth to fourteenth century.[28]

Perhaps the most remarkable pieces of evidence of early adoption of the jews-harp in Britain are a thirteenth-century stone carving of a player in the Chapter House, York Minster,[29] and a small enamel image of an angel playing a jews-harp on the crozier of William of Wykeham in New College, Oxford, and dated *c*.1367.[30] Both clearly show the instrument and the player plucking the lamella.

[28] Kolltveit, *European Archaeology*, p. 70.
[29] Identified in 2013.
[30] See Jeremy Montague, 'The Crozier of William of Wykeham', *Early Music* (November 2002), pp. 540–62, jews-harp, p. 554.

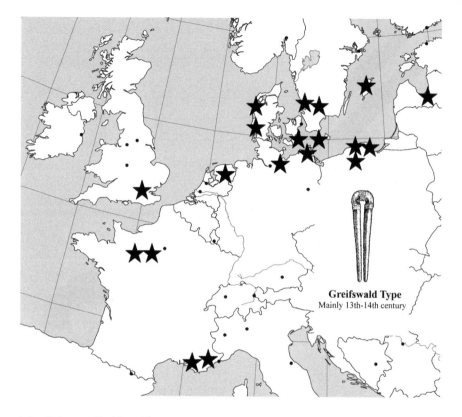

Map 2.4   Greifswald type spread
Source: Drawing by Ann-Turi Ford, by kind permission of Gjermund Kolltveit and Ann-Turi Ford.

By the seventeenth century, the commercial trade was sufficiently well established for England in particular to become the point from which there was worldwide distribution to the Americas, and later to Australia and Africa. Many of the finds from Colonial American sites are of the type designated 'Stafford' by Kolltveit. This is interesting as the 'Stafford' types are very common and, with very few exceptions, only found in Europe in England and Wales. A manufacturer has been identified and we can be very confident that a maker/exporter/trader system was in place between the West Midlands of England and America from at least the early eighteenth century until the middle of the twentieth century.

Suffice to say that, from the fourteenth century onwards, jews-harps were a saleable commodity.

Chapter 3
The Name

Probably, as an ingenious friend suggests, this should be read, the Jaws-harp ...
Thomas Pennant, 1774[1]

Without doubt the single most difficult subject this book has to tackle is the name of the instrument. Of all the thousand names found worldwide, it is only in English that it is called a jews-harp. As to why, the simple answer is that we do not know. The basic facts are that it is neither a Jewish instrument nor part of Jewish musical culture, nor is it a harp – that is, with strings. The theories as to why it acquired the name include misunderstandings, Jewish sellers and, we have to recognise the possibility, an anti-Semitic slur. In fact, the instrument has had many different names over the years, some regional and some commercial. These names can be collated into three distinct groups: the period prior to the eighteenth century, post-eighteenth century and commercial re-branding. Before 1763 three names were common in the English language: jews-harp, jews-trump and trump. After 1763 they were joined by jaw harp, juice harp, gewgaw and, more recently, mouth harp. Commercial names, mainly from late-nineteenth- and twentieth-century America, include Bruce Harp, New Ducie Harp and Snoopy's Harp.

Some of these names are only found in regions. Trump, for instance, is common in Scotland and Ireland. In Stornoway, Scotland, it is known as a *troub* and in Ireland, *trompadh*. Gewgaw is a regional North-East England and Southern Scottish name, but also has Welsh variations of *giwga*, *giwgan* and *biwbo* or *biwba*, though in North Wales it is known as an *ysturmant*.

An analysis of references found to date indicates that the various names jews-harp, jews-trump, trump and the many others, change in the use of name up to and after the mid-eighteenth century. The period 1450 up to 1750 accounts for only 117 of the over 3,000 references from British newspapers, journals, dictionaries and other published works found to date. Nevertheless, of these, 48 per cent use the term 'jews-trump', 24 per cent 'jews' harp' and 22 per cent 'trump', the rest being other names, such as the rarely used name (and only then in dictionaries) 'crembalum'. From 1750 up to 1950, where the base is significantly higher, using the remainder of 2,996 newspaper references shows that 93 per cent use the term 'jews-harp', with 6 per cent for both 'jews-trump' and 'trump', and the others are barely mentioned at 1 per cent and then often only as a reference to older names. The percentage use of 'jews-harp' in all newspapers overall is 90 per cent. After 1950 the situation is very confused and almost impossible to analyse, although 'jaw harp' does become more significant as players and traders became aware of racial sensibilities.

[1] Thomas Pennant, *A Tour in Scotland; MDCCLXIX* (Warrington, 1774), p. 215.

Table 3.1   Selected chronology of name development

Date	Name	Source	Country first used
1481	Jue harpes	*Rates of Merchandizes*	England
	Jue trumpes	*Rates of Merchandizes*	England
1548	Trump	history	Scotland
1549	Iues Trouks	*Rates of Merchandizes*	England
1583–1642	J(I)ewes trump(e)s	*Rates of Merchandizes*	England
1584	Iewes harp	play	England
1591	trompe/ Jewes trump	pamphlet	Scotland
1599	Trompe de Paris/ Iewes harpe	dictionary	England
1628	Jewes harp	natural history	England
1653–1765	Jewes Trumps	*Rates of Merchandizes*	England
1671	Crembala	dictionary	England
1688	Jew's Harp	dictionary	England
1725	Ystrymant	dictionary	Wales
1732	Trompadh	dictionary	Ireland
1749	Jaws-harpical	satire	England
1765	jaws harp	advert	America
1773	Gewgaw	dictionary	England
1784	juice harp	book	America
1800	Trompe de Bearn	dictionary	England
1950	New Ducie Harp	advert	America
1953	Bruce Harp	advert	America
1973	Snoopy's Harp	advert	America
1982	Blues Jaw Harp	advert	America

Etymology Theories

One researcher who went to great lengths to explore the roots of the name and considered its etymology was Frederick Crane. Crane had the conviction that the original name in English was 'trump' and went to some great lengths to have the name adopted by researchers, players and enthusiasts. The problem with this is that 'to trump' in many parts of the UK is a crude colloquial reference to a socially undesirable bodily function, a name that, therefore, has connotations potentially as disagreeable as the more common jews-harp.

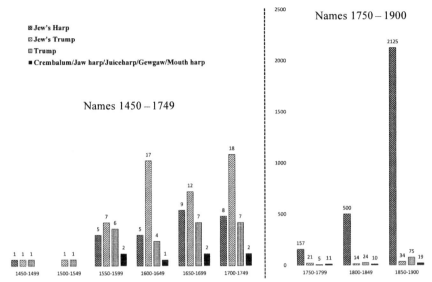

Graph 3.1   Analysis of names

In an article written in 1982, Crane developed the theory that the evolution of the name was trump to jews-trump to jews-harp. His argument was that there is an unbroken tradition of the use of the name 'trump' in Scotland and that it has cousins, 'such as French *trompe*, German *Trumpel*, and Slavonic *drumla*'.[2] Trump, he recognised, could refer to a trumpet, though in an article written in 1996 Crane points to a 'reasonably reliable'[3] mention from c.1450 in an English poem, *Turnament of Totenham*. Lines 15 to 18 have:

> Ther hepped Hawkyn,
> Ther daunsed Dawkyn,
> Ther trumped Tomkyn –
> And all were trewe drynkers.[4]

Crane believed that line 17, 'Ther trumped Tomkyn', refers to the jews-harp, though line 146 also has, 'With flayles and hornes and trumpes mad of tre'.

---

[2]   Frederick Crane, 'Jew's (Jaw's? Jeu? Jeugd? Gewgaw? Juice?) Harp', *VIM*, 1 (1982), p. 40.
[3]   Frederick Crane, 'The Trump in British Literature', *VIM*, 5 (1996), p. 67.
[4]   Thomas Wright (ed.), *The Turnament of Totenham and the Feest. Two Early Ballads* (London, 1836).

Kooper believes that both refer to trumpets.⁵ Another potential use of trump as a description of a jews-harp is found in Robert Wedderburn's *The Complaynt of Scotland* dated 1548. Referring to shepherds, he writes:

> Ther was viij scheiphyrdis and ilk ane of them hed ane syndry instrament to play to the laif. the first hed ane drone bag pipe, the nyxt hed ane pipe maid of ane bleddir and of ane reid, the thrid playit on ane trump, the feyrd on ane corne pipe, the fyft playit on ane pipe maid of ane gait horne, the sext playt on ane recordar the seuint plait on ane fiddil, and the last on ane quhissel.⁶

While we cannot be certain, given the context 'the thrid playit on ane trump' does appear to refer to a jews-harp.

Various arguments have been made for simply calling the instrument a 'trump'. Jeremy Montagu, ex-curator of the Bate Collection of Musical Instruments, Oxford, for instance, suggests, 'Trump is the most logical term for the instrument for it produces the same overtones as the natural trumpet',⁷ while the *Oxford Dictionary of English Etymology* states, 'The notes produced by the instrument are limited, as in the natural trumpet, to the natural harmonic sequences, hence the older name "Jew's trump"'.⁸ The use of the name 'harp' might be linked to the lyre shape of the frame, but this is speculative.

Although there is a certain beautiful logic in the trump to jews-trump to jews-harp theory, there is simply no solid evidence. All three names were used concurrently from at least the end of the fifteenth century and possibly the early fourteenth century. One thing is certain: jews-harp predates jaw harp by at least 300 years.

Theories of Etymology

There have been numerous attempts to justify how jews-harp became the instrument's common name, ranging from the obscure to the ridiculous. Samuel Pegge wrote, 'I conceive the present orthography to be a corruption of the French Jeu-trump, a trump to play with that in the Belgick, or Low-Dutch, from whence come many of our toys, a tromp is a rattle for children'.⁹ Dr Rimbault in *Notes and Queries* suggested that Francis Bacon specifically uses Jue-trump in *Sylva*

---

⁵ Erik Kooper (ed.), *Sentimental and Humorous Romances* (Kalamazoo, MI: Medieval Institute Publications, 2006), p. 189.
⁶ [Robert Wedderburn], J. Leyden, *The Complaynt of Scotland written in 1548, with a preliminary dissertation and glossary* (Edinburgh, 1801), p. 101.
⁷ Jeremy Montagu, personal correspondence.
⁸ C.T. Onions (ed.), *Oxford Dictionary of English Etymology* (Oxford: Clarendon Press, 1978 [1966]).
⁹ Samuel Pegge, *Anonymiana or, Ten Centuries of Observations on Various Authors and Subjects* (London, 1809), pp. 48–9.

Sylvarum published in 1628.[10] The original English publication, however, has 'Jewes harp', while in the French translation of 1631 that section appears not to have been translated, so we have no way of verifying. The nearest phrase comes from *The Great French Dictionary* of 1688, where there is 'Trompe (f) ... *a Jew's Harp, for Boys to play upon. Jouër de la Trompe, to play upon the Jews harp*'.[11]

The same applies to another potential origin of the name from the Low Countries word *jeudgtromp*. English–Dutch dictionaries of the seventeenth century have '*Jeught*: Youth or Adolescence; Tromp: A rattle for little children' and '*Trompet*: Trump or Trumpet', but no reference to the jews-harp as such. A 1754 dictionary has 'a Jews' trump, *een Speel tromp*' and in 1801 there is '*Tromp* (s.f. *Mondtromp*) a Jewers trump or harp'. The last name is most likely a Flemish translation of the English name, there being similar examples in Germany.

Thomas Pennant in *A Tour in Scotland* of 1774 is the first to suggest 'jaws' as an origin, with the footnote, 'Probably, as an ingenious friend suggested, this should be read, the Jaws-harp',[12] though this is not the first use of the name, which can be traced back to 1749, when Bonnell Thornton concocted 'Jaws-harpical'[13] as a humorous device, and its use in American newspaper adverts in the 1760s. 'Juice harp' is an American idea, although it is also found in Australia. In *The Porcupine, Alias the Hedge Hog*, 1784, William Billings of Boston adds a note: 'Our very boys and negroes pretend to understand the original; and they all agree that this word is wrongly translated; for they say it should be rendered thus, juice harp; because, if they play it any considerable time, it makes their mouth water'.[14]

The Jewish Connection

The connection with the Jews can be broken down into three types: humorous, sellers and derogatory. The suggestion that King David's harp was a jews-harp is a recurrent theme first used by Bonnell Thornton's (alias Fustian Sackbut) burlesque, *An Ode on Saint Cæcilia's Day* of 1749. Thornton writes,

> the Judaic, or (as more commonly called) Jews Harp, speaks its origin in its appellation: And I cannot help thinking, that this was the harp which David used, as the sound of the Hebrew Language seems particularly adapted to this instrument. I would therefore advise all painters, engravers etc., not to represent the Royal psalmist with the many-stringed Welsh Harp in his hand, as they have

---

[10] *Notes and Queries* (Oxford: Oxford University Press, 1850), p. 277.
[11] Guy Miège, *The Great French Dictionary* (London, 1688), p. TR.
[12] Pennant, *A Tour in Scotland*, p. 215.
[13] Bonnell Thornton, *An Ode on Saint Cæcilia's Day* (London, 1749).
[14] L.S., *The Porcupine, Alias the Hedge Hog or, The Fox Turned Preacher. Written after the manner of Ignatius Irony, Bartholomew Burlesque, and Samuel Satire* (Boston, MA, 1784).

hitherto done, but to place a monochord lyre in his mouth, such as was used by the Jews in his time, and from then transmitted down to us.[15]

A relatively recent theory is that it got its name from the sellers of the instrument. C.B. Mount appears to have been the first to come up with the idea, in 1897:

> Suppose now that the "trump" had been known in England and Scotland, that it had fallen into oblivion, and was suddenly brought back into vogue by the enterprise of some Jew pedlar selling it around the country – what more likely, in such a case, than that it should be called the Jew's trump or harp?[16]

Given the restrictions on Jews imposed after their expulsion from England in 1290 until the seventeenth century, the pedlar theory looks unlikely, although sellers based on the continent might be a possibility. The *Oxford English Dictionary* expands the theory:

> More or less satisfactory reasons may be conjectured: e.g. that the instrument was actually made, sold, or sent to England by Jews, or supposed to be so, or that it was attributed to them, as a good commercial name, suggesting the trumps and harps mentioned in the Bible.[17]

We do, though, have to consider the name as a racial slur. With the exception of Roycroft, who states in 1671, 'Jewsharp, called Crembala by Comenius, that is to say Trumpet or Harp of the Jews, is in fact so called out of contempt',[18] most early references use the name without comment – that is, it was just a name. It is not until the nineteenth century that *Punch* magazine makes use of the jews-harp as a Jewish symbol, particularly during the period of Baron Rothschild and the Parliamentary Oaths Bill.[19] During the debates surrounding the law that would allow Lionel Rothschild to take his seat in the Houses of Parliament, both politicians and publications used the jews-harp image and name to represent Jewishness, often in a critical or satirical manner. The use of jews-harp in political debates makes for uncomfortable reading. 'More Jews harping on the Dreyfus case'[20] and 'It is clear that in the concert of Europe in all matters relating to the financial affairs of Egypt the leading instrument is the Jew's harp',[21] are typical.

---

[15] Thornton, *An Ode*.
[16] C.B. Mount, 'JEW'S HARP: JEW'S TRUMP', in *Notes and Queries* (Oxford: Oxford University Press, 1897), p. 323.
[17] *Oxford English Dictionary*, vol. VIII (Oxford: Oxford University Press, 1989), p. 232.
[18] T. Roycroft, *Etymoloicon Lingue Anglicanae* (1671).
[19] Crane, 'The Trump in British Literature'.
[20] *Worcestershire Chronicle*, 26 August 1899, p. 4.
[21] *The Times*, 2 October 1884, p. 8.

Figure 3.1   *Punch* cartoon, 18 July 1857
Source: From author's collection.

Names Prior to the Eighteenth Century

Whatever the theories, there is an historical progression with verifiable dates. There is said to be a document using the name 'Jew's trumps' in the early fourteenth century,[22] which would make this the earliest reference to the instrument in the English language to date, though extensive research has not uncovered the original source. There can be no doubt, however, about the authenticity of a customs account book reference dated 1481. On 14 June 1481 a consignment of goods for the merchant William Codde was recorded to have included 'Jue harpes', and another of 'Jue trumpes' on 21 July 1481.[23] This latter name appears to have been the official name of the instrument up to the eighteenth century. The Petty Customs *Rates of Merchandizes* books that establish the value of imported items use different spellings, but the same name of Iues trouks (1549); Jewes trumps (1583 and 1642); Iewes trumpes (1608, 1624 and 1631); Jews Trumps (1653, 1657, 1669 and 1702); Jews-Trumps (1713 and 1765).[24]

Evidence that the word 'trump' in the Scottish region is the jews-harp can be found in the transcript of the trial of Agnes Sampson in 1590, described in *Newes from Scotland*. Sampson confessed that Geillis Duncan 'did goe before them playing this reill or daunce upon a small trompe called a Jewes trump'.[25]

'Iewes harpes' are mentioned by both Sir Walter Raleigh and the Earl of Dudley in the mid-1590s, *The English Irish National Dictionary* of 1732 provides the first reference to the Irish name of 'Trompadh', while other early dictionary references include:

- 'Trompe de Paris, a Iewes harpe' – *A Dictionary in Spanish and English* compiled by John Minsheu (1599)
- 'Zampogno, a jews-harp. Scaccia pensiere' – *Vocabbulario Italiano & Inglese, A Dictionary Italian & English*, Giovanni Torriano (1659)
- 'Jewstrump or Jewsharp, called Crembala by Comenius' – T. Roycroft's *Etymoloicon Lingue Anglicanae* (1671)
- 'Trompe, a Trump, or Trumpet/Trump, or Jewes Trump, a Musical Instrument, Trompe, trompette' – *A New DICTIONARY French and English With Another English and French*, by Guy Miege (1677)
- 'Jewes trumpe or harpe' – the *Nomenclator, or Rememberbrancer of Adrianus Iunius* (1585)
- 'JEWS-HARP, or Trompe de Bearn', in Thomas Busby's *A Dictionary of Music* (1801)

---

[22] *Dundee Courier*, 11 December 1933, p. 11.
[23] Michael Wright, 'Jue harpes, Jue trumpes, 1481', *JIJHS*, 2 (2004), p. 8.
[24] Michael Wright, 'Jews Trumps and Their Valuation, 1545 to 1765', *JIJHS*, 2 (2004), pp. 41–6.
[25] *Newes from Scotland, declaring the damnable life and death of doctor Fian, a notable sorcerer, who was burned at Edenbrough in Ianuary last, 1591* (London, 1591?).

According to *A Dissertation on the Musical Instruments of the Welsh*, the Welsh name was 'Ystrymant', also spelt 'ysturmant'. The dissertation continues,

> [this] implies the mouth in motion; which removes all doubt, the Jews Harp, is a corruption of *Jaws Harp*, or *Jaws Trump*: neither is it to be found in the place of Jewish musical instruments, given to us by *Calvert*. The earliest mention of it, that I can find, is in *Davydd a' Gailym's Ode on the wind*, written about the year 1370, thus "*Ystrymant yr ystermydd*" ...[26]

Ystrymant is also a Walloon word for the jews-harp, and if verified, 1370 would be the earliest reference to the Welsh name we have to date. The 1725 *English and Welch Dictionary* of John Roderick has 'A Jew's Harp, Ysturmant',[27] as does the 1735 edition, though under the title 'A Jew's-trump or Jew's-harp, Ysturmant'.[28]

Use in Literature

Early English playwrights and writers consistently use both jews-harp and jews-trump. In the sixteenth century alone, for instance, John Lyly in *Campaspe* (1584) mentions a 'Iewes harp'; Henry Chettle's *Kind-Hart's Dreame* (1592) has 'Jewes trumpe or harpe'; *Pierces Supererogation or A New Prayer of the Old Asse* by Gabriel Harvey (1593) uses 'Iewes-trumpe'; and Ben Jonson's *Every Man Out of His Humor* (1599), 'Iewes trump'. The use of 'Trump' alone only appears in one work by an English author in William Stevenson's *Gammer Gurtons Nedle* (1575), 'With whewling and pewling, as though they had lost a trump'.[29]

Names from the Mid-Eighteenth Century

Jaw harp originally appears as a comedic device. For around 10 years in the mid-eighteenth century there was a series of burlesque performances in London. In 1749 Bonnell Thornton, the English poet, essayist and critic, wrote a number

---

[26] Edward Jones, *Musical and Poetical Relicks of the Welsh Bards* (London, 1794), p. 107.
[27] John Roderick, *The English and Welch Dictionary: or, the English before the Welch. = Y geirlyfr Saesneg a Chymraeg; ... Containing all the words that are necessary to understand both languages; but more especially, for the translation of the English into Welch* ... (Salop, 1725), p. HA.
[28] John Roderick, *Y geirlyfr Saesneg a Chymraeg; neu'r Saesneg o flaen y Cymraeg. ... A ddechreuwyd ar y cyntaf gan Sion Rhydderch, ag a ddibenwyd yn awr, ynghyd a chwanegiad o lawer cant o eiriau gan y Parchedig Mr. John Williams ... ac Mr. Lewis Evans* ... (Shrewsbury, 1837), p. JE.
[29] William Stevenson, *A ryght pithy, pleasaunt and merie comedie: intituled Gammer gurtons nedle: played on stage, not longe a go in Christes Colledge in Cambridge. Made by Mr. S. Mr. of Art* (London, 1575).

of burlesques and articles where the jews-harp featured, this being typical: 'Hurdi-gurdical, Marrow-bonical. Jaws-harpical and Salt-boxical, Intelligence extraordinary'.[30] The first serious use of jaws harp as an alternative to jews-harp appears in adverts in the *New York Gazette* and the *New York Mercury*, when in 1765 five merchants advertised 'Jaw harps' and 'brass and iron Jaw harps', though the name was dropped after 1769 and only revived in the middle of the nineteenth century.[31]

The use of 'Gewgaw' for a name specifically for the jews-harp first appears in *An Accurate New Spelling Dictionary* of 1773, with 'Gewgaw n.a. Jew's harp, a bauble'.[32]

The *Rural Economy of Yorkshire*, of 1788, under the section 'Provincialisms of East-Yorkshire', provides a specific regional use of the name having a note: 'More especially of the Eastern Morelands and the Vale of Pickering: the Wolds, Holerness, and the Hoawardian hills, use the same dialect, but in a less perfect state – GEWGAW; a Jew's harp'.[33] *The Pitman's Pay, and Other Poems* written in 1843 has, 'The crack o' whuslers i' maw the day,/ Maw gewgaw touch was te the life ;/ And at yen time, 'could nearly play/ "God syev the King" upon the fife !'[34] In *Allan's Illustrated Edition of Tyneside Songs* of 1862, in 'The Stage-struck Keelman' the 'music's a'ranged by Frederick Jimmy Lumphead for nine gugaws'.[35] 'Gewgaw' is still used today in the North-East, locally spelt 'gewgar'.[36] There is a variant *Gewe-Gawe* from the Low Countries, so it is possible the name transferred through trade with that country, and there is a suggestion that jews-harp actually is a corruption of Gewgaw. The other possibility, given the north-east connection with Scandinavia, is that it comes from the Swedish name for the instrument of *munngiga* or 'mouth fiddle'.

Commercial Names

The third group of names falls under the category of commercial expediency. Given the concern with jews-harp as a brand, makers and sellers have tried a

---

[30] Thornton, *An Ode*.
[31] These were Peter Remsen, *New York Gazette*, 6 May 1765, p. 3; Moses Judah, *New York Gazette*, 3 June 1765, p. 1; Peter Goelet, *New York Gazette*, 17 September 1765, p. 3; Abeel and Byvanck, *New York Mercury*, 17 February 1766, p. 3; and Peter T. Curtenius, *New York Gazette*, 18 May 1768, p. 1.
[32] A. Fisher, *An Accurate New Spelling Dictionary, and expositor of the English language* ... (London, 1773), pp. GEO, GIB.
[33] W.H. Marshall, *The Rural Economy of Yorkshire, vol. II* (London, 1788), p. 331.
[34] Thomas Wilson, *The Pitman's Pay, and Other Poems* (Gateshead: William Douglas, 1843), p. 43.
[35] *Allan's Illustrated Edition of Tyneside Songs* (facsimile, Newcastle-upon-Tyne: Frank Graham, 1972), p. 438.
[36] Jonny Handle, personal correspondence, 2014.

number of names, jaw harp being the most common. Others include Johnson Smith and Company, who in 1950 advertised 'The New Dusie Harp – an Improved Jew's Harp';[37] Grossman of Cleveland's 1953 'Bruce Harp'; and in 1973 the latter company's exploitation of the popular animation *Charlie Brown* with the 'Snoopy's Harp'. Finally, there is the 'Blues Jaw Harp' advertised by Coast/Bruno in 1982.[38] None of these appears to have caught on and the search for a suitably politically correct alternative to 'jews-harp' continues. Young players often use the name 'mouth-harp', though this is usually associated with the harmonica. In the end the most commonly used name from the middle of the seventeenth century to the present is 'jews-harp'.

Animals, Objects and Street Names

There have been public houses and taverns, roads and lanes, a bridge, wharf and gate; a farm, field and hill; racehorses, greyhounds and cattle – all of which have been given the name jews-harp. The racehorse Jew's Trump competed in the late 1760s, while Jew's Harp ran at numerous courses in the 1880s and there was a Jaws-harp colt that ran in the 1890s. Two racehorses were given the name in America, racing in 1894 and 1929. The 1870s saw a coursing hound competing all over England and greyhound racing had a Jew's Harp running in the 1930s. None won any major titles, but they did produce offspring that also competed.

There is an iron staple in the shape of a jews-harp that, according to *A Treatise on Carriages* connected 'part of the grasshopper spring, which it raises from the axletree'.[39] Jew's Harp is also a name sometimes given to the shackle with which the chain cable is attached to an anchor on board a ship.

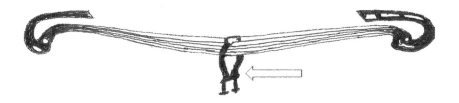

Figure 3.2   Jews-harp staple
Source: Sketch by David Wright from an original in William Felton's *A Treatise on Carriages*, 1794. By kind permission of David Wright.

---

[37] Crane, 'Trolls and Trumps', p. 56.
[38] F. Crane, 'Trumps in American Musical Instrument Trade Catalogs', *VIM*, 11 (2004), pp. 104–16.
[39] William Felton, *A Treatise on Carriages* (London, 1794).

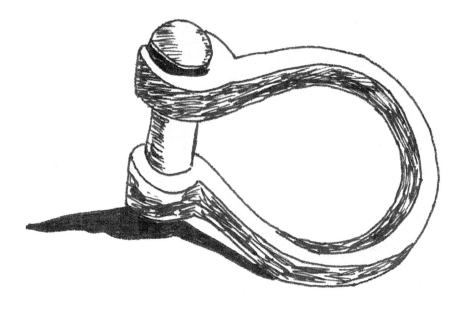

Figure 3.3   Jews-harp shackle
Source: Sketch by David Wright from an original in David Steel's *The Elements and Practice of Rigging and Seamanship*, 1794. By kind permission of David Wright.

Geographic features appear in many parts of England, including an auction lot called Jew's Trump Close that was advertised in 1807 and 1810; a Jews'-Harp Hill west of Bradford on Avon, Wiltshire; Jew's Harp Fields in Staffordshire and Cornwall; Jew's Harp Wood in Wytham Woods, Oxford; Jews Harp Meadow, Orchard and Waterleets in Somerset. Other features are described as being in the shape of a jews-harp, including a public park in Peterborough, an embankment at Tynwald Hill, Isle of Man and terracing at Langley Burrell, Wiltshire.

Streets and Buildings

None of these locations appears to have kept the name, something that applies to streets and buildings. There was a Jew's Harp-Bridge in Lower Watford on the road to Stanmore; Jew's Harp Alley in Deal; Jew's Harp Row, Princess End, Coseley; Jew's Harp Row, Gate, Passage, Fields, Road, Close, Basin and Wharf in London.

Taverns and Inns

The name was used by a number of taverns and public houses. There was the Jew's Harp Beer-House on St Botolph Street, Colchester; The Jews' Harp somewhere between Old Castle Street, Holywell Street and Lyon Inn, Exeter; Jew's Harp Inn, City-road, Newcastle; and a Jew's Harp Public House, Reddal Hill, near Rowley Regis. London had at least three and possibly six public houses or taverns. There is a 1774 mention of the Jews Harp House in Fig Lane,[40] a Jew's Harp Tavern on the Edgware Road; Jews Harp House, Angel Alley, off Bishopsgate Street; Jew's Harp Tavern, Petticoat-lane; and the Jew's Harp on Kingsway. Some of these might refer to the same establishment, as they come from newspaper clippings that are not always entirely accurate.

The one we can be sure of is Jew's Harp Tavern and Tea-House, which with variations of name is thought to occupy a spot close to what is now the lake in the centre of Regent's Park. The extraordinary achievement of the accurate triangulation of the British Isles begun in 1795 provides a slightly more accurate positioning as it required significant points from which measurements could be taken. One of these points was a Jew's Harp Station, which when taking the given measurements from St Paul's (13,522 ft), the Argyll Street Observatory (5,656 ft 8 in.) and St Pancras Church (5,728 ft 1 in.), places the cross-over points close to the Chester Gate on the inner circle of Regent's Park. Whether this pinpoints the tavern itself or a feature close by is uncertain. Overlaying the present pathways of Regent's Park with the plan of 1814, it would appear that the site was within the Inner Circle. The tavern was certainly in an isolated position for most of its existence and may have had a distinctive tower feature of use to the triangulation team. It is also interesting that this establishment was significant enough to be noted on at least six maps from 1741 to 1814, the earliest maps of Roche dated 1741 and 1746, showing it situated on Love Lane, while a road improvement plan of 1756 gives it as being on Clay Street. None of the other maps gives a road name, though there is a distinct similarity between the road layout of the 1741 and 1800 maps. There is one conjectural drawing of a sign drawn *c.*1926,[41] though no specific location for this is given.

This establishment had something of a reputation as a place of dubious entertainment, but it was a recognised place for meetings, suppers, auctions, shooting competitions, bare knuckle fights, sale of carnations, auriculas and tulips (though plant sales did not include the Jew's harp plant or upright-stalked trillium/nodding trillium, *Trillium erectum var. viridiflorum*), and a location for inquests. This last may well have been because the fields surrounding the establishment, known as the Jew's Harp Fields, were notorious for robbers, footpads, suicides and duels. It was also a place for mass meetings and equipment demonstrations, and was one of the proposed landing places for French balloonist Garnerin's descent by parachute on his tour of Britain in 1802.

---

[40] *Public Advertiser*, 29 October 1774, p. 2.
[41] See Crane, p. 145, from C.M. Rounding, *Quaint Signs of Olde Inns* (London: Herbert Jenkins, 1926).

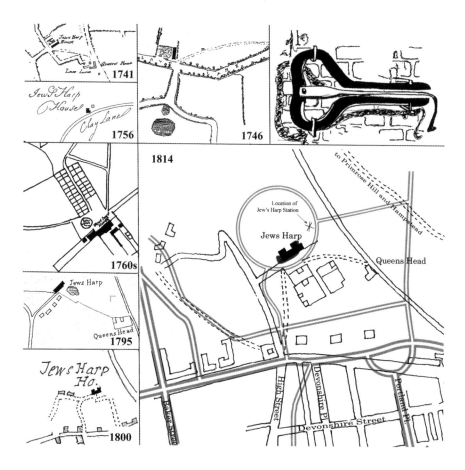

Figure 3.4   Jews Harp House locations from 1741 to 1814, with possible location of site in Regent's Park, and conjectural sketch of a sign for the Jew's Harp Inn

Source: Map drawings by author, sketch by David Wright from a drawing by C.M. Rounding in *Quaint Signs of Olde Inns*, 1926. Sketch by kind permission of David Wright.

Three stories of the Jew's Harp Tavern and adjoining field give us an insight into their importance. The first relates to the visits of the Speaker of the House of Commons from 1728 to 1761 Arthur Onslow:

> There was a house so named situated near the top of Portland-place, but now moved more to the eastward, in consequence of the laying out of the grounds for the Regent's Park. It was long known and resorted to as a tea-garden, &c. by parties on holidays, and well spoken of for good entertainment. Mr. A. Onslow, when Speaker of the House, was wont to go to this house, in plain attire, and

take his seat in the chimney corner in the kitchen, joining the familiarly in the humors of the customers, and was for two or three years a great favorite with the landlord, his family, & visitors, who, not knowing his name, usually spoke of him as "The Gentleman". Mr. Onslow, being seen one day in his state carriage going to the house by the landlord, mine host was somewhat alarmed at the discovery, & hurried home to tell his family what he had discovered, which disconcerted them not a little, knowing with how little ceremony they had hitherto treated him. The Speaker came as usual in the evening to the "Harp", but finding, from the reserved manners of the landlord, his wife, and the children who were accustomed to climb upon his knees and take liberties with his wig, &c. that his name and character had become known to the circle, paid his bill, and without taking any further notice, left the house, to which he never afterwards returned.[42]

Then William Blake the poet mentions the tavern and fields in his epic poem *Jerusalem: The Emanation of the Giant Albion*, written between 1804 and 1820:

The Jew's Harp House and the Green Man,
The Ponds where boys to bathe delight.
The fields of cows by Willan's farm,
Shine in Jerusalem's pleasant sight.[43]

Lastly, the fields next to the Jew's Harp Tavern gained notoriety in December 1795 when they were the chosen venue for a mass protest organised by John Thelwall, a known Republican who had already been tried and acquitted of treason. Protesting against the new laws on seditious gatherings recently passed by parliament during what has been called 'Pitt's Reign of Terror', five to six thousand people gathered to listen to speeches and sign a petition. Though the field was well organised with signing tables and stages, various panics appear to have been spooked by cattle and the appearance of 12 of 'the Horse' from the local barracks and the day ended in a shambles. The strongly pro-government press had a field day, the *Tomahawk Or Censor General* writing, 'A New Song – Charley Fox sent to the Devil (To be sung near the Jew's Harp, Marylebone Fields)'.[44] On 15 December they wrote a scurrilous piece entitled 'The Miscreant's Death', supposedly being the final words of Thelwall, who complained that 'the cowardice of his disciples, at the Jew's Harp Assemblage, had very materially conducted to his destruction'.[45]

---

[42] *Baltimore Patriot*, 15 September 1826, p. 1, and Crane, 'Jew's (Jaw's? Jeu? Jeugd? Gewgaw? Juice?) Harp', p. 59.
[43] William Blake, quoted in Frederick Crane, 'The Trump in British Literature', *Vierundzwanzigsteljahrsschrift der Internationalen Maultrommelvirtuosengenossenschaft*, 5 (1996), p. 86.
[44] *Tomahawk Or Censor General*, 7 December 1795.
[45] *Tomahawk Or Censor General*, 15 December 1795, p. 170.

When the leases ran out for the tenants on Marylebone Park in 1811, the present Regent's Park was created and the Jew's Harp Tavern moved to 1 Redhill Street, also noted as 1 Edward Street. Something of the size and variety of entertainment appears to have remained, it having 100 mahogany and other drinking tables, a ballroom and a music licence, the last of the licences being given in 1928. The building was destroyed by bombing during World War II.

Mentions in Trials

Sixteen different trials make mention of the Jew's Harp House as a location:[46]

Thomas Jewer; theft with violence: highway robbery; 20 October 1773 (not guilty).

Sarah Bridgwater, Jane Bristow; theft: simple grand larceny; 15 September 1779 (guilty – whipped and imprisoned for six months).

Fielding Empson; breaking the peace: assault; 25 April 1781 (not guilty).

Elizabeth Breedon; deception: perjury; 25 October 1786 (not guilty).

James Everard, John Vandebus, Off spring Gregory, Jane Vandebus; theft: burglary; theft: receiving stolen goods; 12 September 1787 (not guilty; guilty – death; guilty – death; guilty – transported to Africa for fourteen years).

Sarah Cornford; theft: simple grand larceny; 15 September 1790 (not guilty).

Dennis Dillon; killing: murder, after fighting with a journeyman-tailor shop-mate; 18 September 1805 (not guilty).

Stephen Adams; theft: housebreaking; 16 September 1807 (not guilty).

John Hopkins, John Jones, Richard Prescott; theft: burglary; 5 December 1810 (guilty – death with a recommendation "to his Majesty's mercy by the jury, on account of their youth and good character").

John Jones; offences against the king: coining; 9 September 1818 (guilty – death).

Edward Parsons, William Dawson; offences against the king: coining; 14 February 1821 (guilty – death).

---

[46] All taken from *The Proceedings of the Old Bailey* website, at www.oldbaileyonline. org, accessed 24 September 2013.

Thomas Bruce, Joseph Waters, Thomas Halfpenny; theft: simple grand larceny; 15 January 1823 (not guilty).

Robert Gardiner, James Aspinall, Hannah Riddel; theft: simple grand larceny; theft: receiving stolen goods; 7 April 1825 (guilty – imprisoned for three months and whipped; not guilty; guilty – transported for fourteen years).

Richard Miller; theft: embezzlement; 12 July 1827 (guilty – imprisoned for three months).

Joshua Gees; theft: simple grand larceny; 13 September 1827 (guilty – transported for seven years).

Mary Perry; theft: simple grand larceny; 14 January 1830 (guilty – imprisoned for eighteen months).

The trial of Richard Carrol in 1782 mentions Jew's Harp Court, which appears to have taken its name from the tavern situated off Angel Alley in Bishopsgate Ward Without, on a site now occupied by the railway lines leading to Liverpool Street Station.

The Name Today

The negative use of a name for, what is after all, just a musical instrument has continued to the present day. Young players, while acknowledging the value of it musically, struggle with the name, though there does not appear to be a suitable alternative. What we now find is that 'jaw harp' is used a lot; Crane's 'trump' is being adopted by the Horniman Museum and a name becoming more popular, particularly by young players, is mouth-harp, one that can be seen as direct translations of the Norwegian *munnharpe* and other European names.

There does not appear to be a sensible solution. The name 'jews-harp' is still recognised throughout the world, but while it remains tainted by the deleterious use of the name, using the term 'jews-harp' will remain controversial.

PART II
Commercial Exploitation

For at least 600 years the jews-harp was imported, distributed, manufactured and exported by traders, makers and entrepreneurs. While of no great monetary value, vast quantities were imported from the Continent and an export trade developed that encouraged manufacturing at a scale such that Britain and Ireland became a major influence in the distribution of the instrument throughout the world.

Chapter 4
Imports and Distribution

Another, who had a Months minde to see the Booths, Jew-trumps ... and other trinkets in Bartholemew Faire ...
Richard Brathwait, 1640[1]

One of the most fascinating questions concerning jews-harps is why these musical instruments were imported and eventually manufactured in Britain in such huge numbers. They had little value and have a very chequered history of acceptance as having any musicality, yet from at least the fifteenth and possibly the fourteenth century vast numbers were first imported and then manufactured by workshops first in England and Scotland, and later in Ireland. Up to the eighteenth century they were part of a sophisticated European trading system that featured an increasing demand by consumers for foreign goods. From at least the eighteenth century and the industrialisation of the West Midlands in particular, jews-harps were recognised as also having a potential for manufacture on these islands. This was triggered by further demand, particularly in North America and later in South Africa and Australia, providing the potential for a profitable business – not a hugely profitable business, but profitable nonetheless.

Part 1: The Commercial Revolution

Evidence for jews-harps being imported comes from archaeological finds and customs records. Kolltveit records 200 pieces found throughout the British Isles and Ireland. and to this list can be added the 240 pieces recorded in the Portable Antiquities Scheme archive and a small number from private collections, providing a total of 462 pieces all told. This is a small percentage of imports and manufactured pieces, the vast majority, and particularly those of iron, having disappeared over time. They do, however, indicate trends, with the caveat that the finds in the Portable Antiquities Scheme in particular are subject to metal detectorists providing location information to the scheme – only one piece has been recorded in Lancashire, for instance, while 26 all told are recorded as coming from the Isle of Wight. Therefore, no inference should be made that the Isle of Wight was a hotbed of players, whereas Lancastrians ignored the instrument.

---

[1] Richard Brathwaite, *Ar't Asleepe Husband?* (1640), p. 121.

58   The Jews-Harp in Britain and Ireland

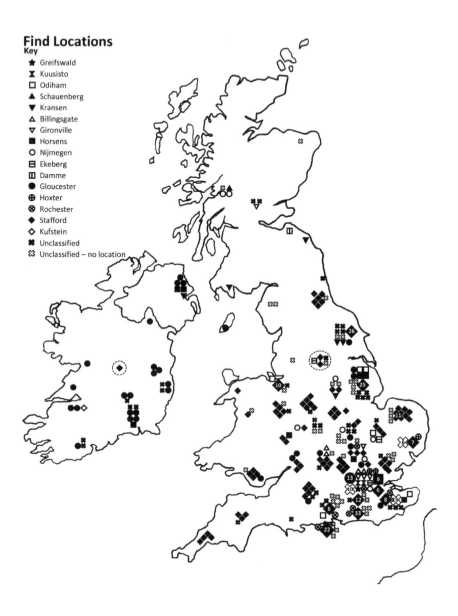

Map 4.1   British and Irish find locations
Source: From the research of Gjermund Kolltveit, the Portable Antiquities Scheme and other sources.

Imports and Distribution

Figure 4.1   Typical finds from around the British Isles
Source: Photograph by author, from author's collection.

There is some dispute regarding the earliest finds. Crane notes that finds in Kent have been dated as Roman or Anglo-Saxon.[2] Using Kolltveit's system not available to Crane, these finds can be identified as 'Stafford' types, which we now know were made during the late seventeenth and eighteenth centuries. This requires us, therefore, to believe that, given these are cast, the same design pattern was used to make the moulds, lost and reconstructed some 1,000 years apart. Details of how the Kent finds were recovered are sketchy, but it looks most likely that they were discarded at the various sites during the later period and are not, therefore, Roman or Anglo-Saxon in origin.

Taking Kolltveit's generalised dating, 32 pieces (7 per cent of the total) of eight types can be identified as being from the thirteenth and fourteenth centuries. While a quarter are from the London area, the spread is nationwide, with seven pieces coming from Scotland. There are just four types of 27 pieces dated fifteenth- and sixteenth-century, one third having been found in the London area, none in Scotland, though six pieces were found in Ireland.

---

[2]   Frederick Crane, *Extant Medieval Musical Instruments: Provisional Catalogue by Types* (Iowa City, IA: University of Iowa Press, 1972).

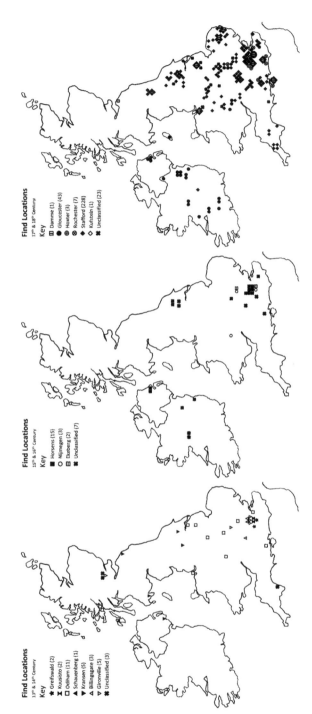

Map 4.2   British and Irish find locations – thirteenth to eighteenth centuries

Almost all of the finds can be dated as seventeenth- and eighteenth-century and are spread throughout these islands. A total of 146 were found in the Home Counties, though there are also substantial finds in Suffolk and Lincolnshire. Of the 403 finds of this latter period, 59 per cent (238 pieces) are types 'Stafford' and 'Rochester'. This is important because, with five exceptions in Europe, these types are only found on the British Isles, the vast majority in England.

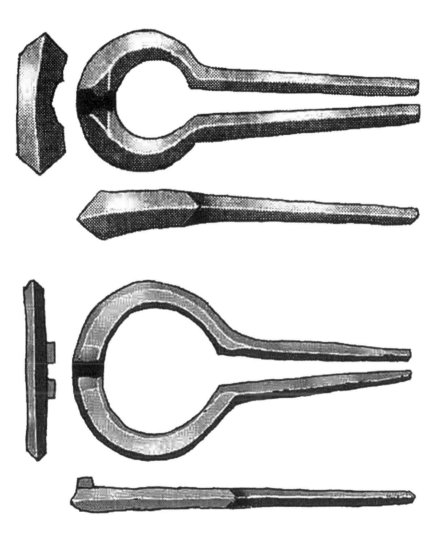

Figure 4.2   'Stafford' and 'Rochester' types
Source: Drawing by Ann-Turi Ford, by kind permission of Gjermund Kolltveit and Ann-Turi Ford.

The implication of this is that there was a manufacturer active at this time, one that has now been identified.[3]

Imports

During the fifteenth century considerable quantities of imports into England and Wales were coming from the Low Countries, the Brabant Fairs being an important source for all manner of goods. *The Overseas Trade of London: Exchequer Customs Accounts 1480–1* records that two cargos of small goods were imported by William Codde, an 'Alien merchant' based in London. Codde's shipment of 14 June 1481 included '4 grs. Jue harpes', while another on 21 July listed '2 grs. jue trumpes',[4] or 864 pieces all told. They were brought in on 'the ship of Peter Jacobson [Jacobisson] called *Trego* of Arnemuiden'.[5] Situated on the Zealand peninsular on the Westerhelde, Arnemuiden, or the 'quay' of Antwerp, was the out-port of that city. Located 45 miles (72 kilometres) to the north-east, it was ideally situated both to supply and to take goods to and from the four great marts: the Pask or Easter Mart of Bergen-op.-Zoom; the Sinxten or Whitsun Mart held at Antwerp; Bamis Mart at Antwerp; and Cold Mart, back at Bergen-op.-Zoom.[6]

Between November 1480 and July 1481 Codde imported nearly 80,000 items divided into 49 different types of goods, mostly small and easily transportable items such as hatbands, knives, leather girdles and glass beads, a list that appears to indicate that Codde specialised in the trade of small, pedlar goods. The first shipment, for example, included:

> 1 basket with 1 doz. copper crosses, 8 doz. small tin bottles, 6 grs. leather girdles, 4 grs. 3½ doz. pouches, 5 doz. red skins [*S*. leather], 4 grs. 1 doz. knives, 3 doz. latten rings, 6 doz. iron rings, 7 doz. writing tables, 5½ grs. lattern girdles, 4 grs. Jue harpes, 2 doz. [*S*. latten] squirts, 12 lbs. stable brushes, 2½ grs. bead-stones, 4,000 glass beads.[7]

Unlike other European countries, pedlar supply was centralised in London.[8] Although there is no evidence that Codde was such a supplier, the list does imply this might be the case.

We know nothing more about Codde other than that he is labelled in the document as an 'Alien' trader. Traders were either designated as 'Denizen' (native English), 'Hanse' of the Hanseatic League, or 'Alien' – that is, everyone else.

---

[3] See Chapter 6.
[4] Cobb (ed.), *Overseas Trade*, pp. 43–4 and 64.
[5] Cobb (ed.), *Overseas Trade*, pp. 43 and 64.
[6] Cobb (ed.), *Overseas Trade*, pp. xxxix–xl.
[7] Cobb (ed.), *Overseas Trade*, pp. 43–4.
[8] Laurence Fontaine, *History of Pedlars in Europe*, translated by Vikki Whittaker (Cambridge: Polity Press, 1996), p. 87.

These terms were written into the record as there could be different rates of custom/ subsidy payable according to which category the merchant fell into.[9] 'Aliens' and 'Hanse' traders were part of an increasing reliance the British Isles had on the supply of goods from manufactories abroad, paid for by the export efforts of clothiers, tanners, cappers and worsted makers.[10] There was the desire in Europe for raw materials, and it is interesting to note that on four occasions between March and August 1481, the *Trego* exported 1,283 cloths, 5,369 goads Welsh straits, 2,818 lb pewter vessels, and no fewer than 24,534 seasoned and summer rabbit-skins. This trade was seen as beneficial to the country as, according to anonymous author W.S., they 'doe bringe in anie treasure'. In contrast, those who 'but exhause our treasure out of the Realm' were the 'mercers, grocers, vintener, haberdashers, mileyners, and such'[11] – that is, importers and distributors such as Codde. The government made a number of attempts to limit these imports, but this does not seem to have been particularly effective, as can be seen by the list of goods given values for import tax found in the *Rates of Merchandizes* books. These books were valuations of goods rather than an amount to pay in import tax, the tax being decided by parliament. In order to know what to charge, however, the Customs Officials needed to have a value for each item. A written document provided guidance to both official and importer, though it generally favoured the latter, and allowed for changes as times demanded, products or imports being added or deleted from the list as necessary.

Of the 12 books reviewed that were published between 1549 and 1765, jews-harps are given a valuation in every one. Their value remained relatively constant over much of the period from 1583 at 10 shillings per gross, only dropping to 5 shillings between 1608 and 1631:

1549 – Iues trounks the grose iiis iiid
1583 – Jewes trumps the gross x,s
1608 – Iewes the gross, containing twelve dozen} v.s
1624 – Iewes trumpes the gross, containing twelve dozen} v.s
1631 – Iewes trumpes the gross, containing twelve dozen} v.s
1642 – Jewes Trumpes, the groce containing twelve dozen} 00.10.00
1653 – Jews Trumps, the groce containing twelve dozen} 00 10 00
1657 – Jews Trumps, the groce containing twelve dozen} 00 10 00
1669 – Jews Trumps the Groce containing twelve dozen} 00 10 00
1702 – Jews Trumps, the groce, cont. 12 doz -10-
1713 – Jews-Trumps, the gross} 0 10 0
1765 – Jews-Trumps, the Groce, cont. 12 Dozen /-/10/-[12]

---

[9] Helen Bradley, personal correspondence.
[10] W.S., 'A Discourse of the common weal' (1581), quoted in Nancy Cox, *The Complete Tradesman: A Study of Retailing, 1550–1820* (Aldershot and Burlington, VT: Ashgate, 2008), p. 19.
[11] W.S., 'A Discourse', in Cox, *The Complete Tradesman*, p. 19.
[12] Wright, 'Jue harpes, Jue trumpes, 1481', pp. 42–4.

The important point to make is that, while goods appear and disappear from the list over this 200-year period, jews-harps are always included, the implication being that there were sufficient numbers being imported for them to deserve to remain on the list. Given that 864 instruments were imported in 1481, a conservative number likely to have been imported into the country between 1550 and 1750 is nearly 200,000 pieces, though this figure seems very low and could be four or possibly 10 times higher, particularly when the export market to the Americas took off in the eighteenth century. The 1784 *Rates Book* has neither jews-harps nor jews-trumps listed, so presumably they were not imported in large enough numbers and were dropped from the list. This date coincides with the beginning of the development of the major industrialisation of jews-harps centred on the West Midlands of England.

In Scotland *The Rates and valuatioun of merchandizes and goodes Importit within the Kingdome of Scotland* of 1612 has 'Jewes trompes the grose contening xii dozen – iii ii',[13] though they did not necessarily acquire jews-harps from England. 'Hollander' ships were discharging their cargo at Carriden, 18 miles from Edinburgh, including 'little drums for bairns'[14] in 1621. 'Odiham', 'Kransen' and 'Gironville' types are all found in Scotland, the latter also being found in London and the south-east Midlands. The 'Odiham' type can be found from Hampshire to Lincolnshire, while 'Kransen' types are only found in the north-east of England.

Information specifically on Wales and Ireland during this period is scarce, with most *Rates of Merchandizes* books referring to England and Wales. Of the nine finds recorded in Wales, six are of the 'Stafford' type, the implication being that Wales falls into the same distribution system as England. Ireland has more finds, mainly of the 'Gloucester' type of the seventeenth century, but with the occasional earlier find. The one reference to Ireland in the *Rates of Merchandizes* of 1669 explicitly states, 'The same to be paid upon MERCHANDIZES Imposed and Exported into and out of the Kingdom of *Ireland*, according to a Book of Rates hereunto annexed'.[15]

European Manufactories

Where the imported instruments were made in Europe is open to speculation. Boccorio in Italy and Molln in Austria can trace their jews-harp-making history back to the early seventeenth century, though the find evidence from the region indicates that forging rather than casting was the production method. These could account for iron finds in the British Isles, but not the cu-alloy cast types.[16]

---

[13] Andrew Halyburton, *The Book of Customs and Valuation of Merchandises in Scotland 1612*, ed. C. Innes (Edinburgh: Her Majesty's General Register House, 1867), p. 315.
[14] *Glasgow Herald*, 12 October 1895, p. 4.
[15] *SUBSIDY OF POUNDAGE, And Granting A SUBSIDY OF TUNNAGE. And other Sums of Money, UNTO His Royal Majesty, His Heirs and Successors: The same to be paid upon MERCHANDIZES Imposed and Exported into and out of the Kingdom of Ireland, according to a Book of Rates hereunto annexed* (1669).
[16] Kolltveit, *European Archaeology*, p. 79.

Nuremberg is another possibility and Thuringia is thought to have had a jews-harp industry, though no evidence has been forthcoming. An 1884 article on children's toys explains, 'From Marburg, in Hesse, come the musical toys – organs, pianos, dulcimers, Jews' harps, trumpets, flutes, horns, &c'.[17] How far back this goes needs investigation. There may be clues in the designs. Kolltveit suggests a chronology of cu-alloy types 'Greifswald', 'Odiham', 'Njimegen' and 'Stafford', all of which have a distinctive angled inner elbow on the bow. The latter two in particular have very striking similarities in the bow-to-arms ratio, the main difference being the thickness and weight of the frame.[18] The vast majority of the 'Greifswald', 'Odiham' and 'Njimegen' types can be found in Northern Europe and there are definite connections with the Hanseatic League routes. This does not answer where they came from, but it might be a clue as to how they were distributed, while the pocket of finds in southern Sweden might indicate a possible manufacturing site.

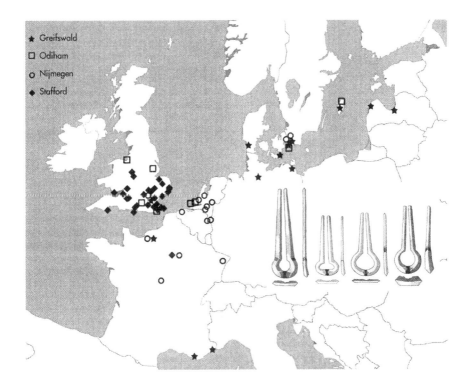

Map 4.3   Cast types found in northern Europe
Source: Drawing by Ann-Turi Ford, by kind permission of Gjermund Kolltveit and Ann-Turi Ford.

---

[17] *Belfast News-Letter*, 30 December 1884, p. 7.
[18] Kolltveit, *European Archaeology*, p. 73.

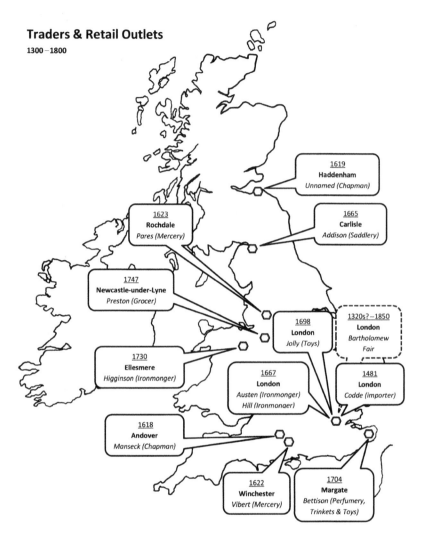

Map 4.4   British and Irish traders up to 1800

Distribution

Once in Britain, the jews-harps had to be distributed. The Westminster Fairs were established in the thirteenth century and attracted numerous French and Flemish merchants,[19] and we have no reason to believe these did not function as

---

[19] Richard H. Britnell, *The Commercialisation of English Society, 1000–1500* (Cambridge: Cambridge University Press, 1996), p. 87, note 52.

distribution centres as well as purchasing points. One of London's most famous of destinations was Bartholomew Fair and we have a number of references in the literature of the seventeenth century that mention an association between jews-harps and the fair, including Ben Jonson's play *Bartholomew Fair*, 'Those six horses, friend, I'll have ... And the three Jew's trumps; and half a dozen o' birds, and that drum';[20] Richard Brathwaite's *Whimzies; or, A New Cast of Characters* with, 'No season through all the yeare accounts hee more subject to abhomination than Bartholemew faire: Their Drums, Hobbihorses, Rattles, Babies, Iewtrumps, nay Pigs';[21] and again in *Ar't Asleepe Husband?* Brathwaite describes someone 'who had a Months minde to see the Booths, Jew-trumps, Hobby-horses, and other trinkets in Bartholemew Faire'.[22]

Relatively few records of local tradesmen survive, but there are nevertheless a few names and the values put on the instrument from the early seventeenth century and late eighteenth century taken from inventories and trade cards:

1618 Thomas Manseck of Andover, Hampshire, Chapman – 3 bone combes ix Jewes harps 00 01 00.

1622 Lambert Vibert of Winchester, Hampshire, mercery – ii doszen of Brasen harpes – iii – 00 03 00. Jewes harpes – viii 00 00 08.

1623 John Pares of Rochdale, Lancs, mercery – Itm three dossen of trumpes all save twoe trumpes 00 00 08.

1665 Robert Addison of Carlisle, Cumberland, saddlery – 2 duz. Jue trumps 00 00 08.

1667 Clement Austen of London, Ironmonger – It 5 dozen of Jews harpes 7.

1667 John Hill of London, Ironmonger – gunlocks harps & Tobacco tongs Lixs viijd 02 19 08.

1698 Alexander Jolly at the Unicorn and Case of Knives in Compton Street, Soho (listed on trade card) – Jews Harps.

1736 Thomas Higginson of Ellesmere, Salop, Ironmonger – jews harps 6d.

1747 Lawrence Preston of Newcastle under Lyme, Staffs, Grocer – Jews Trumps 00 00 06.

1794 Bettison of Margate, Kent, Perfumery Trinkets & Toys (listed on trade card) – Jews Harps.[23]

---

[20] Benjamin Jonson, 'Bartholomew Fair', *The workes of Benjamin Jonson, The second volume* (1614), Act 3 scene 4.

[21] Richard Brathwaite, *Whimzies; or, A new cast of characters. [The epistle dedicatory signed Clitus-Alexandrinus. Followed by] A cater-character, throwne out of a boxe* (London, 1631).

[22] Brathwaite, *Ar't Asleepe Husband?*, p. 121.

[23] Nancy Cox and Karin Dannehi, 'Traded Goods & Commodities 1550–1800', *The Dictionary Project* (University of Wolverhampton), at http://www2.wlv.ac.uk/tradedictionary/ (accessed 15 June 2015): INVEARLY SY1618MNST; INVEARLY SY1622VBRL; INVEARLY NY1623PRSJ; INVMID LY1668ASTC; INVMID

Of particular interest is the difference in price between 'Brasen harpes – iii – 00 03 00 and Jewes harpes – viii 00 00 08' on Lambert Vibert's list. This should not come as a surprise as today there are different qualities of harp with a similar disparity of cost and, as noted, most of the finds from this period are cu-alloy rather than iron – that is, of better quality, which might account for the price difference.

Chapmen, mercers, a saddler, ironmongers and a grocer all appear in the list. Daniel Defoe had no doubt as to the superiority of the English trading system:

> I insist that the trade of England is greater and more considerable than that of any nation for these reasons ... Because England consumes within itself more goods of foreign growth, imported from the several countries where they are produced or wrought, than any other nation in the world ...
>
> ...
>
> [W]e have a very great number of considerable dealers, whom we call tradesmen, who are properly called warehouse-keepers, who supply the merchants with all the several kinds of manufactures, and other goods of the product of England, for exportation, and also others who are called wholesalemen, who buy and take off from the merchants all the foreign goods which they import, these, by their corresponding with a like sort of tradesman in the country, convey and hand forward those goods, and our own also, among those country tradesmen, into every corner of the kingdom, however remote, and by them to the retailers, and by the retailer to the last consumer, which is the last article of all trade.[24]

In Scotland chapmen played a key role in the distribution of goods, 79 being active between the 1590s and 1700, all but one based south of a line from Arbroath to Greenock. There is, however, only one reference to jews-harps from this period – 'patrik thomsoun chapman in hadingtoun ... ss ITem fourtie ellis pearling at ij ss ye ell S*um*ma iiij li. ITem halff ane paipper of huik prennis pryce iij ss iiij d ITem thretteine trumpis pryce yairof ij ss ij d'.[25]

There is a broadside from this early period. 'The Pedler opening of his Packe, To know of Maydes what tis the lack – The second part', c.1620, to the tune 'Last Christmas 'twas my chance', is a list of wares available. The song is 28 verses long, verse 25 being:

NY1665ADDR; INVLATE MY1736HGGT; INVLATE MY1747PRS; London Tradesmen's Cards of the XVIII Century.

[24] Daniel Defoe, *The Complete English Tradesman* ... (London, 1725), Introduction (n.p.).

[25] *1619 Haddington Sheriff Court Book, 4 May 1614–16 Nov 1620* (National Archives of Scotland), SC40/7/14, fols 239v–241r.

Ther's many other things,
as Jewes trumps, pipes & Babies:
St. Martins Beades and Ringes,
and other toyes for Ladyes,
knots and stringes.

As for consumers, there does not appear to be any particular evidence that they occupied urban rather than rural areas. Finds appear in market places, cottages, castles, monasteries, a school, the Thames foreshore – in fact, anywhere there was human habitation.

Part 2: The Industrial Revolution

Developments in manufacturing and markets for goods brought about by the Industrial Revolution had a significant impact on the jews-harp. Centred on the West Midlands, manufactories and small workshops sprang up to satisfy an increasing demand for the instrument. Dublin and Belfast also developed a manufacturing base in the mid–late nineteenth century, particularly as access to world markets meant that specialist makers could invest in new designs and use more sophisticated manufacturing techniques, all intended to satisfy an internal as well as world market. Interestingly, there are relatively few finds recorded from this period. Price lists of one of the early key manufacturers, John Barnsley of Netherton, near Dudley in Worcestershire, show that they were producing seven types and patterns in 1814 for the discerning customer: 'Iron Harps; Tin'd Harps; Brass Harps; New Scotch Pattern; Glasgow Pattern; Aberdeen Pattern and Irish Pattern'.[26] With the exception of the 'New Scotch' and 'Aberdeen Pattern', these were still available in 1822.[27] Identifying these patterns is challenging, though an article from the *Dudley Herald* does provide images of six harps produced by the Barnsley works. By the 1930s, 19 different patterns were being produced by another of the jews-harp-maker families, Troman, some of which are quite exotic and appear to be inspired by ancient lyres. All these types were cast in iron, enabling a variety of shapes, and Troman makes dominated the market in the British Isles up to the 1970s, when the last maker in Birmingham sold the patterns to an American company. Since the 1970s very basic Austrian-made jews-harps have taken over the market and are the only easily purchasable instruments still found in most music shops. With the advent of the internet there has been an explosion of opportunity to purchase jews-harps from all around the world – the exact opposite, in fact, of the situation in the nineteenth century.

---

[26] 1814 price list of John Barnsley.
[27] 1822 price list of several jews-harp makers from Dudley and vicinity.

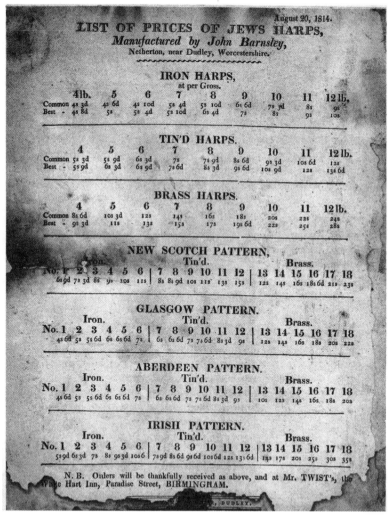

Figure 4.3   John Barnsley price list
Source: By kind permission of David Barnsley.

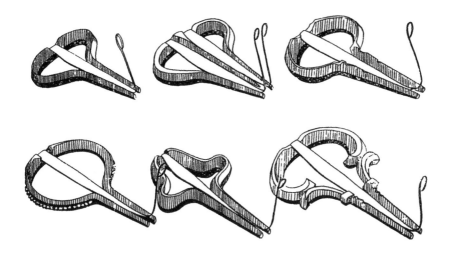

Figure 4.4   Barnsley jews-harps from promotional material
Source: By kind permission of David Barnsley.

Transport Links

The makers Barnsley, Troman and their contemporaries were able to be centred in the West Midlands because of the improvements in transportation brought about by the development of canals and railways. The Barnsleys have a family story about the founder, John Barnsley, carrying a week's production from Netherton to Birmingham, to a 'Mr. Twist's, the White Hart Inn, Paradise Street',[28] from where they were taken by canal to Bristol for export.

Internal distribution was aided by the development of railways. The *Morpeth Herald* and the *Liverpool Mercury* noted that the Railway and Canal Traffic Act of 1888 included the 'unnecessary description of goods, such as Jew' harps, yolk of eggs, railway carriage keys'.[29] The *Dundee Courier* of 1912 encouraged the purchase of *The General Railway Classification of Goods* as '[c]logs, coffin boards, Jews' harps ... – seek what you will, it is set forth within'.[30]

Fairs, Chapmen and Travelling Salesmen

In the early nineteenth century chapmen and fairs still provided points of sale. One Scottish observer in 1851 noted:

---

[28]   1814 price list of John Barnsley.
[29]   *Liverpool Mercury*, 22 June 1889, p. 5.
[30]   *Dundee Courier*, 22 January 1912, p. 4.

There are still those alive in this ancient city who can remember the time when "the Fair o' Dunblane" was a market of no slight importance … Now, although five and twenty years ago … the great centre of attraction for youth of our (then) age was "the Cross". Here were the "sweetie stands", and the "grosart carts", and the "apple carts", and the "gingerbread baskets", and the wonderful "pack" of "John Cheap, the chapman", who could, as we then *imagined*, turn out to view more wonders than all the world beside; he had Jews harps and penny whistles, dancing Toms and four-wheeled horses, pocket knives and peeries – ah! If ever we envied a man in all our lifetime, that man was John Cheap.[31]

The 'Timmer' or timber market was held yearly in Aberdeen at the end of August and was described thus in 1884:

[a] large annual fair, which has of recent years been much distinguished for the abundance of its fruit than for the quality of its "timmer", was held in Castle Street yesterday … In the East end of Castles Street a large proportion of the space was occupied by stands for the sale of all descriptions of toys, including dolls, tin whistles, rattles, Jew's Harps, tin horns, and the innumerable other nick-nacks that excite the juvenile imagination.[32]

Another recollection from the English Midlands in 1895 suggested,

Not so many years ago, the old pedlar's red cart, with its assortment of small wares and shining tin pans, was a familiar spectacle in rural districts, and its coming created considerable excitement in the farmer's household … The small boy of the family, who long had coveted a jew's harp or a pocket comb, produced his hoard of rusty iron and nails, and was made happy by the realisation of his hopes.[33]

At a trial at Birmingham Assizes in 1918 it was mentioned that, '"Hector Rayner Sutherland Leveson-Gower" … formerly travelled about the country selling jews harps'.[34]

Even in the early twentieth century it was noted in the story *The Suspected Boy* that 'a pedlar came by one day and stopped to show his things to the boys, several of whom bought pocket combs, jew's-harps and various trifles of that sort'.[35]

Jews-harps could be used as prizes as well as bought. At a trial in Northampton in 1852,

---

[31] *Stirling Observer*, 31 July 1851, p. 4.
[32] *Aberdeen Journal*, 28 August 1884, p. 2.
[33] *Coventry Evening Telegraph*, 21 November 1895, p. 4.
[34] *Coventry Evening Telegraph*, 20 March 1918, p. 3.
[35] *Bath Chronicle and Weekly Gazette*, 18 October 1930, p. 13.

A stubby little woman with a twist in her eye and a baby in her arms, was charged with having a gambling machine in the *Cheese-fair* ... Within the box were divers sliver pieces of card-board, inscribed with the name of the article to which the lucky prize holder became entitled, such as a "wistle" and a Jew's harp, with the addition of a very questionable illustration drawn with the same free hand.[36]

Newspaper Articles

There are numerous mentions in newspapers of trials of the theft of jews-harps from shop premises. James Wake indicted in 1857 for 'stealing a mop-head, earthenware, and Jew's harps from Mr. Walker, shopkeeper, of Matlock'[37] is typical.

Another reference source is auctions. The *Birmingham Gazette* of 14 August 1826 included an advert by auctioneers Roderick of Temple Street of 'Stock in Trade' that might be of interest to 'Merchants, factors, shopkeepers and others' including 'jews' harps'. Then '50 gross of iron, tinned, and brass Jews' harps' were auctioned on 13 November 1826, '6 gross of 6lb. Jews' Harps' on 6 December 1830, and Knight and Son auctioned 'Jews' harps' as part of the stock of the bankrupt Messrs. Peake and Hall, Liverpool, 16 December 1837. 'Jew's harps' that were part of the cargo raised as salvage from the wreck of the barque *Heroine* were advertised in the *Liverpool Mercury*, 10 June 1853.[38]

One unusual auction advert in the *Sheffield Independent*, 21 May 1867, is addressed to 'Hairdressers, shopkeepers, and others', to sell for the 'Executors of the late Mr. George Taylor ... HAIRDRESSERS' TOOLS, and STOCK-IN-TRADE ... [comprising] Hair and Side Combs, Slates, Sets of Dominoes, Ivory Teething Rings, Whistles, Jews Harps, Rattles, Sealing Wax, and a general assortment of small Articles and Toys suitable for the Trade'.[39]

Adverts placed by music shops appear from the 1870s and the following are typical: W. Longuehaye and Company, Bedford Place, Commercial Road, East London advertised in the *East London Observer*, 24 December 1870, that 'in accordance with Annual Custom at Christmas one portion of the premises has been transformed into an immense FANCY BAZAAR', with 'Musical Instruments, Including Jew's Harps, Trumpets, Trombones'. Heyland's, 23 Bow Street, Sheffield put regular adverts into the *Sheffield Independent* from 1873 to at least 1881 advertising 'MUSICAL INSTRUMENTS of every description, from a penny Jew's harp to a Church Organ, at our Cheerful Friend's'.[40] From 1881 numerous traders used newspaper advertising, including Broadbent's of London Road, Sheffield (1884) and BOGG & SON's (Manchester), 'Jews Harps';[41]

---

36 *Northampton Mercury*, 9 October 1852, p. 3.
37 *Sherborne Mercury*, Dorset, 13 January 1857, p. 2.
38 *Liverpool Mercury*, 10 June 1853, p. 5.
39 *Sheffield Independent*, 21 May 1867, p. 4.
40 *Sheffield Daily Telegraph*, 19 March 1881, p. 6.
41 *Manchester Evening News*, 1 November 1884, p. 4.

MR. EDGAR HORNE'S MUSICAL REPOSITORY, AT DERBY where 'It is evident that this establishment is in a position to supply at a moment's notice any article from a Jew's harp to an Organo Piano';[42] 'GODFREY & CO, HAVING JUST PURCHASED THE WHOLE STOCK ... from MADAME ANDRE, MUSIC SELLER, LITTLEHAMPTON. Who in relinquishing the Business, have decided to offer them at prices so low they MUST be cleared before Christmas – 42 Jew's Harps ... Usual Price. 3d. Our Price. 1d';[43] 'F.R. Dobney, Market Place, Newark – JEWS' HARPS, 1d to 6d.'[44]

The same applied to Scotland: 'At Bird's Music Saloon, 34 Bell Street (Dundee) – Large Arrivals of Melodeons, Mouth Organs, Jews' Harps, Auto-Harps, Brass Whistles, &c.';[45] or in 1904 S. Owens & Sons, Falkirk – 'JEWS' HARPS';[46] Robt. C. Steven, Berwick-on-Tweed, 'JEW's HARPS',[47] and so on.

By the 1930s, when the wireless was making its way into every household, jews-harps were still on the list, as at 'Sherriff's – Gifts – Gramophones ... jew's harps, ocarinas, whistles, tambourines etc.'.[48] Many adverts use the expression 'from a jews-harp to an organ', an indication of the low esteem the instrument continued to have, often with a reference to boys as the focus of the jews-harp market.

Figure 4.5   West Midland jews-harps from the nineteenth and twentieth centuries
Source: Photograph by author, from author's collection.

---

[42]   Derbyshire Times and Chesterfield Herald, 13 March 1887, p. 2.
[43]   Hampshire Telegraph, 24 December 1887, p. 4.
[44]   Newark Directory, 1892, p. 96.
[45]   Dundee Courier, 21 July 1900, p. 1.
[46]   Falkirk Herald, Stirlingshire, 27 February 1904, p. 8.
[47]   Berwickshire News and General Advertiser, 11 October 1904.
[48]   Evening Telegraph, Angus, 16 December 1932, p. 2.

There are not too many adverts from Irish newspapers, though, if the observer from 1897 is correct when he speaks 'from practical knowledge ... that there is scarcely a cabin in Ireland that had not got its musical instrument, violin, flute, jew's-harp, bagpipe, &c',[49] there was certainly a large market. 'THE ESTATE AND INTEREST IN THE LEASES of the HOUSES and PREMISES, 27, 28, 29, 30 NEW ROW WEST, in the City of Dublin', for instance, included '10 Grs Jews Harps'.[50] O'Reily's Manufactory of Wellington Quay, Dublin was selling 'Jews' harps' along with 'Banjos, Guitars, Concertinas, Musical boxes', and so on, under the heading 'CHRISTMAS Presents' in 1883.[51] One of the most interesting adverts is John Haughey's of Lower Bridge Street, Dublin, 'Wholesale Hardware Merchant', in their notice 'to Hardware and Fancy Goods Warehouses: the original Sharkey's Jews' Harps'.[52] Sharkey's was a major jews-harp manufacturer in the latter half of the nineteenth century in both Dublin and Belfast.

Welsh adverts are even rarer. A. Richardson of Central Arcade, Wrexham, advertised 'JEWS HARPS' in 1892[53] and R.J. Heath and Sons of Queen Street, Cardiff advertised 'Jaw harp to Church Organ' in 1909,[54] the only two found so far.

Reminiscences

Recent recollections of where jews-harps could be bought follow a similar pattern. John Wright recalled how, in 1955,

> I was staying with Aunty Doll, in Wellingborough. Used to go there on my bike, stayed the night. In the afternoon I was wandering down just near the station, and there was a kiosk at the side of the road. I was sixteen. They sold all kinds of small instruments, tin whistles, mouth organs and he'd got Jew's harps on a piece of cardboard. I went in and asked the man for one, paid 1s 6d [7½ pence].[55]

Callum Mackay of Stornoway recalled in 2008 that his parents could remember the instruments being available at the saddlers for a penny each. Later, when his first *troub* (jews-harp) broke, he was forced to send away to a joke shop in London for a replacement, until Stornoway's own music shop began to sell the Austrian *maultrommels* in the 1970s.[56] Mrs Mairéad Concannon *née* Flynn, who was born in 1925 and grew up in Clonkeen, Co. Galway, Ireland, thought she might have

---

49   *Morning Post*, London, 7 September 1897, p. 3.
50   *Belfast Morning News*, 11 August 1880, p. 2.
51   *Freeman's Journal*, 18 December 1883, p. 1.
52   *Freeman's Journal*, 11 August 1887, p. 1.
53   *Wrexham Advertiser*, 10 December 1892, p. 2.
54   *Cardiff Directory*, 1909.
55   John Wright interview, 2013.
56   Lucy Wright, *Travels wi' a Trump* (unpublished film for SOAS MA course, 2008).

accessed jews-harps in the local shop or perhaps from the travelling community who went from house to house selling their wares.[57]

Later Developments

By the late twentieth century most music shops throughout Britain and Ireland held jews-harps in stock, though by this time they came from Austria. The popularity of the instrument has dwindled to such a level that up to recent times only basic instruments were available, the market aimed almost exclusively at children. By the early twenty-first century good-quality brass *Dan Moi* from Vietnam began to make an appearance, but it was the internet that made the biggest impact both on the variety of instruments and the quality. High-quality, mass-produced instruments are available from Austria, Hungary, Germany, Sicily, India, Nepal ... the list includes every community that has a tradition of making except Britain. Handcrafted, beautifully made jews-harps at relatively high prices can be found in Norway, France and Sakha-Yakutia. Jews-harps, therefore, are benefiting from new merchandising trends, and importation has again become the main source of supply.

---

[57] Deirdre Ní Chonghaile, personal correspondence.

Chapter 5
Makers

> ... an Englishman has in Troy established a factory of these vibrating instruments; and so brisk has the business been that another factory has been started recently where the common-place Jew's-harps are turned out in hundreds of thousands.[1]

There is a general misconception that jews-harps are simple, basic constructions. Certainly those generally found in music shops are as such, a fact reflected in their cost, but this has not always been so, nor is it entirely true today. A jews-harp is made up of two parts, the frame and the lamella, often referred to as the tongue. The most important parts of the frame are near the tip of the two parallel arms through which the lamella passes to make the sound and the lamella's fixing point at the base of the frame. Other than to hold the instrument to play it, the rest of the frame can be any form, and there have been some quite eccentric shapes, particularly by the nineteenth-century West Midland makers.

The lamella can either be spring steel or a subtly tempered metal strip and filed thinner near the fixing point so that when plucked the part that passes through the parallel frames does so more accurately. The lamella is usually attached by hammering down two flanges, trapping the lamella to the frame. The disadvantage with this system is that once the lamella breaks there is little chance of replacement, which accounts for the finds from sites where the lamella has obviously snapped and the frame thrown away. In more sophisticated harps there is a slot in the base of the frame, the lamella being wedged. The advantage of this system is that the lamellas can be changed if they are broken or are getting out of alignment.

The edges of both the arms and the lamella are also ideally filed either to a sharp edge for a loud percussive sound or are slightly rounded to produce a softer melodic sound. If this sounds complicated, that is because it is. Like any other musical instrument, to make a good one takes skill and knowledge. Instruments readily available today are cheap and, therefore, of a basic construction. Good-quality instruments can be bought, but can cost more than ten times that of a basic type. In this chapter, what will become apparent is that this variety of quality has been part of the production process from the beginning.

The First British Makers

While imports of jews-harp played a significant part in the initial distribution of the instrument throughout Britain, as early as the seventeenth century

---

[1] *Stamford Advocate*, 22 June 1883, p. 1.

manufacturing sites are recorded as being active. It might seem strange to be talking about manufacturing sites rather than local blacksmiths, but, as discussed in the previous chapter, all the evidence points to their production in bulk rather than as one-offs by local craftsmen. A find from Sibertswold in Kent appears to show that an individual blacksmith did attempt to make an instrument, but it is poorly conceived and, as is clear from just the small section remaining, highly unlikely to have achieved a sound.[2] Mícheál Tom Burke Ó Conghaile of Eoghanacht in Ireland speaks of a blacksmith in Mainistir, Árainn, who fashioned silver tongues for jews-harps, probably around the turn of the twentieth century,[3] but this is likely to have been for replacement of broken parts rather than full-blown production.

All the finds we have to date can be identified as either being of a particular type or having characteristics of those types. There is no doubt that a small industry was developed, presumably having been influenced by imports, and it seems possible that the instruments were cast rather than wrought iron. Early finds are copper-alloy, though this changed to cheaper metals when casting techniques and technology were improved by the Industrial Revolution. The advantage of casting is that it allows for multiple pieces of the same style, hence the proliferation of the 'Stafford' type found in England and parts of Wales[4] and the mass production of the nineteenth and early twentieth centuries.

Early Makers

Makers of jews-harps in the seventeenth century are found in both Scotland and England. Piper Haugh in Ayrshire was a village close to Stevenston, sometimes described as temporary and thought, therefore, to have been occupied by itinerant tinkers, though the village appears on maps of the period. There, the 'chief occupation was the making and possibly the playing of trumps or Jew's harps'.[5] A record of 1627 registered the death of one 'Johana Logane, wife of a trump-maker in Stevenston'.[6] Logane is, therefore, the earliest-named maker in the British Isles. Unfortunately there are no archaeological finds relevant to the period, so we have no idea what they were like, how large the facility was or how the workers made the instruments.

---

[2] See Kolltveit, *European Archaeology*, p. 256, cat. no. 181.
[3] Interview by Deirdre Ní Chonghaile, 24 September 2007.
[4] See Chapter 2 for details on types.
[5] William Scott Douglas, *In Ayrshire; A Descriptive Picture of the County of Ayr, with relative Notes on Interesting Local Subjexts, chiefly derived during a recent personal tour* (Kilmarnock: McKie & Drennan, 1874), p. 85.
[6] James Paterson, *History of the Counties of Ayr and Wigton*, vol. V/II (Cunninghame, Edinburgh: J. Stillie, 1863–66), p. 558.

Map 5.1   Location of British and Irish makers

The same applies to Sheffield makers in Yorkshire. According to Harrison, quoted in a Sheffield document dated 1830, at some point after 1600, 'The manufacturers began an ordinary sort of tobacco boxes, and a silly musical instrument called a jew's trump'.[7] Newspaper correspondence in 1874 and 1878

---

[7] *Local Register and Chronological Account of occurrences and facts connected with the town and neighbourhood of Sheffield* (Sheffield, 1830), p. 16.

gives the names of two of these makers. 'The principle manufacturers', according to the *Sheffield Independent*, were 'a family named Taylor, who are called in the parish register and in their wills "trump makers"'.[8] An edition in 1878 gives the name 'Joshua Taylor, born in 1664, died 1698',[9] and a subsequent article suggests:

> it appears as if the frequent mention of trump makers in Sheffield can only be explained by there having been manufacture of various cheap musical instruments, called trump making. Westerby Hatfield … married Hannah Bullas, the rich orphan of a trump maker.[10]

The author labels all musical instrument makers in the area as 'trump maker', and there is an inscription on Taylor's gravestone, 'here lieth the body of Joshua Taylor, the little children's drum maker'.[11]

There was also a seventeenth-century maker working in London. Robert Hewes of St Giles, Cripplegate, is described as both a 'Jews Trumpmaker' and a 'trumpmaker' in records relating to the death in December 1645 of his wife and, we presume, newborn girl child.[12]

The Dominance of the West Midlands

It would appear that by the late seventeenth century jews-harp manufacture had transferred to the West Midlands. Three families seem to have been particularly involved up to the nineteenth century: Sidaway (Siddaway), Barnsley and Troman (Truman).

The Sidaway Family

Originally just one of a number of families identified as West Midland jews-harp makers, a recent discovery has made the contribution of the Sidaway family to the history of the manufacture of the instrument highly significant. A remarkable 'Stafford' find in 2007 from East Yorkshire has the name 'I. SIDAWAY' stamped on the side. We do not know at this time who I. Sidaway was, but five members of the Sidaway family have been identified and we also know of an Ann Siddaway, who, though not a maker herself, married jews-harp maker Samuel Troman on 31 July 1692. The Sidaways were involved in jews-harp manufacture from at least the middle of the eighteenth century, and given the links through marriage with

---

[8] *Sheffield Independent*, 6 July 1874, p. 4.
[9] *Sheffield Independent*, 16 May 1878, p. 8.
[10] *Sheffield Independent*, 5 September 1878, p. 8.
[11] *Sheffield Independent*, 16 May 1878, p. 8.
[12] London Metropolitan Archives, St Giles Cripplegate, Composite register, 1634/5–1646, P69/GIS/A/002/MS06419, Item 003.

the Troman family, and the considerable numbers of 'Stafford' types that are being found, it is possible that the same pattern was shared, though there is no evidence of such a practice at this time.

The implication of this is that, while imports were still being brought into the country in sufficient number to remain on the *Rates of Merchandizes* imports list until the middle of the eighteenth century, a manufacturing industry was growing, particularly in the West Midlands. The Sidaway find, and the number of finds that are clearly 'Stafford' types being recovered in both Britain and North America,[13] shows that the later industrialisation of jews-harps was built upon the foundations of thriving workshops active from at least the early eighteenth and possibly late seventeenth century.

As for the family itself, there is a tantalising reference to a William Siddaway as a jews-harp maker in Rowley Regis in the 1740s who 'bought his iron from the Knight partnership',[14] though, again, there is no more specific information to date. John Sidaway's will is dated 1811 and he is described as a 'Jews harp stock maker', while James Sidaway is mentioned in a pricelist dated 25 July 1822.[15] A William Siddaway is in the 1881 Census as a 'Jew's Harp Maker', though he is likely to have been an employee as there are no records of a business under that name.

Figure 5.1   Sidaway 'Stafford' type
Source: Photograph by kind permission of Ian Chubbock.

---

[13]   The North American finds will be discussed in Chapter 6.
[14]   Marie B. Rowlands, *Masters and Men: In the West Midland Metalware Trades before the Industrial Revolution* (Manchester: Manchester University Press, 1975), p. 145, note 33.
[15]   Frederick Crane, 'Trumps in American Musical Instrument Trade Catalogs', *VIM*, 11, p. 69.

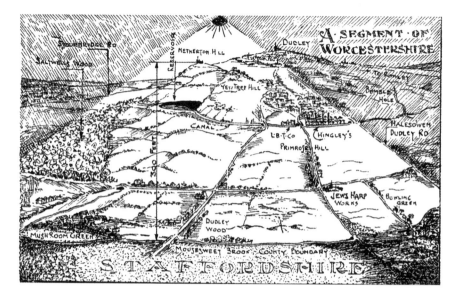

Figure 5.2 Isometric drawing of a segment of Worcestershire indicating the location of the Barnsley jews-harp works
Source: By kind permission of David Barnsley.

The Barnsley Family

The creation of the jews-harp as a mass-produced manufactured item made specifically to exploit a developing world market began with the establishing of a factory in Netherton, near Dudley, by John Barnsley. An undated early-nineteenth-century map of a segment of an unindustrialised Worcestershire clearly shows the location of a jews-harp works between Dudley Wood and Dudley itself. According to the *Birmingham Evening Mail*,

> For many years the Barnsley family had been farmers in the Netherton area, renting their farm from the Earls of Dudley, but they soon realised that local coal and iron ore could be transformed into items then in great demand for trading with the natives in the newly discovered parts of the world ... John Barnsley and Sons Ltd. was in existence as a trading organisation before 1809 – the date on the sole remaining invoice. It was for "Trumps" – Jewes Harpes or Jaws Harps. These were made for sale by the gross to traders from Bristol ...[16]

The *Dudley Herald* article goes into some detail as to working practices:

---

[16] *Birmingham Evening Mail*, 7 September 1970.

The process of manufacture involved the making of wood patterns, moulding in sand, pouring of molten metal into the moulds, filing off burrs, and all for as low a price as three a penny ... Deliveries were carried by the workmen into Birmingham over Black (Bleak) Heath, a walking distance of some ten miles, and yokes were used to support the load. In the early days of the firm the founder himself used to carry the loads on a Saturday to Twist's White Hart Inn, Paradise Street Birmingham, and the workmen awaited his return for their wages ...[17]

Two early price lists show that by 1814 Barnsley's were making seven patterns of jews-harps (iron harps, tin'd harps, brass harps, new Scotch pattern, Glasgow pattern, Aberdeen pattern and Irish pattern). Prices varied from 4 shillings and 3 pence to 35 shillings per gross, prices still only available to the last of the makers, Philip-Crawshaw, in 1974.[18] By 1822, 10 other makers were advertising with John Barnsley, including Benjamin Barnsley, Thomas and Benjamin Lowe, George Smith, James Sidaway, John Wakeman, and David, Nealy, John and Joseph Troman, all located in Upper and Lower Rowley, Dudley Wood and Netherton.

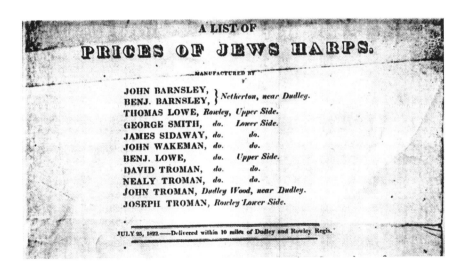

Figure 5.3   Named makers in the Netherton, Rowley Regis area from an 1822 price list (detail)
Source: By kind permission of David Barnsley.

---

[17] *Dudley Herald*, 1 January 1949.
[18] John Wright interview, 2013.

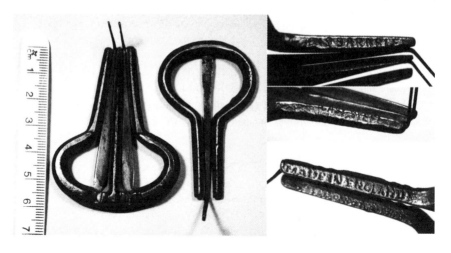

Figure 5.4   Barnsley jews-harps
Source: Photograph by author, with thanks to David Barnsley.

The Barnsley family appear to have had challenging times throughout the period they were involved in the industry. In 1866 Rowland Glegg Barnsley won a Class B medal and certificate at the Dudley and Midland Exhibition, yet by 1869 was filing for bankruptcy, Henry Barnsley having done so a year earlier. Another 'Petitions for liquidation by arrangement notice' for Rowland Glegg Barnsley 'Jew's harp manufacturer' appeared in 1875, though Barnsley still seems to be in business in 1879 and 1881 having transferred to the 'Reliance Works' in Ledsam Street to the west of Birmingham city centre. The year 1888 saw Robert Barnsley, Alfred Barnsley, John W. Barnsley and Ernest Barnsley, trading as John Barnsley and Sons 'engineers, iron founders, pulley-block manufacturers, and Jew's harp manufacturers, Partnership dissolved'. The Barnsleys continued at some level of jews-harp production until the early 1900s.[19]

Families of Makers

There were a number of family businesses and small workshops that appeared throughout the nineteenth and twentieth centuries. Notable are the Jones family, active from the 1830s to the 1890s, and the Watts family, active from the 1890s to the 1930s. In the 1881 census, for instance, 11 members of the Jones family were designated as 'Jew's Harp Maker', ages ranging from 18 to 68. However, the Troman family were the most resilient of the makers, only completely finishing their involvement in the business in the late 1940s.

---

[19] For further information see Michael Wright, 'Trump Manufacture in the West Midlands – Part One: 1800 to 1900', *JIJHS*, 3 (2003), pp. 4–14.

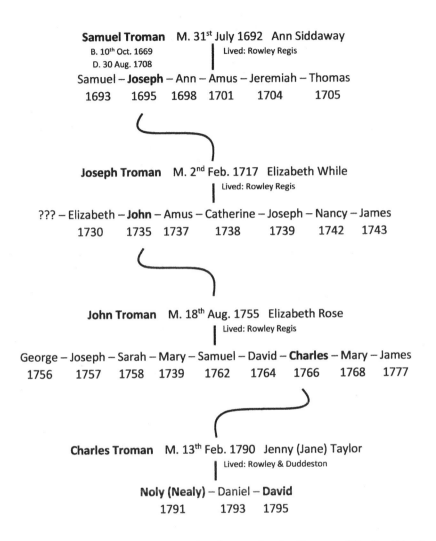

Figure 5.5   Family tree of eighteenth-century Troman makers
Source: Compiled by author, with thanks to Kate Watson.

Figure 5.6 Derek Troman, *c*.1950
Source: By kind permission of Gillian Troman.

The Troman Dynasty

A family tree shows four generations of Troman as jews-harp makers, including Samuel Troman (*c*.1690), Joseph Troman (*c*.1717), John Troman (*c*.1755) and Charles Troman (*c*.1760), all living and working in the Rowley Regis area.[20] While

---
[20] These findings have yet to be verified.

there are at least 24 Tromans named as makers in the nineteenth century and a further ten in the twentieth. As has been noted, the Troman and Sidaway families have been identified as early makers. We are fortunate that Derek Troman, the nephew of the last family maker, David Troman, chose to write his thesis on the family business in 1953 as part of a course he had undertaken in silver-smithing and jewellery at the Birmingham and Midland Institute, now Birmingham Art School.

What is remarkable about the thesis is not just that it gives an insight into the family history, but that Derek Troman's eyewitness drawings provide the only visual representations we have of a typical workshop that could have been around since the Victorian period.

Derek recalls,

> At the end of the eighteenth century, there came, to what we now know as the Black Country, one, Trautmann, a deserter, from the Prussian army. He came from Saxony, where the manufacture of Jew's Harps and harmonicas was in full swing, and settled among the nailers at Rowley. His name became Troman and under the influence of the nailers methods of working, he commenced to make Jews Harps.[21]

Figure 5.7   David Troman's workshop from late 1940s
Source: Drawing by Derek Troman, by kind permission of Gillian Troman.

---

[21]   Derek H. Troman, *Scattia Pensieri: A History of the Jews Harp and its Manufacture* (unpublished thesis, Birmingham and Midland Institute, 1953), n.p.

Figure 5.8   Troman jews-harps
Source: Photograph by author, with thanks to Louise Troman.

Sadly, Derek is no longer alive, left no reference notes, gives no bibliography, and the family have only the vaguest ideas about the business as a whole, which means that, while the Trautmann reference is very interesting, to date no evidence has been found that such a person existed. Even if the dates do not match with the family tree, there may be an element of truth, given that manufacturers are known to have been active in the Saxony region.

By the nineteenth century, however, the Tromans were collaborating with, if not employed by, John Barnsley. In the baptism record of Benjamin Troman's child in the Chapelry of Cradley, Parish of Halesowen in 1812, the father is described as a

'Trump Stock Maker' and later in 1820 as a 'Jews Harp Forger', suggesting that he may have been employed, rather than a maker or manufacturer himself. By 1822 the 'PRICES OF JEWS HARPS' document lists David, Nealy, John and Joseph Troman, implying some degree of independence as makers. It is clear, however, that Tromans were well established in Rowley Regis by 1834, with, according to the 1881 census, 18 members of the family involved with workshops at 32 Hawe Lane, Rowley Regis, 41 Hawkes Street, Aston, 1–6 Court, Birmingham and Long Lane, The Hill, Worcester.

As with the Barnsleys, the Troman family attracted some press interest. The *Northampton Mercury* sent out a warning 'To the Clergy' on 16 May 1825:

> Should John Troman, and Elizabeth Bennett, late of that parish, but now of Hales Owen, apply for that purpose, all Clergymen are desired not to marry them, as he has a Wife living.
>
> The said Troman is about 37 years of age, 5 feet 7½ inches high, or nearly, rather stout made, of a swarthy complexion, has dark brown hair, and profligate appearance; his employment is that of a Jew's-harp Tongue-maker ...
>
> Geo. Thompson, Assistant Overseer of the Poor.[22]

Figure 5.9   Typical workshop in the West Midlands of the nineteenth century
Source: Courtesy of *Black Country Bugle*.

---

[22]   *Northampton Mercury*, 16 May 1825, p. 3.

An action for false imprisonment was made against David Troman in 1871:

> In this action the plaintiff, Thomas Short, jun ... sued the defendant, a jews-harp maker ... for the sum of £10, damages sustained by him through the defendant giving him into custody ... About the 15th of March the plaintiff went to look at some pigeons which the defendant kept.[23]

Troman was found not guilty.

Troman family partnerships were dissolved in 1880 and 1888, and there was a Sales by Auction in 1894, 'of Messrs J and D Troman, trading as T. Troman and Sons, Jews Harp Manufacturers with ... several useful ranges of Shopping and four-roomed Dwelling House at the top of paved yard'.[24]

By the early twentieth century Millicent Troman was heading up the business, altering the methods of production to reflect a changing market. Derek Troman provides an insight into the demise of the industry:

> With the 1914–18 war, came shortages of material; and modern repetitive machinery; but the decline had started. David refused to use machinery, but M. Troman installed many machines. Unfortunately, the machine made Jews Harps, become characterless, toneless toys, and they slowly sank into the category of trash until their death. There are few youngsters who know what a Jews Harp is, and fewer still are the number of adults who can play them.[25]

The quality of jews-harps is commented upon in an article by John Wright. He notes,

> at an earlier period British Jew's harps had been of really excellent quality, however by the 1950s trump-making in England was decidedly on the wane and there was no commercial outlet to revive it.[26]

In 1940 the *Western Daily Press* informs:

> For some 200 years a Birmingham family named Troman has done nothing but make Jew's Harps, and the secret has been passed from father to son in each generation. The present owner of the business is a great-great-grandson of the founder. From a workshop in Curzon Street (Birmingham) 2,000 gross of Jew's harps are turned out every year. Each instrument has to be made by hand, even though some of the smallest of them are sold for as little as a

---

[23] *Birmingham Daily Post*, 13 July 1871, p. 6.
[24] *Birmingham Daily Post*, 4 October 1894, p. 1.
[25] Troman, *Scattia Pensieri*, n.p.
[26] John Wright, 'Jew's Harp: The Classifier's Nightmare – or How I Became Embroiled in All This', *JIJHS*, 5 (2008), p. 14.

penny. Americans seem to buy quite a lot, and the trade is fast developing in South Africa.[27]

The last of the Troman makers had given up by the end of the 1940s and the business was taken over by Sid Philip, creating the company Philip-Crawshaw with his wife. Philip continued until 1975, 'though without tremendous enthusiasm',[28] because of the lack of interest in the instrument other than as a cheap toy.

Two final stories of West Midland makers fall into the category of folklore. According to Phil Drabble, there was 'an old chap called Conquer Pudden, who used to be about the last jews'-harp maker at Dunns Bank',[29] a nickname coming about after an argument with his brother over the fair share of food. Drabble gives no indication of his proper name. Dunns Bank is south-west of Rowley Regis.

Aynock and Ayli (Enoch and Eli) stories figure in a large number of jokes either written or told in the local dialect. In a poem written by J. Westwood it seems that 'Aynock' was a jews-harp maker, as in 'Eynuck bay quite jed', verse 4, lines 5 and 6,

Hast ever sid a jew's harp?
He med um all by Rowley Church.[30]

The Irish Makers

If English manufacturers dominated the market from 1800, they were not the only makers. There is no evidence of Welsh involvement in manufacture, but there was a thriving industry in Ireland from at least the 1830s, one maker transferring to Scotland by the 1880s. *The Dublin Almanac and General Register* of Ireland notes that Patrick Neade was a 'Trump Maker' working at 68 Pill Lane, Dublin, in 1838,[31] moving to 1 Hammond Lane, St Michan's parish by 1841. David Andrews of 2 May Lane, also St Michan's parish, was in their 1841 and 1845 editions as well.[32] An advert, 'ANDREWS, Jew's Harp Manufacturer. Wholesale toy stores supplied. Samples free by post. 41, Matier-street, Belfast',[33] indicates the family were still

---

[27] *Western Daily Press*, Bristol, 1 June 1940, p. 6.
[28] John Wright interview, 2013.
[29] Phil Drabble, *Black Country* (London: Robert Hale Limited, 1952), p. 185.
[30] Roy Palmer, *The Folklore of the Black Country* (Almeley: Logaston Press, 2007), p. 26.
[31] *The Dublin Almanac and General Register of Ireland* (Dublin: Pettigrew and Oulton, 1838), p. 416.
[32] *The Dublin Almanac and General Register of Ireland* (Dublin: Pettigrew and Oulton, 1841), p. 783; *The Dublin Almanac and General Register of Ireland* (Dublin: Pettigrew and Oulton, 1845), pp. 888–9.
[33] *Manchester Courier and Lancashire General Advertiser*, 29 October 1879, p. 2.

involved in the industry in the 1870s, having moved to Belfast. Peter and Joseph Andrews had workshops in 1877 in Dover Street in the area of Shankhill Road to Falls Road, Belfast; Kendal Street in the area Percy Street to Morpeth Street, and Louden Street in the area Dover Street to Boundary Street, also in Belfast.

The Census of Ireland for the Year 1851, General Report states that there were six makers in Dublin, five in Belfast, one in Cork and another in Donegal, though it gives no names or addresses.[34] The same applies to the 1861 *Report* that gives two makers in Dublin, three in Belfast, two in Cork, one in Limerick and another in Tipperary. All are given as aged 15 or above except for the single maker from Donegal.

The Sharkey Family

A major producer, was the Sharkey family. Patrick Sharkey first appears in the 1868 *Belfast, Ulster Street Directory*, with an address in John Street, in the area Donegal Street to North Street, Belfast. Sharkey also had a workshop in Dublin, as the stamps used for indicating the quantities boxed for delivery reveal. Clearly stating, 'JEWS HARPS, 2 Doz. No., BELFAST' and 'JEWS HARPS, 2 Doz. No., DUBLIN', these are believed to date from the 1870s. The family also have a portable stationery box and a very fine, though broken, Sharkey-identified jews-harp.[35]

Figure 5.10   Left: Sharkey dispatch stamps and jews-harp. Right: 'Sharkey' and 'Belfast' stamped on arms of jews-harp
Source: Photograph by author, with thanks to Paul Sharkey.

---

[34] *The Census of Ireland for the Year 1851, part VI, General Report*, p. 415. At http://www.histpop.org/ohpr/servlet/AssociatedPageBrowser?path=Browse&active=yes&mno=40 9&tocstate=expandnew&display=sections&display=tables&display=pagetitles&pageseq=1 &assoctitle=Census%20of%20Ireland,%201851&assocpagelabel= (accessed 10 June 2015).

[35] Paul Sharkey, personal correspondence.

Figure 5.11   James Sharkey in 1892, aged 21
Source: Photograph by kind permission of Paul Sharkey.

The *Freeman's Journal* had a notice in 1887, 'to Hardware and Fancy Goods Warehouses; the original Sharkey Jews' Harps to be had from John Haughey, Wholesale Hardware Merchant, 8 Lower Bridge street, Dublin',[36] though according to the 1881 census, Patrick and his brother, James, had at least partially moved the business to 11 Caithness Street, Glasgow. By 1891 they had been joined by the son of James, also James, their premises including 229 South Speirs Wharf, St George in the Fields. By 1901 James the elder is described as a 'Master' and his son a 'Maker' and their address is given as 15 Rodney Street, St George in the Fields. In 1955 a decedent was shown an old wooden box, containing a jews-harp and several moulding jigs and parts for making them. The harp exists, but the moulding jigs are lost.[37]

There is one coincidental reference to a James Sharkey, a soldier, charged with stealing 50 cigars at the Aldershot Petty Sessions, 1882. His accomplice is said to have had two 'jews harps' in his pocket. Both were found guilty,[38] and it is unlikely that there is any connection with the family.

Emigrants to America

An unnamed maker from Ireland gave an enlightening interview to the *New York Mail and Express*, reprinted in the *Bismarck Daily Tribune* in 1886, as 'THE JEWSHARP – A FEW FACTS OF INTEREST TO THE AVERAGE SMALL BOY, – A Man Who Works Extensively at the Manufacture of the Youngster's Delight – How Really Fine Instruments Are Made'.[39] Extracts from the article include price and quality, tone and volume, along with insights into the interviewee's working practices. He was, he said,

> engaged in the business for over forty years, thirty-five of which I have spent in this country. My father and brother were in the business before me, and are now at work at the old trade in Belfast, Ireland …

> I suppose I could finish on an average six or eight first-class instruments in a day, and perhaps twice or three times as many of the less expensive ones. The lowest price which I charge for a harp is 15 cents and the highest $2. The latter are made with German silver frames, and the tongue is of finer steel. The frame, however, does not have anything to do with the musical tone of the instrument, and it is usually made of iron, which is afterward "tinned". I have all my frames cast and "tinned" at a foundry and then finish them up here.

---

[36] *Freeman's Journal*, 11 August 1887, p. 1.
[37] Dave Miller, personal correspondence.
[38] *Aldershot Military Gazette*, 4 November 1882, p. 5.
[39] *Bismarck Daily Tribune*, 10 June 1886, p. 4.

Most of the harps are made for out-of-town trade, and a large number are sent west every year. For the last two years business has been very dull, and it seems as if jewsharp playing was waning in popularity. In Ireland and Scotland the instrument is very popular, especially among the Scotch, who take about two-thirds of all the jewsharps made in Belfast.

Naming the maker is problematic as there are not many named makers from Ireland working in America who fit the description of the interviewee. The Sharkeys have no family history of makers other than Dublin, Belfast and Glasgow; David Andrews is a candidate, given the date of around 1850 when we know Andrews was active, and there are the five unnamed makers from the 1851 register. Other makers in New York were English. Thomas P. Pascall was a native of England, though there are no records of him as a maker before setting up in New York City. A John Smith is noted in the 1881 census as living at 35 Bowling Green, Dudley, Worcestershire as a 'Jews Harp Maker'. He emigrated to America by 1882, setting up a 'manufactory of jews-harps in Troy', New York State, where 'the process of manufacture comprises of no fewer than thirty separate operations'.[40] The *Stamford Advocate* noted,

> an Englishman has in Troy established a factory of these vibrating instruments; and so brisk has the business been that another factory has been started recently where the common-place Jew's-harps are turned out in hundreds of thousands.[41]

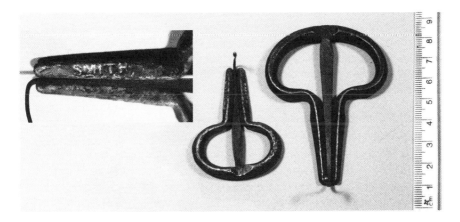

Figure 5.12   Smith harps
Source: Photograph by author from the John Wright collection, with thanks to Catherine Wright-Perrier.

---

[40] *Manchester Evening News*, 13 October 1882, p. 2.
[41] *Stamford Advocate*, 22 June 1883, p. 1.

His sons William and John continued the business, the family having a high reputation for making very fine instruments, and though no longer produced, they are much sought after even today.

What About the Workers?

There are a number of references to employees at the various works. Thomas Hopewell was a 'jews harp maker for Benjamin Tromans'[42] in 1843, and John Brookes in 1850. George Shaw worked for Nealy Troman in 1845, Edward Jackson for William Troman in 1846. The 1881 Census shows 20 persons described as 'Jews Harp Maker', mainly males living in and around Birmingham, where the Barnsley and Troman works had transferred to from the Dudley/Rowley Regis area. Ages range between 13 and 66 years old, nearly half being in their 20s and 30s. William Cox was registered as a 'Jews Harp Filer' and with Josh Sweetland was 14 years of age. Three of those listed are female: Blanche Hammond and Mary A. Moore, also both aged 14, and Charlotte Troman, aged 35, all living in Birmingham. The 1891 census gives Elizabeth Wootton, aged 16, and Norah E. Fothergill, aged 21, as an 'Employed Jews Harp Maker', along with Alfred Bellamy and Ebenezer Ingley. George Stokes is registered as 'Jews Harp Maker' living in Stourbridge, some 14 miles west of Birmingham and could have been an outworker.

Inquests and trials provide more names of makers. Edwin Jones, aged 18, was accused of assault in 1881.[43] William Hodgson, 'jew's-harp maker' aged 13, was convicted of stealing coal in 1889.[44] At the inquest of Samuel Perry aged 54, of 22, Coplow Street, Birmingham, a 'journeyman Jews' harp maker'[45] in November 1895, it was said he had 'used to complain bitterly of being short of work',[46] though his death was deemed accidental when he fell off a roof.

As elsewhere in Britain, working relations had its problems and disputes broke out between owners and workers, as the *Birmingham Gazette* reported in 1824:

> *Importance of Jews Harps* – Amongst the *turn outs* of workmen which have recently taken place, is one of the *journeymen Jews harp makers*, at Wolverhampton, who put forth a long statement of the grievances for which they now seek redress. One of those was stated to be the manufacturing of the tongues of these delectable instruments, out of steel-wire instead of hammered steel, "to the injury of the workmen, and the great detriment of the public".[47]

---

[42] St Giles Church Records.
[43] *Worcestershire Chronicle*, 8 January 1881, p. 6.
[44] *Birmingham Daily Post*, 15 March 1889, p. 3.
[45] *Birmingham Daily Post*, 27 November 1895, p. 7.
[46] *Daily Gazette for Middleborough*, 2 December 1895, p. 4.
[47] *Birmingham Gazette*, 2 December 1824, p. 2.

Unfortunately, there is no further information, but this is a fascinating reference as it tells us something of the value both owners and workers put on the instruments they were producing. The paper, you will note, cannot resist a slightly negative side-swipe with 'these delectable instruments'.

Later in 1895 at the annual dinner of the Musical Instruments Trades Protection Association, 'it was stated that even the makers of penny whistles and jews'-harps have gone in for "strikes"'.[48] Again, there is little evidence of the circumstances at this time.

The Process

Derek Troman's account of the work process in his dissertation, combined with John Wright's visits to Sid Philip's workspace in the late 1960s, provide the only detailed explanation of a manufacturing business with a history of at least two hundred years. In this section, Troman's description, from his unpaged dissertation *Scattia Pensieri*, will be followed by additional information from Wright, as noted during my interview with him in Angers, on 20 July 2013.

Casting the Frame

> Casting was originally done in the workshops, but eventually it was found to be cheaper to have castings done by some outside firm, who specialised in it. When done on the premises, the frame castings were placed in pots with Hæmatite ore, and fired for three weeks, to make them malleable, this entailed rising at 4 a.m. to light, or make up the fires. Often they worked till very late at night. When the castings were cold they were put in revolving barrels, known as shaking barrels, with leather scrap and oil. The leather scrap came from Walsall, and was called Mosings – pronounced mousings. (Troman)

> What he [Philip] showed me were the original patterns cast in brass. Half the patterns were cast into sheets of what looked like Mazak, and these were then pressed into a sand mould. You'd repeat the imprints into two half-moulds. Then bring the two together, and run the molten metal in … He had problems with frames. He had big problems getting true castings without bubbles. [To remove the "flash"] they "barrelled" them. In fact it was an oblong box lined with steel sheeting with an electric motor to turn it. They opened the boxes up and put wood-shavings in. They put these castings in and then turned the lot for a few hours. It took the flash off from the castings and smoothed them. (Wright)

Castings were also finished off by outworkers:

---

[48] *Yorkshire Evening Post*, 17 January 1894, p. 3.

old Bill Troman of Club buildings, Rowley, with hands so large that he was paid in crowns, [would] tramp into Birmingham, twice a week, to deliver his out work, of filed up castings, to Gt. Brook St. (Troman)

Various methods were used to make the frames more marketable, sometimes to the detriment of its usefulness as a musical instrument:

> Many types were decorated with file cuts on the faces, electro plating was also popular in gold, copper, tin and brass, although for many years, a tinning pot and brass dip was kept at Gt. Brook St. The most common finish was blueing and varnishing, the Harps being on a hot-plate, thus acquiring their blue colour. (Troman)

> [S]ome of the frames ... were nickel-plated – some of the older ones. The chromium plating was awful, especially as they plated the whole finished harp with the tongue already fitted which deadened the sound. (Wright)

Making the Tongues/Lamellas

> The tongues were cut on a press, to a long, tapering shape, the size being depend[ent] upon the size of the Jews Harp frame ... The tongues were hammered at their wider end, to give them a certain amount of soring, or width of spring.

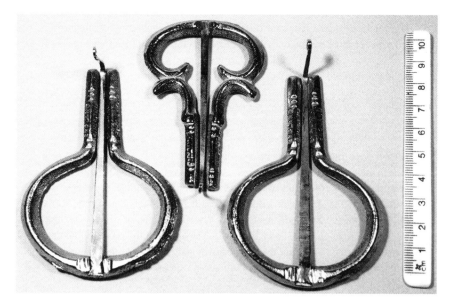

Figure 5.13 Nickel-plated jews-harps from the last period of makers in the British Isles
Source: Photograph by author, from author's collection.

Making use of materials at hand, bundles of tongues were put into the heating furnace, the bundles being made from a number of tongues placed in a Harp frame and tempered blue. After tempering came pickling in acid to remove the scales. The two components, frame and tongue, were now ready for assembly.

For the better quality Harps the tongues, were filed to a feather-edge at a bench on a peg, similar to a jewellers peg. In fact it was an Elm block about 6 inches long and two inches deep, with a file cut, down the centre and screwed to a bench. (Troman)

Figure 5.14   Sid Philip, the last British maker, working on a lamella (tongue) at his workshop in his house, c.1968
Source: Photograph by John Wright, by kind permission of Catherine Wright-Perrier.

[Sid Philip's] wife described tempering the tongues. She said you just used to leave them in the coal fire, and they watched the colours change – straw colour, basically. It went up the strip, travelled up the strip. (Wright)

Fixing the Tongue/Lamella

The stool on which an assembler sat, also bore a resemblance to a silversmith's stool, as did the tree-trunk, with slightly domed stake, set in a hole in the top.

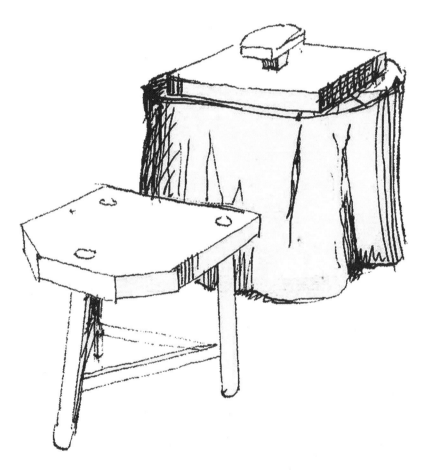

Figure 5.15   Stump, stool and stake
Source: Drawing by Derek Troman. By kind permission of Gillian Troman.

This was surrounded by a flat steel on the tree-trunk top. This steel became indented on each side of the head, in time, as the setter dropped his hammer, first in one side, then the other. The tongue was first hammered on the wide end to give it a "u" section, and this was dropped into the undercut slot, in the casting, with the apex of the "u" uppermost. When given a sharp blow with the hammer, the edges of the tongue were forced into the undercuts, and welded in. Thus the tongue was attached to the frame. But one must remember that the two ends of the frame were still quite a distance from the tongue, and had to be hammered up to the tongue. These two processes of welding and hammering up, were known as "knocking-in" and "knocking-up". The turning up of the tongue and the finishing, were the last things to be done. (Troman)

Equipment

It is interesting to note, that the press upon which (the tongues) were cut, in David Troman's workshop, was probably the original one from Rowley; for the thread of the shaft was brazed on wire, showing that it was made before the lathe came to the Midlands. It is more than likely that the frame of the press was made in the anchor forges of Cradley or Rowley. (Troman)

[Philip] had two steel blocks he used as anvils; by his wall in the living room he had a bench, quite high, and on that bench he had two steel blocks ... He had two, and the essential thing about those steel blocks is that they should not ring – don't ring like an anvil – "Donk". And he had two. One was better than the other. One was nineteenth century and had no ring to it at all, the other was later and had a slight ring to it, but he didn't like that one. But I've seen blocks like that in Austria let vertically into a tree trunk. You get the same thing, no ring. Don't ask me why they want that, but the main thing was to fix the tongues; to fix the *spring*, as he called it. He had a very narrow hammer he used, just the width of the base of the tongue ... (Wright)

Quality Control

According to Harold Parsons,

Rowley itself used to be prominent in the production of jew's harps, but the world monopoly of this musical instrument has now passed to Aston, Birmingham, where it is claimed that each one made has to stand up to a rendering on it of "The Blue Danube" before being passed as fit for sale.[49]

One final feature on all West Midland products was a notching system to identify the maker. These were discovered by Frederick Crane:

---

[49] Harold Parsons, *The Black Country* (London: Robert Hale Limited, 1997), p. 24.

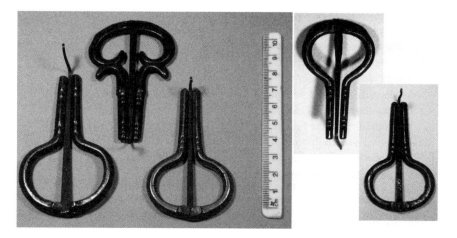

Figure 5.16   Notching on jews-harps indicating makers
Source: Photograph by author, from author's collection.

The grooves appear in one or two clusters, one of these located on the arms not far from the point where they leave the bow, the other (if any) located farther down the arms. For a shorthand, I indicate the cluster pattern with the number of grooves in the first cluster, followed by a slash and the number of grooves in the second cluster; e.g. 3/2.[50]

The sequences noted are: 1/0; 2/0; 2/2; 2/3; 3/0; 3/2; 3/3; 4/3. Three have been identified: 3/2 and 3/0 are Troman, presumably from different workshops; 3/3 are Barnsley.

The End of Manufacture

By the mid-1970s the company Philip-Crawshaw was the last of the British makers still active, though having problems not only with getting a decent price for the harps, but also in the manufacturing process:

> He had problems with frames. He had big problems getting true castings. The last time I saw him his project was to get them cast in India, and that never came to anything. The problem was castings without bubbles.[51]

---

[50] Frederick Crane, 'Catalog of the F. Crane Trump Collection, Part 1 – England', *JIJHS*, 2 (2004), p. 63.
[51] John Wright interview, 2013.

In 1975 Grossman of Cleveland, Ohio, bought the assets of the company. Unfortunately, there is no record in their archive of the sale and, though they sold 'England'-marked jews-harps in 1977 and there are adverts showing Birmingham-style instruments in 1982, cheaper Austrian imports became the standard type and are still in their catalogue at the time of writing.

All told, 169 individuals and partnerships working in England, Ireland and Scotland have been identified as jews-harp makers, dating from 1627 to 1975. Today there is one maker, Jonny Cope, who is working on the Norwegian wrought-iron style of instrument, and there may be others, but, as noted at the beginning of this chapter, the market relies on imports. The internet has enabled players to acquire excellent instruments and music shop traders to continue with the supply of the basic Austrian types. There are also opportunities to collect the vast numbers of different shapes and types that can be found from all over the world – though whether from Britain, will be up to another generation. As Derek Troman ends his thesis, 'with my father and uncle, sons of David Troman, will go the secrets of a forgotten craft'.

Chapter 6
Exports

... for we do not massacre, we are such good Christians as only to cheat ...
Horace Walpole, 1755[1]

While the Scots and Irish have taken to the jews-harp as a musical instrument, incorporating it into their musical culture, the English have not. In England, foreign players were and are welcomed with enthusiasm, but the English on the whole have not proved keen. This did not, however, stop the English in particular from exploiting the instrument's potential as an exportable good, an opportunity that drove the development of businesses and manufactories whose main target were foreign markets, focusing on North America, Australia, New Zealand and South Africa.

Colonial Expansion and Market Exploitation[2]

Up to the end of the eighteenth century, European imports were the main source of supply for traders, while the Americas were the main customers for exports. Jews-harps were cheap, easy to transport, novel and, crucially, unknown in any part of the American Continents. The Spanish introduced *trombes* to South America in the sixteenth century and they were taken up by various indigenous people, such as the Mapuche of Argentina. The English, however, focused their efforts on North America, particularly on the fur trade, where jews-harps were one of many different goods used for barter. It would appear, however, that generally jews-harps were a popular item in the United States well into the 1930s.

As with many aspects of the history of jews-harps, their importance as barter goods should not be overstated. They had a value, but a small one. Sir Walter Raleigh in his voyage to Guyana in 1595 suggested, 'Wee should send them Iewes harpes: for they would giue for euery one two Hennes',[3] while the Earl of Dudley wrote:

> yet if they would bring him hatchets, kniues, and Iewes harps, he bid then assure me, he had a Mine of gold, and could refine it, & would trade with me: for

---

[1] Peter C. Mancall, *Deadly Medicine: Indians and Alcohol in Early America* (Ithaca, NY and London: Cornell University Press, 1996), p. 39.
[2] For an extensive description, see Wright, 'The Jews Harp Trade in Colonial America', *The Galpin Society Journal*, LXIV (March 2011), pp. 209–18.
[3] Richard Hakluyt, *Voyages and Discoveries: Principal Navigations, Voyages, Traffiques and Discoveries of the English Nation, vol. III* (New York: American Geographical Society, 1928), p. 665.

token whereof, he sent me 3. or 4. Croissants or halfe moones of gold weighing a noble a piece or more, and two bracelets of silver. Also told there of another rich nation, that sprinckled their bodies with the pouder of golde, and seemed to be guilt, and furre beyond them a great towns calld El Dorardo, with many other things.[4]

The Fur Trade

Gold may have been the primary interest of these early adventurers, but by the eighteenth century the fur trade attracted a more pragmatic approach to trade. According to Axtell, 'The Indians of the Eastern Woodlands [experienced] a consumer revolution every bit as revolutionary as that experienced by their European suppliers',[5] resulting in a burgeoning distribution network that was started by the French and exploited by the early New England colonials:

> [At] the heart of the stem lay the idea, deeply embedded in English imperial thought since Elizabethan period, that the purpose of colonies was to produce goods valued in the empire ... Hundreds, perhaps thousands of colonists became involved in the distribution of goods throughout the empire, from the palisades and finely stuccoed homes of the gentry to the longhouses and winter camps of the Indians who traded furs and skins.[6]

Colonists were keen to exploit the locals, as observed by Horace Walpole in a letter to Richard Bentley:

> At present my chief study is West Indian History. You would not think me very ill-natured if you knew all I feel at the cruelty and villainy of European settlers: but this very morning I found that part of the purchase of Maryland from the savage proprietors (for we do not massacre, we are such good Christians as only to cheat) was a quantity of vermillion and a parcel of Jew's Harps.[7]

The same was true of Virginian trader Captain Fleet,

> [He] was accustomed to trade with the savages living on the Potomac River before the arrival of the Maryland colonists at St. Mary's ... and in the new colony, he continued to be interested in the fur trade. We find him embarking on a trading expedition in "the good vessel called the Deborah" [taking with him] six dozen and two of trucking axes, two dozen and two of howes,

---

[4] Hakluyt, *Voyages*, p. 108.
[5] James Axtell, *Beyond 1492: Encounters in Colonial North America* (Oxford and New York: Oxford University Press, 1992), p. 129.
[6] Mancall, *Deadly Medicine*, p. 39.
[7] Brian L. Mihura, 'The Jew's Harp in Colonial America', *VIM*, 1 (1982), p. 63.

nineteen yards of Dutch cloth ... sixteen pairs of Irish stockings, one chest containing some beads, knives, combes, fish hooks, jews-harps, and looking glasses ...[8]

According to Kevin McBride of the Mashantucket Pequot Museum and Research Center, we can be reasonably certain that English and Dutch traders responded fairly quickly to native demand and desires for certain trade items, and if native people didn't want jews-harps, they would not have been carried.[9]

Sir William Johnson, Superintendent of Indian Affairs, was at the forefront of this trade and recorded that six jews-harps could be exchanged for 'a large Racoon' skin. To put this in context the same list shows that two large racoons could be traded for 1¼ lb of black or white Wampam, or 'Wire by the fathom if thick, while a small racoon bought Small knives for Women',[10] or flints. Johnson's lists of Indian goods included 'Jews Harps small & large'[11] and '20 Groce of the Smallest brass Jews Harps', which are given a value of 10s.[12]

Generally there has been very little research into the jews-harp in the United States, though those archaeological finds available for scrutiny indicate that supplies were coming from Europe. There are a few types that might have been made locally, but the vast majority can be identified as European in origin, with 'Gloucester', 'Rochester', 'Bruck', 'Ekeberg' and 'Stafford' types all identified. The Sidaway 'Stafford' type is particularly interesting as of the finds identified to date 83 are 'Stafford', 70 alone being found at Fort Michilimackinac, situated on the Straits of Mackinac between Lake Huron and Lake Michigan. In addition there are 19 iron and seven brass jews-harps found during historical excavations at Louisburg and some 200 finds from a Seneca Indian site near Rochester, five of which are displayed in the local museum and are variations on the 'Stafford' type. If the other pieces are of the same type, that would make this collection the largest found to date.

Fort Michilimackinac was part of the French trading post system, serving as a supply depot for traders in the western Great Lakes. Relinquished by the French to the British in 1761, it was abandoned in 1780 in favour of Fort Mackinac, situated on the more defensible Mackinac Island. The 135 finds were discovered in what is considered to be part of the French period of the fort. If this is so, given that the vast majority of 'Stafford' types are, as established, of English manufacture, the question is, where were they getting them from?

---

[8] Raphael Semmes, *Captains and Mariners of Early Maryland* (Baltimore, MD: The John Hopkins Press, 1937), p. 65.
[9] Kevin McBride, personal correspondence.
[10] Alexander C. Flick (ed.), *The Papers of Sir William Johnson, vol. VII* (Albany, NY: The University of the State of New York, 1931), pp. 894–5.
[11] James Sullivan (ed.), *The Papers of Sir William Johnson, vol. III* (Albany, NY: The University of the State of New York, 1921), p. 334.
[12] Flick (ed.), *Papers*, pp. 780 and 782.

Map 6.1 Seventeenth- and eighteenth-century North American find locations

While Montreal appears to be a major distribution point, were jews-harps imported directly from Britain, or through a trading channel in New England, such as the Albany traders in New York State, a major trading centre for New England merchants? Trade with the Native Americans was taken seriously, as this piece in the *Pennsylvania Packet*, 10 March 1781, shows:

Intelligence Extraordinary

Great complaints having been made of the bad quality of the sixty thousand pounds worth of Jews harps and razors, sent out last year by Mr. contractor Knox for our Indian allies in North America! The lords of the treasury, that they may not be again deceived, it is said, have been pleased to appoint (with a salary of 200l. a year) doctor Duncan Moffat, one of the American refugees, to be essay-master of all the Jews-harps, fifes, bagpipes, and other instruments of wind music, that may in future be sent out; and that he, the said doctor, or essay-master, shall personally make trial of every such Jews harp, &c. and see that it accords and sounds well to the tune of Yankee Doodle, before it be shipped to our great and good allies, the brave savages in the western world![13]

Dr Moffat had recently qualified from St Andrew's University. The most startling statistic is that of £60,000 for jews-harps and razors, which, even if we say nominally that jews-harps only made up 1 per cent, is a considerable number of jews-harps at 10 shillings for 20 gross – £600 buying nigh on 3.5 million items. How Dr Moffat coped with testing so many can only be guessed at, but it does imply that playing a tune like 'Yankee Doodle' was both achievable and desirable.

It is difficult to assess what value the Native Americans put on such items as jews-harps, but once acquired it appears that the instruments were popular, as a description taken from Lewis and Clark expedition of 1804–1805 indicates:

> They [Yankton Sioux] put all the presents that they got together, and divided them among their whole party equally. The Indians after the goods were divided, was very merry; they play'd on the Jews harps & danced for us for beads that we gave them.[14]

Traders in New England

Trader goods appear to have been imported into America and distributed through general merchandise stores and ironmongers established in the developing New England Colonies. In all 166 traders can be traced as advertising in 41 newspapers or supplements from 1733 to 1783 alone. The number of traders advertising jews-harps during this period went from five in the 1730s, centring mainly on Philadelphia, to 17 in the 1740s, again mainly in Philadelphia but also spreading north to Massachusetts. There were 54 in the 1750s centred on Philadelphia and Boston, with a growing trade in New York and reaching north to Portsmouth, New Hampshire; 78 in the 1760s, when New York almost equals Philadelphia with 19 traders to their 21 and the spread is from Portsmouth in the north to Savannah in Georgia in the south; dropping to 47 in the 1770s to early 1780s, when there were more pressing issues than the sale of jews-harps.[15]

Until the mid-1760s all the sales are variously described as 'Jews harps', with or without capitals and sometimes hyphenated: iron and brass 'jews harps'; brass and iron 'Jews harps'; brass, iron, and 'tin'd Jews harps', and 'a neat assortment of black and white stony batter Jews harps'. Why 'stony batter' is not clear and while there is a Stoneybatter district of Dublin, Ireland, as yet there is no evidence of jews-harp making in Ireland until the 1830s.

[13] *Pennsylvania Packet*, 10 March 1781, p. 4.
[14] Joseph Whitehouse, *Lewis–Clark Expedition, 1804*, at www.lewis-clark.org (accessed 15 June 2015).
[15] See Wright, 'The Jews Harp Trade in Colonial America', pp. 214–16.

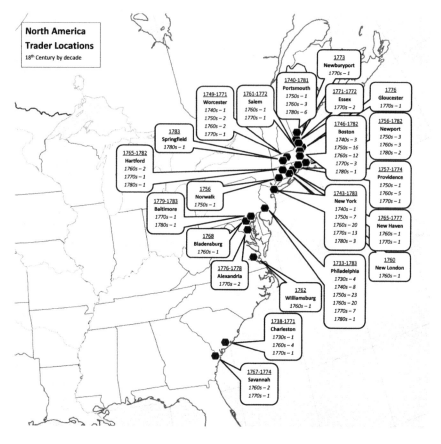

Map 6.2   Eighteenth-century North American trader locations

The use of the name 'jaws harps' in adverts appears to have only been fashionable during this period for a short time between May 1765 and October 1768, when it was used by five traders: Peter Remsen selling 'Jaws-harps' (1765);[16] Moses Judah, 'jawharps' (1765);[17] Peter Goelet (1765–67), 'brass and iron Jaw harps';[18] Abeel and Byvanck, 'brass and iron jaw harps' (1766);[19] and Peter T. Curtenius, 'brass and iron jaw harps' (1767).[20] Even then they all used the name 'jews-harp' in other adverts, in some cases on the same day in different publications. Employing the term 'Jaws harp' in this context is the first use of such a name intended for a mass clientele.

[16] *New York Gazette*, 6 May 1765, p. 3.
[17] *New York Gazette*, 3 June 1765, p. 1.
[18] *New York Gazette*, 17 September 1765, p. 3.
[19] *New York Mercury*, 17 February 1766, p. 3.
[20] *New York Gazette*, 18 May 1767, p. 1.

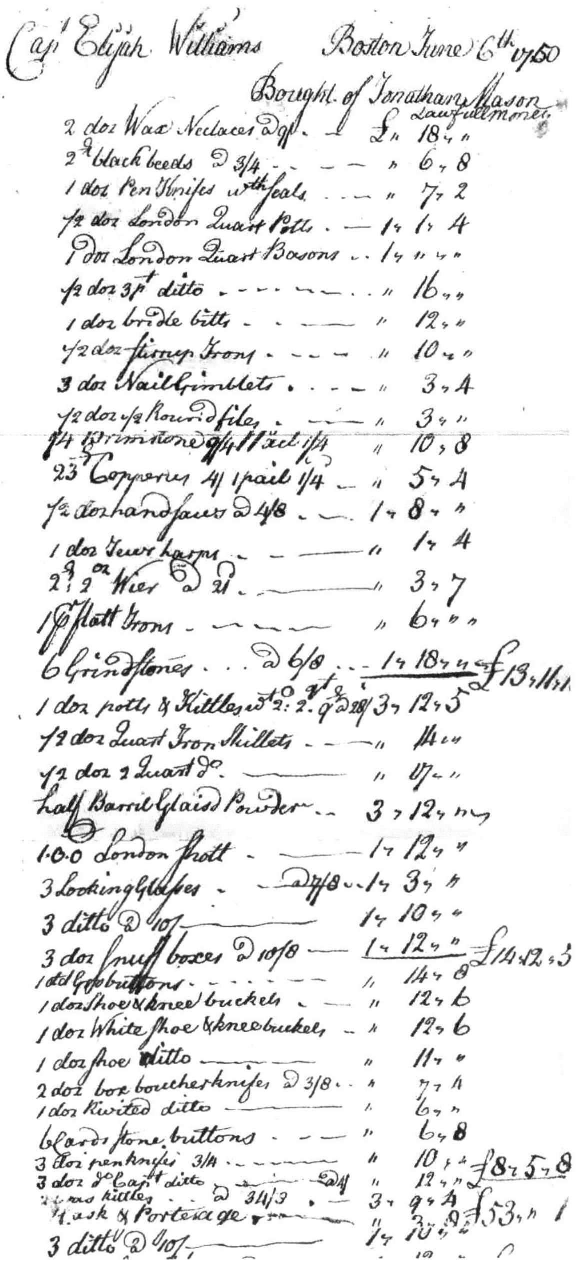

Capt Elijah Williams Boston June 6th 1750
Bought of Jonathan Mason
Lawfull money

2 doz Wax Neclaces @ 9/	£ ,, 18 ,, ,,	
2 q black beeds @ 3/4	,, 6 ,, 8	
1 doz Pen Knifes with seals	,, 7 ,, 2	
½ doz London Quart Potts	1 ,, 1 ,, 4	
1 doz London Quart Basons	1 ,, ,, ,, ,,	
½ doz 3 pt ditto	,, 16 ,, ,,	
1 doz bridle bitts	,, 12 ,, ,,	
½ doz stirrup Irons	,, 10 ,, ,,	
3 doz Nail Gimblets	,, 3 ,, 4	
½ doz ½ Round files	,, 3 ,, ,,	
14 Brimstone @ 4/ 11 ... 1/4	,, 10 ,, 8	
23 Copperas 4/ 1 pail 1/4	,, 5 ,, 4	
½ doz hand saws @ 4/8	1 ,, 8 ,, ,,	
1 doz Jews harps	,, 1 ,, 4	
2 q 2 or Wier @ 21	,, 3 ,, 7	
1 pr flatt Irons	,, 6 ,, ,, ,,	
6 Grindstones @ 6/8	1 ,, 18 ,, ,,	£13 ,, 11 ,, 1
1 doz potts & Kittles wt 2: 2. q @ 28/	3 ,, 12 ,, 5	
½ doz Quart Iron Skillets	,, 14 ,, ,,	
½ doz 2 Quart do	,, 17 ,, ,,	
half Barril Glaisd Powder	3 ,, 12 ,, ,,	
1.0.0 London shott	1 ,, 12 ,, ,,	
3 Looking Glasses @ 7/8	1 ,, 3 ,, ,,	
3 ditto @ 10/	1 ,, 10 ,, ,,	
3 doz snuff boxes @ 10/8	1 ,, 12 ,, ,,	£14 ,, 12 ,, 3
1 doz Gs buttons	,, 14 ,, 8	
1 doz Shoe & knee buckels	,, 12 ,, 6	
1 doz White shoe & knee buckels	,, 12 ,, 6	
1 doz shoe ditto	,, 11 ,, ,,	
2 doz box boucher knifes @ 3/8	,, 7 ,, 4	
1 doz Rivited ditto	,, 6 ,, ,,	
6 Cards stone buttons	,, 6 ,, 8	
3 doz pen knifes 3/4	,, 10 ,, ,,	
3 doz do Capt ditto @ 4/	,, 12 ,, ,,	£8 ,, 5 ,, 8
brass kittles @ 34/3	3 ,, 9 ,, 4	
Cask & Porteradge	,, 3 ,, 8	£53 ,, ,, 1
3 ditto @ 10/	1 ,, 10 ,, ,,	

Figure 6.1 Elijah Williams invoice from 1750

Source: Courtesy of Pocumtuck Valley Memorial Association Library, Deerfield, MA.

Figure 6.2 'Gloucester' and 'Stafford' types found at Sutler's Store, Fort Edward, NY
Source: Photograph by kind permission of David Starbuck.

Trade moved with frontier expansion. Deerfield was on the border of the English and French Colonies, close to the disputed Ohio valley and their store stocked jews-harps. Finds have been made at Fort William Henry, Fort Edward, Fort Gage, Fort Ticonderoga and Fort Pontchartrain (Detroit), all actively involved in the French–Indian War, 1754–1760. Excavations at forts Pontchartrain and Edwards have found Sidaway 'Stafford' types, which, given that Fort Edward was mainly manned by Provincial troops and Rogers' Rangers, does rather imply a New England supplier of English imports.

Ports of Origin and Places of Manufacture

London, Bristol and Liverpool are consistently referred to in the adverts as ports of origin for all goods shipped, though James Stuart of Philadelphia alone mentions Glasgow.

The usual reference begins 'Just' or 'Lately imported in the vessels [name]'. Birmingham is mentioned by two traders: George Deblois of Salem, Massachusetts, 'Lately arrived from BIRMINGHAM ...'[21] and Sause's, New York, 'a large and general Assortment of GOODS', which he had just imported from London and Birmingham.[22] London, though, is the port of origin referred to most often in the adverts, at 52 per cent, (compared with Bristol, 25 per cent, and Liverpool,

---

[21] *Boston Gazette*, 28 September 1761, p. 3.
[22] *New York Gazette*, 9 November 1778, p. 3.

14 per cent), and appears to be the most likely source. Gilbert Deblois' supplier certainly seems to have been based in the capital, as he was selling 'London sewing and knitting needles, pins, brass and iron jews-harps, fish hooks'.[23] From the archaeological evidence it would appear that London merchants obtained their jews-harps from both English and Mainland European makers.

The Impact of the Industrial Revolution

British makers were quick to exploit the markets opening up worldwide, and the improvements in technology and transport brought about by the Industrial Revolution enabled them to feed that market. This export trade continued throughout the nineteenth and twentieth centuries up to the 1970s.

In 1874 the wholesaler John F. Stratton of New York was advertising 'English Harps, Irish Harps, Scotch Club Harps, Lacquered, Solid Brass Irish Harps' at prices from $0.34 to $2.49 per dozen.[24] Individual maker's marks are often visible, one make often identifiable being Troman instruments with their distinctive 3/2 notches. C.J. Whitney & Co. of Detroit, advertising in 1875, was selling P. (Philemon) Jones harps, described as 'The celebrated Jones Harp, The Finest Harp Manufactured'. As well as 'Scotch and Wrought-iron Lacquered' harps there are 'Extra Syrian' and 'Extra British Vibrators', the 'Syrian' being a frame style. They also sold 'Jones Harps in pairs, specially tuned for Doubles and Duet playing', and the American-made T.P.P. harps by Thomas P. Pascall of New York and a native of England.[25]

Pascall and John R. Smith of Troy, New York, had emigrated from England, Smith in 1881 from the Dudley area. Smith harps were and still are particularly well regarded, their prices reflecting their quality. Grossman of Cleveland in 1932 sold 'Standard Pattern – Bright Finish, Gold Bronze – Finest English Make and "Horseshoe" Pattern – Blued and Varnished' for between $0.70 and $4.40 per dozen, while Smiths harps were valued at between $3.00 and $10.80 per dozen. According to the Michigan *Kalamazoo Gazette* in 1897,

> The Trade in Jew's Harps. The cheapest jew's harps come from Germany and Austria, the medium and finer grades from England, and the very finest are now made in this country. Of the total production, two-thirds or more are made in England ... The total sales of jew's harps in this country are not so large as they formerly were.[26]

Grossman appears to be the main, if not the only, importer of English harps from the 1950s to the demise of the Birmingham industry in the 1970s. In 1973 they

---

[23] *Boston Evening Post*, 9 August 1756, p. 3.
[24] Crane, 'Trumps in American Musical Instrument Trade Catalogs', p. 71.
[25] Crane, 'Trumps in American Musical Instrument Trade Catalogs', pp. 67–116.
[26] *Kalamazoo Gazette*, Michigan, 19 October 1897, p. 8.

were advertising 'Jaw harps – England's Finest ... Built by English craftsmen who have been engaged in the art of building Jaws Harps for many generations, hence their leadership in quality'.[27] Prices were considerably higher by this time at $10.20 and $34.20 per dozen, though not for the manufacturer, Philip-Crawshaw, who they bought out two years later.

Quite a few adverts mention Irish harps. In 1924 J.W. Jenkins Sons, a retailer of Kansas City, was selling English, Irish and Smiths harps. Whether 'Irish' in this context refers to the pattern or the country of origin is impossible to know from the information we have at the moment. There was a particular Irish pattern, but, given there was also a major jews-harp manufacturing presence in Ireland in the nineteenth and possibly early twentieth century, these could be Irish imports.

One thing is certain: the jews-harp remained popular well into the twentieth century. However, by 1930 the US government was getting concerned:

> In 1935 the Department of Commerce of the United States reported that all the Jew's harps of the world were then being made by one firm in Birmingham, England, that one order just given from the United States to this firm was for 160,000 instruments, and that the firm in question, though making 100,000 a week, was unable to keep up demand owing to a lack of skilled "tongue-setters".[28]

As noted on many occasions throughout this book, jews-harps, while not having any specific role, appear during momentous events. During the American Civil War, 1861–1865, the Northern Anaconda Plan called for a blockade of Southern States ports, encouraging blockade runners to run goods through for considerable profit. In 1863 there was a cargo sale in Charleston, South Carolina:

> Direct Importations ex. Steamships Banshee and Pet. BY WILKES MORRIS, Auctioneer, On Friday, 29th instant, commencing at 10 o'clock, a.m., I will sell at my Sales Room, No. 2 granite Row, Wilmington, N.C., the following desirable articles, imported in above named Steamers: (including) 1 cask Awls, Needles, Thimbles, Jew's Harps, Tacks, Looking Glasses, &c.[29]

Australia and New Zealand

North America, however, was not the only export destination during the nineteenth and twentieth century. Australian and New Zealand trade can be traced back to the 1820s, and, as with the colonisation of New England, jews-harps can be found as part of goods used to buy land. The New Zealand Company is said to have

---

[27] Crane, 'Trumps in American Musical Instrument Trade Catalogs', p. 93.
[28] Percy A. Scholes, *Oxford Companion to Music* (London: Oxford University Press, 1970), pp. 542–3.
[29] *Charleston Mercury*, 22 May 1863, p. 2.

purchased the site of Wellington and the shores of Port Nicholson in 1839 for about £350 worth of 'miscellaneous goods – knives, Jews'-harps, slate pencils, fireworks'. However, the Maoris soon discovered that the wily 'European had "bested them". They were not the people to put up with such chicanery. Disputes arose, concerning this and many similar transactions'.[30]

Goods were imported into Australia with the specific intention of trading further east. An advert from 1848 is to 'CAPTAINS OF VESSELS AND SHIPPERS TO NEW ZEALAND AND THE SOUTHERN ISLANDS. BLUED AMERICAN WEDGE AXES. Falling axes Handled tomahawks, Jews' harps, &c'.[31]

Traders had been established and were importing goods by 1823. For example:

> AT DEANE's Store, Bridge-street, [Hobart] the following valuable Articles are just landed from the late arrivals, and will be offered for SALE, at the usual low prices [including] brass & iron butt hinges, hoes, jews' harps, shingle, batten, rafter, and spike nails ... Wheat at 8s. per bushel, and other colonial produce taken in payment.[32]

Goods were shipped from England and shipwreck was always a danger:

> The whole of the GOODS and SHIP'S MATERIALS; raised by means of the diving apparatus from the wreck of the barque Heroine, sunk off Lyme Regis, while on her voyage from London to Australia, with a general cargo; [including] brass Jew's harps ...[33]

Large quantities of jews-harps were coming from the Midlands. In 1873, according to 'TRADE OF BIRMINGHAM AND DISTRICT', 'Heavy orders have just come to hand for jew's harps, one firm alone having received an order for nearly 100 gross for the Australian market'[34] – that is, 14,400 instruments. An auction in Sydney in 1930 was selling 50 gross jews-harps,[35] from which we can imply that the market was still very strong throughout the region well into the twentieth century. The retail sale value in the 1930s varied from 6d (2½p), 9d (4p) and 12d (5p) each.

South Africa

There is considerable evidence of a thriving trade in South Africa that continued well into the twentieth century. The *Western Daily Press* in 1940 wrote, '[the]

---

[30] *The Braidwood Dispatch and Mining Journal*, 19 March 1904, p. 1.
[31] *The Sydney Morning Herald*, 16 December 1848, p. 1.
[32] *Hobart Town Gazette and Van Diemen's Land Advertiser*, 10 May 1823, p. 1.
[33] *Liverpool Mercury*, 10 June 1853, p. 5.
[34] *Sheffield Independent*, 3 March 1873, p. 2.
[35] *The Sydney Morning Herald*, 17 September 1930, p. 2.

Jew's Harp, a heart-shaped metal framed instrument, or weapon held between the lips, and popular in the streets years ago, is still in demand ... Americans seem to buy quite a lot, and the trade is fast developing in South Africa'.[36]

As with the Americas, there is no indication that jews-harps were known on the African continent before European intervention and there appears to be two areas in particular where jews-harps are found in use – Nigeria and South Africa. There is a guinea corn one from Nigeria, made by children with a small hollow cut in the pith as the resonator and a projecting tongue of the cortex for plucking. Other Nigerian instruments are 'locally made but based on European models from which they derive, called *bambaro*'.[37] The inspiration for these may well be Austrian types.

As in the Americas, they were useful as barter goods:

> a commercial traveler in Africa, who, failing otherwise to attract the attention of the natives, mounted a rock and played on his jew's-harp so effectively that the natives became infatuated with the instrument, and gladly exchanged a pound of ostrich feathers for a jew's-harp.[38]

British exports appear to be mainly to South Africa, and we can trace that trade back to at least the mid-nineteenth century, though there is mention of a French explorer, François LeVaillant, in the eighteenth century sharing his jews-harp with the local bearers.[39] This trade continued up to the demise of the industry. A newspaper from 1949 describes a house-servant 'playing upon the jew's-harp, an instrument upon which they excel', being particularly popular in KwaZulu-Natal, where they were noted as being 'particularly good at playing them'.[40]

Evidence of the jews-harp's popularity can be seen in a remarkable photograph discovered by Angela Impey:

> By the mid- to late 1800s the jews harp had been thoroughly adopted by young Nguni women in the KwaZulu-Natal region. A vital clue to this is contained in a photograph lodged at the Marianne Hill Monastery Archives in Durban, South Africa. This image, dated 1900–1908, includes two Zulu women, one of whom is wearing a jews harp on a string around her neck. The other is holding an *umqangala* mouthbow.[41]

---

[36] *Western Daily Press*, 1 June 1940, p. 6.
[37] Jeremy Montagu, personal correspondence.
[38] *Repository*, 10 September 1885, p. 2.
[39] Frederick Crane, 'Monsieur Le Vaillant Wows the Hottentots', *VIM*, 4 (1994), pp. 38–44.
[40] *Hull Daily Mail*, 12 November 1949, p. 4.
[41] Angela Impey, 'Sounding Place in the Western Maputaland Borderlands', *Journal of the Musical Arts in Africa*, 3 (2006), pp. 63–4.

The photograph distinctly shows a Troman Baroque-style jews-harp.[42]
The following section has been taken from an article by Angela Impey and Michael Wright, 'The Birmingham–KwaZulu-Natal Connection' in the *Journal of the International Jew's Harp Society* and is from the section written by Angela Impey:[43]

> British ships traded in agricultural implements and non-essential stuffs from the Delagoa Bay, Mozambique, their trading activities linked with the Portuguese networks southwards into the Zulu-speaking areas, so it is possible that jews-harps became part of the local musical culture by the mid-nineteenth century. Later jews-harps were likely to have been made available in South Africa by way of a number of sources. Weekly advertisements published in the *Zululand Times* from 1907 reveal that commercial music stores such as Jackson Bros., Durban, traded "musical instruments of every description". While jews-harps may not have been identified specifically, the Jackson Bros. advertisement provides evidence of a vigorous trade of musical instruments from England, Europe and America to South Africa at that time.

> In recent times jews-harps were sold at "concession stores" that were located on the gold mines in Johannesburg, run mostly by Jewish immigrants from Lithuania. These were general dealerships-cum-eating houses that were customarily located near to mine compounds.[44] The "concession stores" played an important role in introducing western instruments to rural Africans and these included also guitars, violins, concertinas, accordions and mouth organs, and it was through the networks of migrant workers that many new musical practices were disseminated throughout the southern African region. Rural trader, Alec Frangs, who ran a store in the Donnybrook area of southern KwaZulu-Natal from 1926, claims that jews-harps were amongst the musical instruments sold to Zulu people. It's also interesting to note that by the 1950s, Hohner South Africa began to import jews-harps through the Schwartz company in Molln, and distributed them through retail outlets in the cities of Johannesburg, Durban and Port Elizabeth. Instruments were traded as "impulse buys" by way of wholesale companies, whose distribution networks extended deep into the countryside across the entire southern African region. The portability of jews-harps was readily adopted by Nguni women as there already existed a repertoire of mouth bows in their musical cultures.

---

[42] See Michael Wright and Angela Impey, 'The Birmingham–KwaZulu-Natal Connection', *JIJHS*, 4 (2007), p. 44.
[43] Wright and Impey, 'The Birmingham–KwaZulu-Natal Connection', pp. 44–8. I am grateful to Angela Impey, SOAS, for information on the use of jews-harps in KwaZulu-Natal.
[44] See Joseph Sherman (Ed.), *From a Land Far Off: A Selection of South African Yiddish Stories* (Cape Town: Jewish Publications, and Joseph Sherman, 1987), and Joseph Sherman, 'Serving the Natives: Whiteness as a Price of Hospitality in South African Yiddish Literature', *Journal of Southern African Studies*, 26(3) (2000), pp. 505–22.

Figure 6.3   Mampolwane Ngomonde, Usuthu Gorge, South Africa
Source: Photograph by Angela Impey, by kind permission of Angela Impey.

In an interview recorded in 2003 by Impey, a woman recalls,

> We grew up with our mothers playing *is 'tweletwele* [jews-harps]. These songs were there before we were born. Then we were able to buy them. They were only a tickey or half a cent, and bread was also a half cent. And sugar. We bought them at KwaMatata [store] in Swaziland and Ndumo.[45]

The two main suppliers to Africa from the UK appear to be John Barnsley of Netherton and the Troman family, from Rowley Regis and Birmingham. A third maker, Isaac Watts, also supplied instruments for export, according to a descendent, Frank Southall:

> Isaac Watts was making and exporting jaw's harps from Albion Street, Birmingham, before 1910 ... Most of the export business was to natives in various parts of Africa where it was ultimately found that they used to make necklaces of the jaws's harps, hence the great demand.[46]

---

[45] Impey, 'Sounding Place', p. 64.
[46] Frank Southall, personal correspondence.

Exports 119

Figure 6.4   Top: Letterhead. Bottom: D & B Troman business card
Source: By kind permission of Gillian Troman.

There was a regular shipping of goods to South and West Africa, though specific details are scant and something as small as a jews-harp may well have been hidden under the general title of hardware. One ship owner, H.R. James, had ships plying their trade to Cape Town in the mid-1880s and is a possible source. Research continues.

Adoption by Locals

One of the more interesting aspects of the South African trade is how the instrument was adopted into an established musical tradition. According to Impey,

> Known most commonly as *isitolotolo*, and in the area of my research as *is'tweletwele*, it is assumed that the instrument was readily adopted by young Nguni women as its construction and performance practice were similar to those of existing mouthbows. Like them, the jews harp exploits the physical properties of the mouth both to produce a melodic phrase and to resonate and amplify a wide range of harmonics. Jews harps were similarly used by young

women as walking instruments, much of the performance repertoire becoming interchangeable with that of mouthbows.[47]

These songs were inherited from grandmothers and aunts, and feature three main thematic concerns. First, they profile natural landmarks (e.g. rivers, mountains) and fauna (e.g. cattle, birds, locusts), which were used as metaphorical devices to communicate socioeconomic concerns. Secondly, they chronicle relationships and social events (e.g. greetings, sightings, proposals of love and songs of moral regulation). Thirdly, they comment on labour migrancy, lamenting the departure of their men ... but celebrating also their return, which was inevitably complemented with gifts and food.[48]

The full story is both tragic and inspiring, but beyond the scope of this book.

---

[47] Impey, 'Sounding Place', p. 62.
[48] Angela Impey, 'Songs of Mobility and Belonging', *Interventions: International Journal of Postcolonial Studies*, 15(2) (2013), p. 263.

PART III
Cultural Aspects

The jews-harp has had an impact on all parts of British and Irish culture – art and architecture, film, television and radio, literature, poems and jokes, crosswords and puzzles and, of course, musical culture. Visual representations include enamels, stone carvings, paintings, etchings, drawings and cartoons. The shape of the jews-harp is noted in architecture, landscapes and objects; stories have been written extolling its virtues and its irrelevance; jokes written, some anti-Semitic, others dismissive; while crossword puzzle clues vary from the obvious to the almost totally obscure. Songs mentioning jews-harps have been composed, but in the end it has to be the players, both professional and casual, who will decide the demise or revival of the instrument.

Chapter 7
Art, Architecture and Mass Media

> Some of the Principle Inhabitants of Ye Moon, *as they Were Perfectly Discover'd by a Telescope brought to ye Greatest Perfection since ye last Eclipse, Exactly Engraved from the Objects, whereby ye Curious may Guess at their Religion Manners, &c.*
>
> William Hogarth, 1724[1]

There are a surprising number of artworks depicting jews-harps: enamels, stone carvings, paintings, etchings and cartoons. The instrument has been used for decoration, in illustration, in political comment and satire, as an architectural term and as inspiration for young artists. New discoveries continue to be made, the latest providing the earliest representation of a player found to date.

Figure 7.1   Thirteenth-century carving in the Chapter House, York Minster
Source: Photographs by kind permission of David Wright and Jim Spriggs, reproduced with permission of the Chapter of York.

---

[1]   Sean Shesgreen (ed.), *Engravings by Hogarth* (Dover Fine Art, 1973), n.p. (italics in original).

Stonework[2]

The Chapter House of York Minster was begun in the 1260s and was completed before 1296. It is octagonal in shape with 42 seats for the Chapter when in session, above each of which are four sculpted heads. Between each seat are other carvings of larger heads, animals and grotesques. Between the seats of 'Dunnington' and 'The Dean' there is a remarkable stone carving only recently observed,[3] which clearly shows a jews-harp player and the playing action. There was some concern this might be a Victorian reconstruction, but, according to Master Stonemason John David,

> The conclusion is that it is an original C13th stone. The very slight doubt I initially had was that the piece of stone is slightly lighter than the stone above. But when one looks about, there is colour variation amongst the other pieces of stone. The column below was replaced in the 1840s and its capital renewed which one might think would have given the opportunity to insert a new niche springer from below. However, the capital behind is original and the stone also sits on this, so a new piece of vaulting which bears the carving could not of been inserted from below. All the tool marks are similar to other original work.[4]

After re-visiting the site a year later, John David states quite clearly 'it is original.'[5] Measuring approximately 40 cm in height, this is the earliest visual representation of the jews-harp not only in Britain, but in Europe, where the earliest dateable image previously recorded is on a seal found in Switzerland, dated 1353.[6]

Two other medieval carvings are either definitely not of a player or questionable. An Exeter Cathedral carved angel is often described as a jews-harp player, but in fact it is a trumpet player with the trumpet broken off leaving the circular mouthpiece and the hands apparently in a jews-harp-playing position. Secondly, a corbel carving in St Sepulchre Church, Northampton has been described both as a jews-harp and as a pan-pipe player.[7]

There is an architectural feature on Saxon churches that is given the name 'Jew's Harp Pattern'. This was described in 1859 by George Atkinson:

> At Scartho, on this impost is sculpted an ornament or moulding, which is never found, I believe, but in works of the Saxon period. I have never seen it named or

---

[2] I am grateful to David Wright for much of the research in this section.
[3] Thanks particularly to Gill Wright.
[4] John David, personal correspondence.
[5] John David, personal correspondence.
[6] Frederick Crane, *A History of the Trump in Pictures: Europe and America* (Mount Pleasant, IA: Frederick Crane, 2003), p. 3.
[7] Jeremy Montagu, retired curator of the Bate Collection of Musical Instruments, believes it is a jews-harp. Hélène La Rue, late of the Pitt Rivers Museum, now deceased, favoured pan-pipes.

noticed in architectural books. In outline it has much the shape of a Jew's harp. It is found on the oldest parts of Stow church, on the impost of the belfry window of St Peter at Gowt's, on a string course in the east end of the nave at Barnetby le Wold and on the face arch at Nettleton.[8]

Noted in the *Kelly's Directory* of 1889, 1896, 1905 and 1913, the Nettleton church of St John is described as having 'a doorway reputed to be Late Saxon, and bearing a characteristic ornament termed the "Jews' harp" found on the remains of this period in other Lincolnshire churches'.[9]

Other Imagery

A coat of arms mentioned in 1797 of a window in the village of Stoke, Newark Deanery, had a 'Paly of six argent and azure, on a bend of 3 Jews' harpes, or such like, Sable, this is oft'.[10] The window in Stoke was replaced during the Victorian period and there are no images, but a Scopham family coat of arms from Lincolnshire clearly depicts a 'JEWS HARP, as borne in the arms of *Scopham*',[11] though what connection there is between the Scopham family and the jews-harp is unclear.

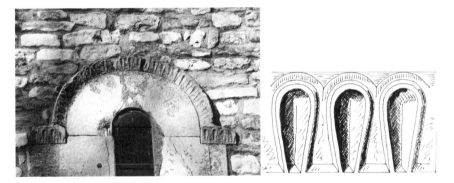

Figure 7.2   Left: 'Jew's Harp Pattern' in situ at Stow Minster, Lincolnshire. Right: Schematic sketch
Source: Photograph by kind permission of David Wright.

---

[8] George Atkinson, *On Saxon Architecture, and the Early Churches in the Neighbourhood of Grimsby. A Paper Read at the Meeting of the Lincoln Diocesan Architectural Society* (Lincoln: W. & B. Brooke, 1859), p. 31.
[9] *Kelly's Directory* (1889), p. 354.
[10] 'Parishes: Stoke by Newark', *Thoroton's History of Nottinghamshire, vol. 1: Republished with large additions by John Throsby* (1790), pp. 345–51, at http://www.british-history.ac.uk/report.aspx?compid=76007 (accessed 15 June 2015).
[11] William Berry, *Encyclopaedia Heraldica, Complete Dictionary of Heraldry, vol. III* (London: Sherwood, Gilbert and Piper, 1828–1840).

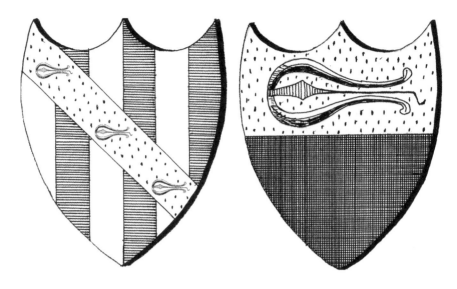

Figure 7.3   Left: Conjectural drawing of Scopham stained glass window in St Oswald's Church, East Stoke Church. Right: The Scopham crest

Enamels, Miniatures, Paintings and Etchings

Dated c.1360, on either side of the head of the William of Wykeham crozier in the Chapel of New College, Oxford, there are 10 small silver-and-enamel plaques, each measuring approximately 38 mm × 19 mm and depicting a variety of musical instruments from a triangle to a portative organ. An angel playing a jews-harp distinctly shows the playing style: the jews-harp is 3.5 mm long and exquisitely drawn, while the finger of the angel is plucking the lamella outwards. There is another late medieval miniature from the *Bucolics and Georgics of Virgil*, dated 1411–1412 in a manuscript at Holkham Hall, Norfolk, though this is most likely French in origin.

A number of jews-harp representations were created in the seventeenth and eighteenth centuries, including an oil painting, *Boy Playing a Trump*, by Sir Peter Lely, a coat of arms by Randle Holme III and a carving by an unknown artist. From the eighteenth century there is an engraving attributed to Egbert van Heemskerck II and William Henry Toms, and two drawings or etchings by Hogarth.

William Hogarth

The two Hogarth works are particularly interesting. *The Beggar's Opera Burlesqued*, prints of which were made the year of the first performance of John Gay's opera in 1728, depicts the characters with animal heads:

Art, Architecture and Mass Media 127

The actors are given the heads of braying, mooing, barking, meowing animals. Harmony is flying away to join the Italian opera ... The orchestra, prominent in the centre foreground, consists of a bladder-and-string, a dulcimer, a trump (jews-harp), a salt box, and bagpipes – all regarded as ridiculous by the highbrows.[12]

Burlesques using these instruments became a popular entertainment from the late 1740s to 1760s.[13]

Hogarth's *Some of the Principal Inhabitants of ye Moon* was originally drawn around 1724, and reproduced as an etching later in the century.

This iconoclastic emblem, executed in a surrealistic style, is a daring attack upon the English ruling class from a middle-class point of view ... A bishop is resting his limbs on a luxurious pile of cushions; his head, a Jew's harp, operates a money-making machine by means of a prayer book tied to its crank. The machine, shaped like a church steeple, is topped by a weather vane, which like the moons on the king's orb and sceptre, is a symbol of inconstancy. This device pours money into a chest bearing a coat of arms that reveals the hierarchy's preoccupation with food.[14]

Figure 7.4 *The Jew's Harp*, engraving by David Wilkie, with detail
Source: Author's collection.

---

12 Crane, *History of the Trump*, pp. 89–90.
13 See Chapter 8.
14 Shesgreen (ed.), *Engravings*, n.p.

David Wilkie

A surprising number of paintings, drawings and etchings were inspired by the jews-harp during the nineteenth century. The most famous and most commonly reproduced is David Wilkie's *The Jew's Harp* of 1807. Wilkie painted genre subjects of everyday life and surroundings, and in this case depicting a Scottish villager playing a jews-harp for a girl and a young child. The painting may have been inspired by an earlier work, *Pitlessie Fair*, where he has a detail of children, one of whom is playing the jews-harp, the pose being very similar to the village player in the later work. The engraving is by John Burnett. Wilkie published prints after the painting, and they apparently sold for substantial prices, with prints selling at 10 shillings and 6 pence in 1809,[15] helping to spread his reputation. The painting was bought by Dr Annesley in 1812 for 25 guineas and is now in Sudley House, Liverpool.

The engraving inspired a poem, used as an illustration on a broadside dated 1821 and 1828:

THE JEWS HARP

"Music hath charms" So said the sage:
And music pleases youth and age.
Behold the sire, in tuneful strains,
His children's mark'd attention gains!
Well pleas'd, they tell the notes he raises,
And oft are eager in their praises:
Not David's harp would yield more pleasure
To them;– 'tis sweet beyond all measure:
Sly Brush too in his turn's elated,
Nor deems the music overrated.[16]

The Jews-Harp as a Theme

Altogether there are 14 works found so far simply called *The Jew's Harp*, *Jew's Harp*, *The Jew's Harp Player* or *The Player on the Jew's Harp*. All told, 48 drawings, sketches, watercolours and paintings by British artists have been identified, many by amateur artists, their works no longer in existence. Those that are available appear to fit into a sentimental genre style of artwork popular during the Victorian period, with works by F.W. Jopham and George Paul Chalmers typical of this approach.

---

[15] *Northampton Mercury*, 30 November 1809, p. 1.
[16] Broadside Ballads Online from the Bodleian Library, Johnson Ballads 370, at http://ballads.bodleian.ox.ac.uk (accessed 15 June 2015).

Art, Architecture and Mass Media 129

Figure 7.5 *Girl with Jews Harp*, by F.W. Jopham
Source: From the Frederick Crane Collection, by kind permission of Lois Crane.

In a similar vein, Daniel Maclise portrayed an Irish lass playing a jews-harp, the origin of which was recounted by Leith Ritichie:

> It was almost dark before I reached the Roundwood road; and this was in part the fault of a harp whose plaintive tones allured me into a cottage. In the annexed engraving the reader will see both harp and harper, the latter a young peasant

girl, and the former an instrument composed of iron ... This may be said to be now the only instrument of the Irish peasant, and it exemplifies in a striking manner the degradation of this country.[17]

The antithesis of this style would be the often caustic woodcuts reproduced in *Punch* magazine, where the jews-harp is used as a symbol of Jewishness or, at best, something of little musical value. 'Po' little Mo" is typical of the former, where a stereotypical image of a Jew symbolically holds an enlarged jews-harp.[18]

Recent Artworks

There is a small, though ever-increasing, number of more recent artworks. Lindsay Porteous, a trump player from Culross, Fife, Scotland was painted by his mother, Nora, in 1988, and he commissioned a stained glass representation from Robert Mercer in 2012.

There is a series of drawings of the accomplished player John Wright by Denis Cantiteau, drawn after Wright's death in 2013. Jews-harps appear in a number of humorous cards, mainly personal to players. One commercial one comes from 1904, depicting an Irish boy player and a girl in tears saying, 'Oh! Hush sad harp, that dreary tone'.[19] Lindsay Porteous' brother, Nigel, sends hand-drawn Christmas card cartoons regularly, subjects including a jews-harp playing highlander, punk and Santa Claus; David Wright sends fellow player and brother, Michael, personalised birthday cards; while Jonty Clark caricatured Michael Wright in 2014.

Artists and photographers continue to explore the visual possibilities. Jonathon Cope is inspired by the making process, while Mark Ware takes a more abstract approach.

Paul Gardner is a graphic artist. He explains,

> I use an iPad to create and manipulate images. The strong geometric shape of the Munnharpa is almost a "design classic" and Bauhaus inspired inasmuch as its form follows its function. I'm also inspired by the historical personality of this little instrument. It pops up, here and there, in paintings, carvings and texts but only very momentarily. I like its elusiveness.[20]

So, albeit on a limited scale, the image of the jews-harp continues to hold a fascination for a new generation.

---

[17] Quoted in Crane, *History of the Trump*, p. 12.
[18] Crane, *History of the Trump*, pp. 130–33.
[19] Crane, *History of the Trump*, p. 139.
[20] Paul Gardner, personal correspondence, 2014.

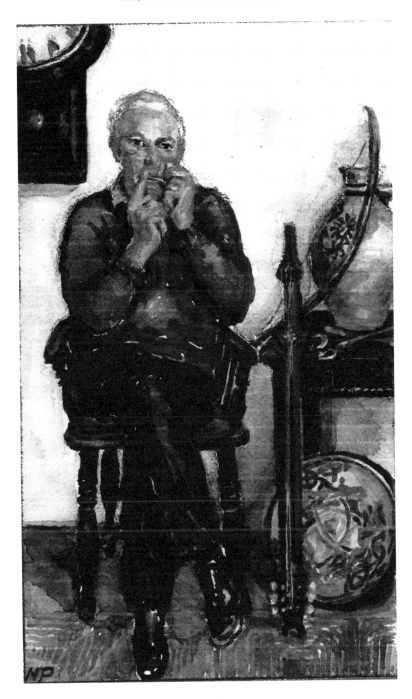

Figure 7.6 *Lindsay Porteous*, by Nora Porteous
Source: By kind permission of Lindsay Porteous.

Figure 7.7 *Jews-harp in the forge*, by Jonathon Cope
Source: © 2014 Jonathon Cope.

Figure 7.8 CD cover concept, by Mark Ware
Source: Author's collection.

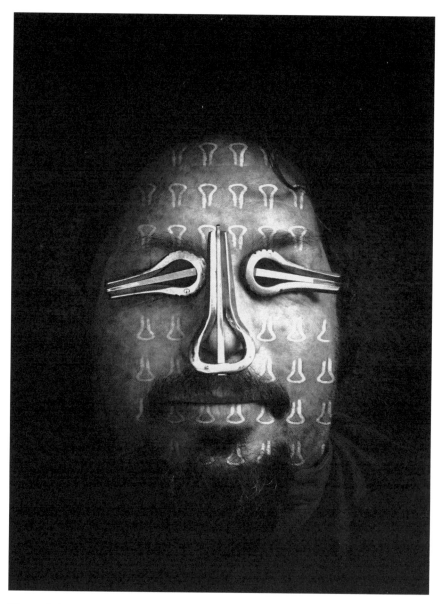

Figure 7.9   *Self-portrait with harps*, by Paul Gardner
Source: By kind permission of Paul Gardner.

Figure 7.10 Caricature of Michael Wright, by Jonty Clark
Source: © 2014 Jonty Clark.

Chapter 8
The Jews-Harp in Popular Culture

And there will be black-nebbit Johnnie, The tongue o' the trump to them a'.
Robert Burns, *c*.1795[1]

There is a story in British newspapers that appears to have originated in Cincinnati, Ohio, USA, referring to a merchant tailor, Platt Evans, but given a local Yorkshire setting:

> Any one who lived in the West Riding will remember Emerson, the tailor, one of the oldest and best of his craft, as well as the jolliest – always as ready to take a joke as to give one. It used to be considered the "fair thing" to send persons to his shop for articles at variance with what usually constitutes the stock-in-trade of members of his profession. One day, one of his friends encountered a greenhorn, who inquired of him where he could purchase a Jew's harp. Of course he was directed to Emerson's shop as the establishment where they kept the largest assortment at the most reasonable prices. Our friend proceeded to the place indicated, and found Emerson (who by the way is troubled with an impediment of speech) [who] gravely approached his new customer with a pair of glove-stretchers, and observed in a mild tone, "W-we shall h-have to t-take your mum-mum-measure", whereupon he inserted the stretcher into his mouth, spreading open his countenance to the full extent of the "stretch", and with a face indicating the utmost seriousness remarked to the astonished customer, "Y-young man, we-we haven't gur-gur-got any of y-your size".[2]

The Cincinnati version appeared in 1859, 1874, 1875 and 1881 in newspapers from Exeter to Falkirk. In fact, various amusing tales fill spaces in newspapers over the years. A mother encouraging her little boy to be good so he could go to heaven told him, 'he would be "like the angels, who have harps in their hands". "Mamma," responded the urchin, wistfully gazing into his mother's eyes, "mamma, if it makes no difference to God, I would rather have a Jew's harp!"'[3]

Then there are two stories from Paris, France and Ceredigion, Wales:

---

[1] Robert Burns, 'The Election: A New Song. Tune – Fy, let us a' to the Bridal', *The Heron Ballads, or The Election Ballads*, 2 (British Newspaper Archive, Literature Network, 1795–1796), verse 2.
[2] *Kentish Gazette*, 20 December 1859, p. 7.
[3] *Burnley Express*, 11 September 1880, p. 3.

"See that poor, afflicted boy sitting in front of your shop. No doubt his tooth is dancing with pain – an ulcerated tooth, perhaps, See how he holds his jaws with both hands and sways from side to side. Poor fellow." "My dear, you are badly mistaken. The lad is perfectly happy. He is playing a Jew's harp."[4]

A clergyman, who was anxious before his return home to buy some toys for his school children, entered a well-known establishment in St. Mary-street and asked the shopman how he sold "Jews' harps". "Sell them, sir?" replied the latter, "we do not keep such things." "But I saw them in your window," persisted the reverend gentleman. After further discussion, the divine discovered that what he took for Jews' harps were only some patent curling pins.[5]

The jews-harp appears in humour and satire, stories and sayings and literature – in fact just about any part of popular culture. Some of it is undoubtedly anti-Semitic, particularly in England. Much of it, however, is witty and innocent fun.

"Onions cut in half will absorb the smell of new paint." Yes, and a cornet will drone out a jews-harp. Life is full of queer things.[6]

What musical instrument does the syrup of a current tart remind you of? Why, the Jew's harp (juice-sharp) of course.[7]

Witness at Southend: "She spends all her time listening to United States film actors in the cinema, and talks like a Jew's harp."[8]

"Here is one line," said the Editor, "in which you speak of 'the music of the cider press'. How would you imitate the 'music' of a cider press?" "With a juice harp," answered the poet.[9]

Why is a Jew's Harp like a good Dinner; Because it makes a Man's mouth Water.[10]

---

[4] *North Devon Journal*, 11 March 1886, p. 2; *Bury and Norwich Post, Suffolk*, 19 April 1887, p. 6; *Shields Daily Gazette*, 3 September 1904, p. 3.
[5] *Western Mail*, South Glamorgan, 2 October 1895, p. 5.
[6] *Hampshire Telegraph*, 4 August 1888, p. 11.
[7] *The Era*, London, 5 September 1864, p. 5.
[8] *Nottingham Evening Post*, 13 December 1933, p. 10.
[9] *Hull Daily Mail*, 8 May 1906, p. 1.
[10] *A new tea-table miscellany or, bagatelles for the Amusement of The Fair Sex. To which are added, A Collection of Conundrums with their solutions* (London, 1750), p. 200; *The pleasant companion or, merry & complete favourite jester, containing all the fun, all the humour, all the learning, and all the judgement which so lately flowed from the two universities* (London, 1775?), p. 170.

Figure 8.1 *World's largest mouth harp*, by Nigel Porteous
Source: By kind permission of Lindsay Porteous.

Specimen Bricks from the Dictionary of the Future. – Accordion: a pair of bellows which have accidentally swallowed a jew's harp.[11]

Sayings and Proverbs

Sayings and proverbs are particularly prevalent in Scotland and Ireland. 'The tongue of the trump' analogy quoted from Robert Burns is used by Sir Walter Scott in *The Bride of Lammermoor*, *The Monastery* and *Redgauntlet*, and another expression, 'But never look like a sow playing on a trump for the luve o' that, man' occurs in *Rob Roy*.[12] Kelly's *A complete collection of Scottish proverbs explained and made intelligible to the English reader* of 1721 gives two examples: 'Like a Sow playing on a Trump. Spoken when People do a Thing ungracefully' and 'You have lost the Tongue of the Trump. That is, you want the Main Thing'.[13]

---

[11] *Morning Post*, London, 5 December 1879, p. 3.
[12] Sir Walter Scott, *Rob Roy* (Edinburgh: Archibald Constable and Co.; London: Longman, Hurst, Rees, Orme, and Brown, 1818), vol. 2, p. 256.
[13] James A. Kelly, *A complete collection of Scotish proverbs explained and made intelligible to the English reader* (London, 1721), pp. 232 and 389.

The Irish have a similar saying, 'Ye ha'e tint the tongue o' the trump', and there are many variations on a theme: *Nárbh fhiú trumpa gan teanga* ('He isn't worth a tongueless Jew's harp'); *Is fuath liom cláirseach gan téada, Is fuath liom bréaga gan binneas, Is fuath liom trumpa gan teanga, Is fuath liom táilliúr gan deimheas* ('I hate a harp with no strings, I hate lies without sweetness, I hate a jews-harp with no tongue, And I hate a tailor without shears'); *Na trí ní is lú a bhfuil úsáid iontu, Trumpa gan teanga, Cnaipe gan lúbán, Madra alla gan fiacail* ('The three most useless things: A jews-harp with no tongue, A button with no buttonhole, A [hunting?] dog with no teeth'); *Trí rudaí nach bhfuil aon mhaith iontu, súgán gan casadh, trumpa gan teanga, cat dall* ('Three useless things: a súgán [rope] with no twist, a tongueless jews-harp, a blind cat'); *Ceithre ní gan mhaith, sagart gan Laidin, muileann gan criathar, trumpa gan teanga, madra alla gan fiacail* ('Four useless things: a priest without Latin, a mill without a screen/sieve, a tongueless jews-harp, a [hunting?] dog without teeth'). Finally, *'Is iomaí sórt ceoil atá ann', mar a dúirt an fear a raibh an trumpa maide aige* ('"There are many types of music", said the man with the wooden jews-harp').[14]

Viv Legg, of a traditional Romany singing family in Cornwall, remembers that, when she was a child, her mother would scold her wrong-doings with, 'You little jews-harper!'[15] In a similar vein, there is this from the *North Devon Journal*, recorded during the trial of Clara Ellen Alford: 'dressmaker, as old offender, at Barnstaple Court on Saturday ... Merely because a somewhat plump policeman ventured to laugh she called him a hungry-looking Jew's harp!'[16] There does not appear to be any particular reason for either usage.

Plays

Sixteenth- and seventeenth-century plays used the jews-trump, either for comic effect or, as with the proverbs, as an analogy, though as Crane points out,

> Whatever may have been the now unknown reason for associating the instrument with the Jews, the association would be, for some centuries to come, a common reason for bringing the name of the instrument into a literary text.[17]

In Mr. S. Mr. of Art's rustic farce *Gammer Gurtons Nedle* there is a description by the character Diccon the Bedlam (fool?):

---

[14] Donla uí Bhraonáin (ed.), *Seanfhocla Chonnacht* [Proverbs of Connacht] (Dublin: Cois Life, in association with Foras na Gaeilge, 2010), *passim*.
[15] Viv Legg, personal correspondence.
[16] *North Devon Journal*, 22 November 1906, p. 3.
[17] Crane, 'The Trump in British Literature', p. 71.

That ever I saw a sorte, in such a plyght, As here within this house appereth to my sight, There is howlynge and scowlyng, all cast in a dumpe, With whewling and pewling, as though they had lost a trump. Syhing and sobbing, they weeps and they wayle I marvell in my mynd, what the devill they ayle ...[18]

In Henry Chettle's satire on current abuses, *Kind-Hart's Dreame*, 'There is another Iugler, that beeing well skild in the Iewes Trumpe, takes vpon him to bee a dealer in Musicke: especiall good at mending Instruments ...'[19] Ben Jonson, referring to a character overly devoted to acquiring money, has Carlo Buffone say, 'I thought he had beene playing o' the Iewes trump',[20] while Thomas Dekker lists instruments associated with different languages:

Very base-viall men most of 'em: besides whole swarmes of welsh harpes, Irish bag-pipes, Iewes trompes, and french kitts. All these made I together play: But their dambd catter-wralling, frighted me away.[21]

The Clown in *The Faire Maide of the Inne* by Fletcher and Massinger, says, 'No, no, I will not steal it; but my dear Jews-trump, for thou are but my instrument, I am the plotter'.[22]

A woman reminiscing on the help she gave a young man who no longer visits her in Thomas Randolph's play *Hey for Honesty, Down with Knavery* grumbles:

Anus – Ay, but erst he would have come every day to my door.

Chremylus – perchance a-begging?

Anus – No, only to hear the melody of my voice.

Chremylus – Like enough; it could not choose but please him to hear what excellent music your Jew's- trump could make, now all your teeth are out.[23]

---

[18] William Stevenson, –1575; John Bridges, –1618, *A Right Pithy, Pleasant, and Merry Comedy, entitled Gammer Gurton's Needle. Played on Stage not long ago in Christ's College in Cambridge. Made by Mr. S., M.A.* (London, [1575]), p. 4.
[19] Henry Chettle, 'Kind-Hart's Dreame: Containing Five Apparitions with their Invectives Against Abuses Reigning', in *Early English Poetry, Ballads, and Popular Literature of the Middle Ages, vol. V* (London, 1841).
[20] Ben Jonson, *Every Man Out of His Humor* (1599), act 3, scene 6.
[21] Thomas Dekker, *If it be not good, the Diuel is in it. A nevv play, as it hath bin lately acted, vvith great applause, by the Queenes Maiesties Seruants: at the Red Bull. Written by Thomas Dekker* (1612), act 2, scene 1, at http://quod.lib.umich.edu/cgi/t/text/text-idx?c=eebo;idno=A20066 (accessed 15 June 2015).
[22] J. Fletcher and P. Massinger, *The Faire Maide of the Inne* (1626), act 2, scene 1.
[23] Thomas Randolph, *Hey for Honesty, Down with Knavery* (1651), act 4, scene 4.

And from R.M.:

> Hee may for his ompudence resemble most fitly the tongue as a Iewes-trumpe; which though repulst by the finger, returns with more eagernesse to his full Twang.[24]

Literature

Novels of a later period have similar views as in *Joseph Andrews* and *Tristram Shandy*:

> O Love, what monstrous tricks dost thou play with thy votaries of both sexes! ... Again, when thou pleasest, thou canst make a mole-hill appear as a mountain; a Jew's harp sound like a trumpet; and a daisy smell like a violet.[25]

> I'll stake my Cremona to a Jew's trump, which is the greatest musical odds that ever were laid ...[26]

One of the more bizarre stories comes from Charles Kingsley's *The Water Babies*, published as a serial between 1862 and 1863. A contemporary review suggests that 'Professor Kingsley's "Water Babies" grows in interest, and when the reader will take the trouble to look underneath its surface, he will be repaid by discovering remarkable beauties of thought and teachings'.[27] One story refers to 'The History of the great and famous Nation of the Doasyoulikes, who came away from the country of Hardwork, because they wanted to play on the Jews'-harp all day long':

> In the first picture they saw these Doasyoulikes living in the land of Readymade, at the foot of the Happygolucky Mountains, where flapdoodle grows wild ... They were very fond of music, but it was too much trouble to learn the piano or the violin; and as for dancing, that would have been too great an exertion. So they sat on ant-hills all day long, and played on the Jews'-harp ... [After 1,000 years] they had forgotten even how to make Jews'-harps by this time ...[28]

Within 2,000 years they devolve into apes – a reversal of the Theory of Evolution.

---

[24] R.M., *Micrologia: Characters or Essayes, of Persons, Trades, and Places Offered to the City and Country* (London, 1629).
[25] Henry Fielding, *The History of the Adventures of Joseph Andrews, and of his friend Mr. Abraham Adams* (1742), Book 1 Chapter VII – Philosophical Commentary.
[26] Laurence Sterne, *The Life and Opinions of Tristram Shandy, Gentleman* (Harmondsworth: Penguin Classics, 1985), p. 365.
[27] *Cambridge Chronicle and Journal*, 27 December 1862, p. 3.
[28] Charles Kingsley, *The Water Babies* (London, 1912), pp. 196–8.

The House of the Seven Gables, by Nathaniel Hawthorne, also mentions the jews-harp, in a description of a female character:

> Stretching out her long, lank arm, she put a paper of pearl-buttons, a Jew's harp, or whatever the small article might be, in its destined place, and straightforward vanished back into the dusk, as if the world need never hope for another glimpse of her.[29]

In 'The Adventure of the Empty House' from *The Return of Sherlock Holmes*, Sherlock identifies a villain in the following way: 'because I recognised their sentinel when I glanced out of the window. He is a harmless enough fellow, Parker by name, a garrotter by trade, and a remarkable performer upon the jew's harp'.[30] George Bernard Shaw in a discussion on the crumbs tossed to the oppressed classes suggested, 'Bathrooms and pianos, smart tweeds and starched collars, reach numbers of people who once, as "the unsoaped" played the Jew's harp or the accordion in moleskins and belchers'.[31] Other writers and playwrights who mention the instrument include William Blake, Lord Byron, Tom Stoppard and James Joyce, who gives his own slant in *Ulysses*: 'Alone, what did Bloom hear? The double reverberation of retreating feet on the heaven-born earth, the double vibration of a jew's harp in the resonant lane'.[32]

Patrick O'Brian is noted for his well-researched representations of the Royal Navy of the Napoleonic Wars period, and mentions jews-harps in four of the Aubrey–Maturin series:

> By the time of the evening singing, after a purely formal beating to quarters ... The cook obliged them with a ballad of eighty-one stanzas about Barton, the Scotch pirate, accompanied by three Jew's harps ...[33]

> They are a sad lot in the wardroom here: German flutes by the dozen and not a true note between 'em. Jew's harps are more their mark. And all the mids' voices broke long ago; in any case there's not one can tell a B from a bull's foot.[34]

> The *Nutmeg of Consolation* received her Captain without ceremony, instantly hoisted in his gig, slipped her moorings, and as her little band (a tromba marina,

---

[29] Quoted in *Dunfermline Saturday Press*, 8 December 1860, p. 4.
[30] Arthur Conan Doyle, 'The Adventure of the Empty House', in *The Return of Sherlock Holmes* (London: George Newnes, Ltd., 1905), p. 17.
[31] George Bernard Shaw, *Man and Superman; A Comedy and a Philosophy* (Westminster: Archibald Constable & Co, Ltd., 1903), p. 208.
[32] James Joyce, *Ulysses* (London: Egoist Press, 1922), p. 689.
[33] Patrick O'Brian, *Far Side of the World* (London: Harper Collins, 1984), p. 118.
[34] Patrick O'Brian, *The Reverse of the Medal* (London: Fontana Books, 1987), p. 21.

two fiddles, an oboe, two Jew's harps and of course the drum) played Loath to Depart she made her way out through the shipping with the last of the tide and a fair but very faint breeze.[35]

The *Surprise* had always been a tuneful ship and much given to dancing, but never to such a degree as this evening, when the crowded forecastle saw the ranks of country-dancers advance, retreat and caper in perfect time despite the swell, while fiddles, horns, Jew's harps and fifes played with barely a pause on the bitts and even perched on the windward cathead.[36]

This latter scene was reproduced in the film *Master and Commander: The Far Side of the World.*

Folklore

Traditional tales have been identified from Northern European and Scandinavian countries, mainly from Norway. Most of these relate to unearthly beings or forest spirits and all bar one give the jews-harp magical properties.[37] Tales from the British Isles and Ireland are few and far between, but there are, however, two English tales from Cornwall. 'The Giant of Towednack' tells how the giant goes home with presents, taking 'a large brass jew's harp from his pocket for Tom and several smaller ones and whistles for the children'.[38]

'The Fairies of Eastern Green' has a smuggler waiting for horses to transport his goods. He hears music; and on venturing nearer, he beholds this sight:

perched on a pretty high bank in their midst, a score or so of little chaps; many of them blew in mouth-organs; some beat cymbals or tamborine; whilst others played on jew's harps, or tweeted on May whistles and feapers.[39]

A German tale was translated into English as 'The Queen who could not bake gingerbread nuts and the King who could not play the Jew's harp'. The story tells how they contrived to be happy together in spite of these sad deficiencies.[40]

---

[35] Patrick O'Brian, *The Nutmeg of Consolation* (London: Harper Collins, 1997), p. 98.
[36] Patrick O'Brian, *Clarissa Oakes* (London: Harper Collins, 1997), p. 53.
[37] See Frederick Crane, 'Trolls and Trumps', *VIM*, 9 (2000), pp. 7–26 and 'Trolls and Trumps', *VIM*, 11 (2003), pp. 18–21.
[38] William Bottrell, *Stories and Traditions of Penwith* (Penzance, 1870).
[39] William Bottrell, *Stories and Folk-Lore of West Cornwall, Traditions and Hearthside Stories of West Cornwall Third Series* (Penzance, 1880; facsimile reprint 1996 by Llanerch Publishers, Felinfach, 1996), p. 93.
[40] *Glasgow Herald*, 10 April 1886, p. 8.

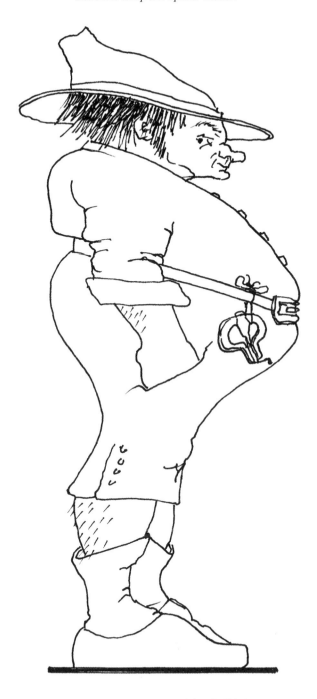

Figure 8.2   *The Giant of Towadnack*, by Michael Wright
Source: Author's collection.

'Prince Ritto; or, the Four-Leaved Shamrock', by Fanny W. Currey, is described thus by the *London Standard*:

> a genuine fairy story of the delightful country where they eat fern seed and walk invisible; where Ritto, or anybody else who is lucky enough to find a four-leafed shamrock in a wood, may easily learn how to harness dragon flies with ropes of cobweb to chariots of flower blossoms ... to steal honey from the busy bee, to ring no end of chimes from the bells of flowers, to play on a Jew's harp made of bees' wings ...[41]

The dark side of fairy lore is covered by 'The Four Hunters and the Four Glastigs' from Scotland. There is a tradition that because the jews-harp is made of metal it can ward off evil spirits. Whether this covers the whole of the British Isles is debateable, but there is no doubting the belief as described in the story from Perthshire from which comes a magical tale of hunters approached by fairy women, called glastigs. The only one to survive is a jews-harp player. There are small variations of the story – two or four hunters, for instance – but the basic story is the same. The hunters make for a bothy or shelter and all but one regret the lack of female companionship. Their request is answered by the arrival of two or four beautiful women and the story continues:

> When the hunter sitting at the fire noticed this, he drew his dirk from the scabbard, and laid it across his knees. Then he took two trumps out of his pocket, and began to play on them. The woman standing before him noticed this and said: "Good is the music of the trump, Saving the one note in its train. Its owner likes it in his mouth, In preference to any maid." The hunter, however, did not acknowledge that he heard her, but continued playing on the trumps as before.[42]

By the time dawn breaks, the hunter had held off the temptress. Left alone, he discovers the corpses of his companions, their blood having been drained from their bodies.

> The place was afterwards known as the Glen of the Green Women. Glenfinlas is a tract of forest ground in the Highlands of Perthshire, near Callander. It belongs to the Earl of Moray. The scenery in the vicinity is amongst the finest in Scotland. The full title of the ballad is "Glenfinlas; or Lord Ronald's Coronach" – *coronach* being the lamentation for a deceased warrior – *Cassell's Illustrated British Ballads*.[43]

---

[41] *London Standard*, 22 December 1877, p. 2.
[42] James MacDougall, *Folk Tales and Fairy Lore in Gaelic and English* (Edinburgh, 1910), p. 251.
[43] *Exeter Flying Post*, 5 October 1881, p. 6; variation of story published in the *Dundee Courier*, 19 January 1879, p. 7.

The Jews-Harp in Popular Culture   147

Figure 8.3   *The Performer*, by Nigel Porteous
Source: By kind permission of Lindsay Porteous.

Rhymes and Poems

There are also a few alphabet rhymes. In 'Another Alphabet on a Single Rhyme',

> I is for Idol that leads us astray;
> J is for Jew's Harp that urchins oft play …[44]

In 'The Angry Author's Alphabet',

> I an inebriate, shouting and slanging;
> J a Jew's harp, which a street boy was twanging.[45]

---

[44]   *Hereford Times*, 8 February 1862, p. 6; *Berwickshire News and General Advertiser*, 28 June 1892, p. 4.
[45]   *Daily Gazette for Middlesbrough*, 21 November 1892, p. 4.

There is one poem in praise of a local football team, under 'Athletic Notes. By "Sportsman" ... An eccentric bard on the victory'. Verse 4 reads:

> Then with drum, and fife, and Jew's-harp,
> Double B, and sweet bassoon;
> Let us sing, not flat but B sharp,
> To the fame of Burnley "Toon".[46]

Stories appear in poetry form, even if, as in this case, it is a parody of Homer's *Iliad*, introduced as 'Homer travestie, being a new burlesque translation of the ten first books of the Iliad, By the translator Thomas Bridges':

> Be that as't may, away they went,
> And reach'd the great Achilles tent,
> They found him sitting on his rump,
> Playing upon a brass Jew-trump;
> The music seem'd to please him much,
> Because he grinn'd at ev'ry touch.
> Only Patroclus tarry'd near him;
> No mortal else would stay to hear him.
> So taken was he with his airs,
> They stole upon him unawares.
> No sooner did he 'spy them come,
> But up he started off his bum;
> And whipp'd the trump into his pocket
> So quick, 'twas ten to one he'd broke it ...[47]

There is also 'The story of Aeneas and Dido burlesqued from the fourth book of the Aeneid, of Virgil':

> Given him by Apollo, whose sharp
> Snout he presented with a Jew's harp ...
> Apollo was so delighted
> With his Jew's harp from morn to night he'd
> Still laugh and strum, and strum and laugh,
> So gave him in return this staff:
> A staff which had such wond'rous pow'r,
> The like was never seen before ...[48]

---

[46] *Burnley Express*, 18 February 1893, p. 8.
[47] *Literature and Language, Volume 2* (London, 1764), p. 235.
[48] *Literature and Language* (Charlestown, SC, 1774), p. 108.

Figure 8.4 *Scots Trump Player*, by Nigel Porteous
Source: By kind permission of Lindsay Porteous.

Various odes were written incorporating the jews-harp either in passing or on the instrument itself, as in this case, 'ODE upon a JEW's HARP', sent in a letter to James Boswell by Andrew Erskine:

New-Tarbat, Nov. 23, 1761.

Dear BOSWELL,

... I have often wondered, Boswell, that a man of your taste in music, cannot play upon the Jews harp; there are some of us here that touch it very melodiously, I can tell you. Corelli's solo of Maggie Lauder, and Pergolesi's sonata of The Carle he came o'er the Craft, are excellently adapted to that instrument; let me advise you to learn it. The first cost is but three halfpence, and they last a long time. I have composed the following ode upon it, which exceeds Pindar as much as the Jews harp does the organ.

ODE upon a JEW's HARP.
I.
SWEET instrument! which fix'd in yellow teeth,
So clear so sprightly and so gay is found,
Whether you breathe along the shore of Leith,
Or Lowmond's lofty cliffs thy strains resound;
Struck by a taper finger's gentle tip,
Ah softly in our ears thy pleasing murmurs slip!
II.
Where'er thy lively music's found,
All are jumping, dancing round:
Ev'n trusty William lifts a leg,
And capers like sixteen with Peg;
Both old and young confess thy pow'rful sway,
They skip like madmen and they frisk away.
III.
Rous'd by the magic of the charming air,
The yawning dogs forego their heavy slumbers;
The ladies listen on the narrow stair,
And Captain Andrew straight forgets his numbers.
Cats and mice give o'er their batt'ling,
Pewter plates on shelves are rattling;
But falling down the noise my lady hears,
Whole scolding drowns the trump more tuneful than the spheres![49]

---

[49] Mr James Boswell; Mr Andrew Erskine, *Letters Between the Honourable Andrew Erskine and James Boswell, Esq.* (London, 1763), pp. 25–7.

There were more serious poems by war poets Patrick MacGill in 1915 and Sidney Keyes and Alun Lewis c.1942. Patrick Moore's collection was published as *Soldiers Songs*, and includes 'The Return'. Here is verse 2:

> When a Jew's harp breaks the silence, Purring an old refrain,
> Singing the song of the soldier, "Here we are again!"
> Here we are! Here we are!
> Oh! here we are again!
> Some have gone west,
> Best of the best,
> Lying out in the rain,
> Stiff as stones in the open, Out of the doings for good.
> They'll never come back to advance or attack;
> But, God! don't we wish that they could![50]

Sidney Keyes was killed in action in Tunisia in 1943, just 20 years old. With Keith Douglas and Alun Lewis, he is regarded as one of the outstanding poets of World War II. Lewis died on active service in Burma in 1944. This poem, 'Poets in the Storm', is credited to them:

> Just here you leave this Cardiganshire lane,
> Here by these milk churns and this telegraph pole,
> Latch up the gate and cut across those fields.
> Some things you see in detail, those you need;
> The raindrops spurting from the trodden stubble
> Squirting your face across the reaping meadow,
> The strange machine-shaped scarab beetle,
> His scalloped legs clung bandy to a stalk,
> The jew's-harp bee with saddlebags of gold,
> The wheat as thin as hair on flimsy slopes,
> The harsh hewn faces of the farming folks,
> Opinion humming like a nest of wasps,
> The dark-clothed brethren at the chapel gates;
> And farther on the mortgaged crumbling farm ...[51]

Crossword Puzzles and Games

Not surprisingly the name of the instrument appeared during the war as crossword puzzle clues, as in this provided in *Picture Post* of 1943: '11 across: You won't

---

[50] Patrick MacGill, *Soldier Songs* (London, 1917), p. 91.
[51] In *The Times Literary Supplement*, London, 11 August 1945, p. 378.

find this instrument in a Nazi orchestra (4 and 4)';[52] or from the *Western Morning News*, '10. Hitler does not play them (2 words) (4, 5)'.[53]

The Times used the instrument in crosswords and quizzes on at least 10 occasions, some references more obscure than others. Here are some mentions in 'Word-Watching', described as '[a] daily safari through the language jungle' and compiled by Philip Howard. In each instance, readers had to guess the correct definition from three possibilities:

> Guimbard: a. A wandering minstrel; b. A greave; c. A jew's-harp.[54]
> [The answer is, of course, c.]
>
> Vibrissa: a. A Jew's harp; b. A nostril hair; c. An ankle bone.[55]
> [The answer is b.]
>
> Crembalum: a. Osmins eunuch in Il Seraglio; b. A Jew's Harp; c. An antiphon in Plainsong.[56]
> [The answer is b.]

The *Times Two* crossword also featured the jews-harp:

> Down: 5. Instrument plucked in mouth (4,4)[57]
>
> Down: 1. An old Jew's harp in need of repair, I understand (8)[58]
> [The solution: Pharisee.][59]
>
> Across: Not a jew's-harp (8)
> [The solution: Psaltery.][60]

More family-focused quizzes include 'Fireside Questions for the Family':

> How many strings have: (a) a double bass; (b) a guitar; (c) a ukulele; (d) a tromba marina; (e) a Jew's harp; (f) a side-drum; (g) a balalaika?[61]

---

[52] *Picture Post*, 20 March 1943, p. 26.
[53] *Western Morning News*, Devon, 9 April 1936, pp. 2 and 15.
[54] *The Times*, 1 August 1989, p. 18.
[55] *The Times*, 2 December 1993, pp. 48 and 44.
[56] *The Times*, 9 January 1988, p. 22.
[57] *The Times*, 10 June 1999, p. 52.
[58] *The Times*, 24 June 1997, p. 26.
[59] *The Times*, 25 June 1997, p. 26.
[60] *The Times*, 19 January 1939, p. 5.
[61] *The Times*, 24 December 1949, p. 7.

There is also 'Can You Tell – ?'

> What is the name of the form of metal lyre which is held between the teeth and played by plucking its vibrating tongue?[62]

> What is a Jew's harp? Answer: A Jew's harp is a primitive musical instrument consisting of a metal frame which is pressed against the teeth. The reed is plucked.[63]

One final reference comes from *The Leeds Times*, 1871. It purports to be taken from a love letter produced in a breach of promise case:

> A Model Love Letter. – Breach of promise cases usually produce laughter; especially when the love letters are read is the risibility of the court excited. We have been favoured, from a thoroughly trustworthy source, with a letter which was not read the other day when a cause for breach was tried in one of the Midland counties … We print the epistle more as a warning than an example … "Your laugh rings in my ears like the jews-harp strain, or the bleat of a stray lamb on the bleak hill-side."[64]

---

[62] *Nottingham Evening Post*, 16 November 1931, pp. 3 and 16.
[63] *Evening Angus*, 2 March 1935, p. 7.
[64] *The Leeds Times*, 30 December 1871, p. 3.

Chapter 9
Players

It never ceases to amaze me how varied the instrument can be in terms of construction and playing style.

Jonathan Cope, 2010[1]

Jim Spriggs, York

Plough Sunday is the last Sunday before Epiphany, i.e. about two weeks after Christmas. There was a tradition, probably post-Restoration, for a plough to be taken into church to be blessed at the altar steps before being put back to work on the land. This tradition was revived in a number of parishes after the 2nd WW, in order to encourage men to go back to farming.

Figure 9.1   Plough Sunday, Bolton Percy, Yorkshire, 1990s
Source: By kind permission of Rob Guest, from a snapshot.

---

[1] Jonathan Cope, personal correspondence.

The Yorkshire Longsword team I belong to helped to provide the entertainment after the service, in our case at St Helen's, Bolton Percy, near York … when we have too many men for a particular dance, they stand out and play an instrument, in my case the jews harp. The tunes used are the usual common folk tunes that go with this type of dancing: "The Girl I left Behind Me"; "Buffalo Girls"; "the Keel Row"; etc.[2]

Ward Cooper, Wednesbury, West Midlands

I guess I'd be about five, I suppose, when I first saw a jews-harp in my grandfather's house, and that was in Wednesbury. That would have been about 1968, something like that. I remember the day because there was a big family gathering in the house and my dad played guitar and my granddad produced this jews-harp out of his pocket and he says, "Have you ever seen one of these before?" And he just started playing it, twanging away and my dad joined in on the guitar. My dad was a singer in a band – an amateur, rock-and-roll band – but he was also into Irish folk music. I remember them playing an Irish folk song that my dad played and was singing – I think it was "Paddy on the Railways" – and my granddad was accompanying him on the jews-harp.

In the time when I saw him on stage, when my dad was singing and playing guitar, they were playing Irish folk-songs and I distinctly remember my dad singing one verse of the melody of the song, the chorus I think it was, and then he stopped and strummed the guitar and my granddad played the melody – the same time as what my dad had just sung, he played the tune. He was good.[3]

Johnny Handle, Hexham, Northumberland

Aa met Bob in the early 1960s. Aa was oot hikin in the Hills around the Ingram Valley. It was a wintry kind o' day, and Aa woz wet through te the gills, lookin' forward te getting on the bus, dryin' oot, and hevvin a good meal at Newcastle, cos Aa'd et all me bait. Aa' just cum on te the main Wooler-Newcastle road, when Aa saw the tail lights of the United bus dissapearing through the fallin' snow!! Ne bus for two hours!! So Aa walked doon the road a bit (Sarely put oot) and there shinin' in the dark was a "Blue Star". The pub at Powburn!

In Aa got, ordered a Pint and sum Chicken Soop (Aa kin still mind the smell te this day. it was heaven) and heard, in the Back Room, a fiddle and Jews Harp gannin. Went In and there was Bob Clark and Ivor Smith, playin' away. So Aa stopped and

---

[2] Jim Spriggs, personal correspondence. See Appendix: Notes: Track 1.
[3] Interview with Ward Cooper, Oxford, 30 October 2013.

lissened tiv Ivor fiddlin' away, and Bob fiddling a bit hissel' and deein' odd bits on the Gewgar. Aa wish Aa cud mind what they played, but it was a long time ago.[4]

The Earliest Players

The importation, making and distribution of jews-harps as a musical instrument is irrelevant if the instrument is not incorporated into the musical culture of the country. As indicated, the Scottish and Irish appear to have adopted the jews-harp more readily than the rest of England and Wales, with the exception of Northumberland. While there is the carving in York Minster and an early image of a player on the crozier of William of Wykeham, in New College Oxford dated c.1360, there is no indication that the instrument had any particular musical status other than a recognition of its existence at that time. Other instruments on the crozier depict shawms and trumpets, but also triangles and cymbals, so we gain no further information concerning its use. Early references to players are non-existent until the very end of the sixteenth century. Dated 1549, *The Complaynt of Scotland* appears to be the first description of a player:

> Thir scheipirdis aude there vyuis sang mony vthir melodi' sangis, the quhilkis i hef nocht in memorie. than efter this sueit celest armonye, tha began to dance in ane ring, euyrie ald scheiphyrd led his vyfe be the hand and euyrie yong scheiphird led hyr quhome he luffit best. Ther was viij scheiphyrdis and ilk ane of them hed ane syndry instrument to play to the laif. the first hed ane drone bag pipe, the nyxt hed ane pipe maid of ane bleddir and of ane reid, the thrid playit on ane trump, the feyrd on ane corne pipe, the fyft playit on ane pipe maid of ane gait horne, the sext playt on ane recordar the seuint plait on ane fiddil, and the last on ane quhissel.[5]

Up to recent times, shepherds took jews-harps with them to play while relaxing during the lambing season. According to Johnny Handle,

> Many a time the sheep woz gathered for lambin in ootbye deserted farmhooses, and the like, te save roondin them aal a lang way doon from the High Fell valleys. So the shepherds wad pack aal the gear they needed, wot wi clathes, Beddin', medicines and that, te stay in these ootbye neuks for upwards of three weeks or mare. NE room for fiddles or melodeons. So they tyeuk their Moothies, whistles and Gewgars te while away the hoors of bein midwives ... And if they med a new tune or twee then wen they got back te their farms they cud put it te the fiddle or melodeon te see how it wad gan.[6]

---

[4] Johnny Handle, personal correspondence.
[5] [Wedderburn], Leyden, *The Complaynt of Scotland*, p. 101.
[6] Johnny Handle, personal correspondence; he adds, 'Bob Clark, Billy Atkinson (Moothie), Will Taylor, and Jimmy White, telt te me in the 1960s and 1970s'.

The seventeenth-century song, 'The Shepherds Delight / Both by Day and by Night', to the tune 'Now the Tyrant has Stole my Dearest away', mentions the jews-harp:

With Bagpipes and taber, and Hoby sometimes,
We dance and skip and sing, and our natural Rymes;
Two Jews-trumps well play'd on, with Violin soft,
Makes spirits to rise, and our bloods mount aloft.

Geillis Duncan

It is not, however, until 1590 that we have the first British named player. Geillis Duncan was accused of witchcraft and was one of the 'witches' who gathered at North Berwick churchyard as part of an alleged conspiracy to murder King James IV. At the examination of Agnes Sampson, December 1590, she confessed, 'She passed there [North Berwick kirk] on horse back convoyed by ... Couper and lighted at the kirk yard. Gilli ... them on the trump. John Fian led all the rest'.[7]

Figure 9.2   Entrance port of the ruined North Berwick Kirk
Source: Photograph by author.

---

[7] 'Examination and Confession of Agnes Sampson', quoted in Lawrence Norman and Gareth Roberts, *Witchcraft in Early Modern Scotland: James VI's 'Demonology' and the North Berwick Witches* (Exeter: University of Exeter Press, 2000), p. 147.

The trials of Sampson and Barbara Napier provide more detail: 'They danced along the kirk-yard, Gelie Duncan played to them on a trump, John Fian, misselled, led all the rest' (Sampson)[8] and 'upon Allhallow Even lastwas, 1590 years, to the frequent convention held at the kirk of North Berwick, where she danced endlong the kirkyard, and Gelie Duncan played on a trump. John Fian, miselled, led the ring' (Napier).[9]

> These confessions made the king in a wonderful admiration, and he sent for said Geillis Duncane, who upon the like trump did play the said dance before the King's Majesty: who, in respect of the strangeness of these matters, took great delight to be present at their examinations.[10]

This, sadly, did not save her from execution.[11]

Donald McIlmichall

Trials also provide the names of the next two players. In 1677, Donald McIlmichall was accused and found guilty of the theft of a cow and of consorting with evil spirits. At his trial at Inveraray, Argyll, he confessed to meeting with a group of dancers. He judged them 'not to have bein *wordlie* men or men ordayned of god' and reported that they 'enquyred if he wes baptized and that he said he wes'. Subsequently,

> he mett them in Leismore and at the Shian of Barcalden and still saw the old man that seemed to be cheif being ane large tall corporal Gardman and ruddie and he was engadgeit to conceal them and no to tell other. Bot that he told it to the forsaid Robert Buchanan once fer which he was reproved and stricken be them in the cheik and other pairts, and that he mett them still on ilk Sabaths nights and that he playd on trumps to them quhen they danced.[12]

The word 'trumps' implies that McIlmichall either had two or more instruments available or that he played two at the same time, a technique used to change key when necessary within a tune. This is not an unusual skill, commonly used in Austria, and also by the third named player, Peter Kelly, original name Mackhuen.

---

[8] Robert Pitcairn, *Criminal Trials and Other Proceedings before the High Court of Justiciary, vol. II*, Bannatyne Club Publications 42, Maitland Club Publications 19, 3 vols (Edinburgh: printed for the Maitland Club, 1831–1833), p. 239.

[9] Pitcairn, 'The Trial of Barbara Napier's Assizers for Wilful Error', in *Criminal Trials, vol. II*, pp. 245–6.

[10] *Newes from Scotland*, p. 14.

[11] For a full account of the events, see Michael Wright, 'The Jew's Harp in the Law, 1590–1825', *Folk Music Journal* 9(3) (2008), pp. 349–71.

[12] J.R.N. Macphail (ed.), *Highland Papers, vol. III* (Edinburgh: Scottish History Society, 1914–1934), p. 37.

Peter Kelly

Kelly was accused of murder in 1729 and a number of reports and trial witnesses testified to his skill at playing two jews-harps and to the dissolute life he led:

> he had an excellent Hand at playing upon 2 Jews Harps at once, which involv'd him in bad Company and exposed him to keep ill Hours ... the Day before this Murder was discovered, he had a Wedding at his House, and the Prisoner was there, and said till 12 at Night, and further, told a long Tale, or compound of Mirth and Madness, as their throwing the Stocking, drinking, dancing, and playing upon the Jews Harps, which he said, the Prisoner had pawn'd for 3 d. and he lent him Money to fetch them, and that the Prisoner got drunk and carried the Bridegroom's Wig home – William Graham.[13]

> [H]e had been profligate in his Life, Whoring, Drinking, and idling away his Time, and neglecting his Business, so that his Wife and Children were forc'd to go begging, while he went about from house to house, playing upon his two Jews-Harps at once, in doing of which he was very ingenious, and obtruding himself upon all Companies in Ale-houses, and often none of the best, who gave him Drink, and sometimes a little Money for his Musick – James Guthrie, Ordinary of Newgate Gaol.[14]

> It seems he play'd with great Dexterity upon two *Jews-Harps* at a time, and this serving to entertain People of as loose and idle a Disposition as himself, he thereby got a good deal of Money, or least Drink, which was to him all one ... – anon.[15]

Both McIlmichall and Kelly were hung.[16]

Mention in Trials

Jews-harps or locations named after the instrument appear in many trials, the *Proceedings of the Old Bailey* alone with 42 cases between 1729 and 1850. So far

---

[13] *Proceedings of the Old Bailey*, at www.oldbaileyonline.org, version 7.0 (accessed 24 September 2013), ref. t17290226-9.

[14] James Guthrie, *The Ordinary of Newgate his Account, of the Behaviour, Confession, and Last Dying Words of the Malefactors, Who Were Executed at Tyburn, on Monday the 24th of this Instant March, 1729* (London, 1729), n.p.

[15] Anon., *The Lives of the Most Remarkable Criminals: Who Have Been Condemn'd and Executed; For Murder, Highway, House Breakers, Street-Robberies, Coining, or Other Offences; From the Year 1720, to the Present Time, vol. III* (London, 1735), p. 96.

[16] That all these three players were tried and executed for one crime or another had nothing to do with their playing the jews-harp, but it was thought important enough, or unusual enough, to mention it in their trials. For a full account of the events, see Wright, 'The Jew's Harp in the Law, 1590–1825'.

around 80 cases have been traced countrywide, of which 32 refer to a location. What is striking is the age of the accused and the severity of the sentences. Of the 23 cases where ages are given, 17 are under 21 years of age and seven are under 16. John Bailey, for instance, was sentenced to transportation for seven years in 1822 for 'theft and simple grand larceny'. At his trial with Goodman Solomon it was stated by ironmonger Augustus Finch that 'the two prisoners came in and asked for a penny Jew's harp'. Bailey's defence was, 'He went with me to buy the harp, and as we came out this piece of brass laid on the step – I picked it up and shewed it him; and said, "Let us go to an iron shop and see if they will buy it"'. Bailey was 10 years old and Solomon, who had the same sentence of transportation, was 15 years old.[17] William Groom is said to have taken 'a Jew's-harp out of his pocket, and began to play on it' when arrested for theft. He was 14 years old and 'Transported for Seven Years. – Convict Ship'.[18]

Boys

While there is the occasional reference to girls owning or playing jews-harps, there are numerous references suggesting jews-harps were a boy's musical instrument. The *Berkshire Chronicle* of 1857 commented, 'The boys of London are as peculiar in their locality as the palm is to the east' and that they were 'addicted to singing, whistling, and screeching; early adepts of the Jew's harp'.[19] The *Manchester Evening News* in 1885 noted:

> The boy's pockets challenges the wonder of every person who has never been a boy, as well as those who have once been boys ... [including] a brass clock wheel, an out-of-date key, a Jew's-harp, a slate pencil ... all can be carried in one pocket.[20]

On a similar theme, the poem, 'A Boy's Pockets – What they contain (sometimes)' lists the following items:

> A pistol with caps and a junk of lead,
> A "gross big" screw and a rag that's red!
> An old Jew's harp that hath lost its strains –
> Such are the "treasures" a boy retains ...[21]

---

[17] *Proceedings of the Old Bailey*, t18221023-13.
[18] *Proceedings of the Old Bailey*, t18400203-743.
[19] *Berkshire Chronicle*, 4 April 1857, p. 7.
[20] *Manchester Evening News*, 21 February 1885, p. 4.
[21] *Western Times*, Devon, 21 July 1905, p. 7.

Under the heading 'What Boys do for a Prize', the *Tamworth Herald* tells:

> [A] schoolmaster once promised to give a beautiful machine [bicycle] to the boy who proved himself most worthy of it ... One genius confidently claimed the bicycle because he had learnt the Jew's-harp, the tin whistle, and the trombone, and was indignant when the schoolmaster passed him over.[22]

'The Strike of School Children', in *The Graphic, London*, described in some detail a schoolboy protest march:

> The schoolboy strike which broke out recently in Scotland, at Edinburgh, and Dundee, and afterwards affected Cardiff, Middlesborough, West Hartlepool, and various metropolitan districts, originated during the strike of dockers at the East End of London. The schoolboys simply imitated the dockers by the strike in which they took part, and they parodied, in their evening demonstration about the streets, many of the features of the docker's daily procession ... The tallest boy in the column walked at the head of the procession carrying a pole ... Behind him came the band, composed of about a score of lads beating trays, kettles, and triangles, and a few blowing flutes or playing jews' harps.[23]

Disruption of one kind or another does not seem far from boys' minds. There are disturbances in church services and general nuisance complaints. Here is one such concern, sent to the editor of the *London Standard*:

> the human, or rather, inhuman boys who infest some parts of Kensington, and make day as well as night hideous with concertinas, whistles, jew's harps, and – what is three times worse than all three instruments of torture put together – their own raucous renditions of the refined lyrics of the music hall.[24]

Sean Breadin from Durham recalled from the 1970s a tale of disruption caused in church:

> A friend once told me of a Jew's Harp craze that occurred in a Newcastle high school in the early 1970s; the rougher elements would use [jews-harps] for comic effect & mischievous distraction during suitably solemn moments in assemblies, classes & even church services, the instruments being small enough to conceal from irate pedagogues. One wonders just how localised this craze was ...[25]

---

[22] *Tamworth Herald*, 14 July 1900, p. 3.
[23] *The Graphic, London*, 19 October 1889, pp. 7–8.
[24] *London Standard*, 12 November 1895, p. 6.
[25] Sean Breadin, personal correspondence.

Regional Players

Altogether we know of just over 200 named players: 105 English; 89 Scottish; nine Irish or Irish-American and a couple of references to Welsh players. There were also 18 named European players who performed in the British Isles. In addition there are up to 100 unnamed players mentioned in newspapers and other sources.

Players can be divided into those of whom it was noted could play, often in obituaries; amateur performers, including competition participants; professional and semi-professional stage acts; and, later, recording artists. Stage and professional performances occur throughout the nineteenth century, the most famous being Austrian player Karl Eulenstein.

Karl Eulenstein

Born in 1802 and gaining a reputation in Europe for playing up to 16 jews-harps, Eulenstein came to England in 1826 and was heralded by critics and audiences alike as he 'raised it [the jews-harp] in the science of music ... So unprepared is the mind for the exquisite effect produced that description would be difficult'.[26] Performing in selective concert venues and to discerning audiences, including King George IV, Eulenstein toured the country gaining a reputation for playing the jews-harp more skilfully 'than any other player before or since ... on [this] simple instrument the harmony he produces is quite astonishing'.[27] 'Delicious sweetness'[28] and 'elegance and melody, the compass and variety ... he gives to his instrument'[29] are typical comments in newspapers of the time. His death was noted in 1890 and he is referred to in a number of articles in the 1930s and 1940s, such was his high reputation. Tunes mentioned are Rossini's 'Di tanti palpiti', 'Kathleen O'More'[30] and 'A Rondo. A la Paginini', while the *Hull Packet* noted of his playing,

> [there are] three distinctive qualities of tone – the deep notes of the first octave may be compared to the sounds produced from the reed pipe or clarionet; the intermediate and the lighter notes resemble the human voice, and some organa; the harmonious are precisely those of musical glasses.[31]

Eulenstein and Geillis Duncan were not the only performers to play before royalty. *The Morning Post* tells that a certain Mr Warren performed before his

---

[26] *Northampton Mercury*, 12 June 1826, p. 10.
[27] *The Times*, 29 June 1826, p. 3.
[28] *Leamington Spa Courier*, 16 August 1830, p. 4.
[29] *Cheltenham Looker-On*, 13 May 1833, p. 2.
[30] See Appendix: Notes: Track 2.
[31] *Hull Packet*, 25 March 1828, p. 4.

Majesty [William IV] with great éclat: 'His power over that little instrument is truly astonishing'.[32]

Generally, there seems to have been a ready acceptance of European players rather than local musicians in musical circles in Britain, a readiness that applies today, though now extended to World Music.

Scottish Players

One of the greatest players was Angus Lawrie of Oban, a champion piper who specialised, if the recordings are anything to go by, in march, strathspey and reels (MSRs). The live recording of 'Dornoch Links' and 'Lochiel's Away to France' (marches), 'The Shepherds Crook' (strathspey) and 'Lochiel's Away to France' (reel), is one of the finest of the MSR performances the author has heard.[33] A total of 15 tracks of Lawrie are available online through the Tobar an Dualchais project website, along with 17 other players including other Scottish trump players, Lindsay Porteous from Culross,[34] Duncan Williamson, Katherine Dix and Arthur Middleton.

John Wright met Lawrie in 1965 after listening to the recordings held in the Vaughan Williams Memorial Library, Cecil Sharp House, London. 'I could not believe my ears! I've been trying to do the same thing ever since,' he recalled in 2013, continuing,

> Very hard to understand what he's doing ... he seemed to breathe the whole time but there was something that changed and that seemed to correspond to separating odd and even harmonics ... I worked it out afterwards and at present I think it comes from raising the tip of the player's tongue to touch the roof of the mouth. When I originally tried to imitate Lawrie's technique in 1965 I used to use the tip of my tongue just to separate the notes. That was wrong, but in a funny way the wheel has turned full circle now. In fact what I do is a bit like diddling. But actually these days when I play tunes I throw in all the articulation techniques I know.[35]

Other Scottish players of note are 'Curly' Mackay, Willie Kemp, the piper Allan McDonald from Edinburgh, Brendan Power, Don Black, Calum Campbell, Norman Chalmers, Ewan MacPherson, Willie, Allan and Gordon McKenzie from the Elgin district, Jim Clark from Aberdeen, Dave Gould from Sutherland, Kenny Dan MacDonald, Emily MacDonald and Callum Mackay from Stornoway. Mackay learned as a child in the 1950s inspired by the playing of a neighbour, Peter MacLeod,

---

[32] *The Morning Post*, London, 7 July 1835, p. 3.
[33] The reader might like to visit the Vaughan Williams Memorial Library, Cecil Sharp House, London for the BBC recording. There is also the website http://www.tobarandualchais.co.uk/ (accessed 15 June 2015).
[34] Lindsey Porteous has almost singlehandedly promoted the trump in Scotland for the last 50 years.
[35] Wright, interview, 20 July 2013.

who gave him his first instrument aged nine. The troub (local name) was a man's instrument, not played by women or girls, and was often shared between families. Despite jews-harps not being readily available in Mackay's youth, it seems every man and boy owned one. Tunes he plays include 'Miss McLeod's Reel'.[36]

Competitions

In and around Dundee between November 1934 and August 1937, no fewer than 37 competitions were reported in the local press. Twenty venues were mentioned and 45 players named. They were part of a series of competitions that included diddling, whistling, singing, recitations, melodeon, harmonica and fiddle playing, pie and scone eating and beauty and ankle competitions.

Figure 9.3   'Diddlers who competed at the Forfar Ploughing Association's diddling competition. A prizewinning trio of two Jew's harps and an accordion'
Source: *Dundee Courier*, 11 January 1936. Photograph courtesy of DC Thomson.

---

[36]   Wright, *Travels wi' a Trump*.

A. Stark of Dundee was particularly successful on the jews-harp, winning on six occasions with one second; Allun and Charles Suttie gained two firsts, six seconds and two third places; George Smart and his brother J. Smart won four firsts with two third places; W. Blair had six placings including one first; W. Kidd of Dundee, two firsts and three placings; and W. Miller, two firsts and a second place.

These were very popular events. At the Forfar and District Ploughing Association event in Forfar, 'The hall was packed, and, despite the fact that extra seats were taken in and dozens of people were standing, several hundreds more had to be turned away'.[37] Unfortunately, no tunes are mentioned.

Since the revival, jews-harp competitions have been held at various festivals from the early 1970s, the first c.1971 at Kinross with Fife folk singer John Watt as the judge and Lindsay Porteous the winner. The festival moved to Auchtermuchty, the last competition there being in 2013. The Traditional Music & Song Association of Scotland also hold trump competitions at Keith Folk Festival and Kirriemuir.

Welsh Players

There are three references to Welsh players. One comes from 1904: 'The haunt of a Cardiff hermit has been disturbed with extraordinary results ... His chief amusement when indoors, where he never burnt a light, was playing a Jew's harp to amuse the rats, with which the place literally swarms'.[38] The hermit is not named. Another is dated 1914, referring to a yearly tradition:

> In Pembrokeshire early on new Year's morning one's rest is disturbed by the discordant sounds of such musical instruments as mouth organs, Jew's harps, &c, and the singing of boys with lusty voices of the verse:
>
> Rise up on New Year's morning
> The cocks are all a-crowing:
> And if you think it too soon,
> Rise up and look at the stars and moon.[39]

A short story written by Owen Wynne Jones under the pseudonym 'Glasynys', was published in *Cymru Fu*, c.1862. Apparently from the Montgomeryshire area, it is a very detailed description of an evening spent at a farm in a valley somewhere around the Vale of Towy:

> We two are seated in a pair of armchairs, one of black oak and the other of white sycamore. Opposite us, around the fire, was my Uncle Rolant, engaged in conversation as he attended to his jew's harp ...

---

[37] *Dundee Courier*, 11 January 1936, p. 3.
[38] *Evening Telegraph*, Angus, 15 June 1904, p. 3.
[39] *Nottingham Evening Post*, 1 January 1914, p. 4.

After settling the candles in their proper places, and attending to the fire, and seeing that everything was in order, the man of the house favoured us with a solo performance on the jew's harp ... which was followed by combined efforts on the jew's harp, the harp, the *crwth*, and the clarinet, together with Delo Wmffra's contribution on the fife and the tambourine. The house re-echoed to the noise, and everyone played his part as he should.[40]

Figure 9.4   Thomas McManus, *c*.1968
Source: Photograph by John Wright, by kind permission of Catherine Wright-Perrier.

[40] D.M. and E.M. Lloyd (eds), 'A Merry Evening at the Hafod', *A Book of Wales* (London and Glasgow: Collins, 1953), pp. 159–60. See Appendix: Notes: Track 3.

Irish Players

The antiquarian Thomas Dineley suggested in his journal of 1681 that the Irish 'are at this day much addicted (on holidayes, after the bagpipe, Irish harpe, or Jews harpe) to dance after their country fashion'.[41]

Twentieth-century Irish players we can name include John Campbell of Newry, County Antrim; Patrick Devaune; John Camand; Sweeney (no pre-name); Máirtín Sheamais Ó Fátharta; an American living in Ireland, Rick Epping; and an Irishman living in England, Thomas McManus. There are undoubtedly others. Thomas McManus had a distinctive technique:

> He used to wrap his thumb and forefinger around the frame and cup his hand in a "C" to make a resonator ... [and] slid his hand along his fingers so he could control the actual strength of the beat by the angle of the finger. It was quite a complicated way of playing.[42]

There are quite a few Irish recordings, including Patrick Devaune, 'St Patrick's day in the morning'; Sweeney playing 'Christmas Eve' and 'Craigh's Pipes';[43] and John Campbell of Newry, 'Love will you marry me', 'Maggie Picken', 'Fishing for Eels',[44] 'The Frost is Over' and 'The Shaskeen'.[45] John Campbell (1933–2006) was a renowned storyteller and plays 'The Shaskeen' on a video recording that is in the Irish Traditional Music Archive's 'Inishowen Song Project'. He gives an amusing account of local 'character' Johnny Haley, who taught him to play, and follows on with an explanation of how to play the jews-harp:

> You only need two fingers and one thumb on that hand to hold it [holds up left hand]. And you only need one tooth. Hold it up against the tooth. And you only need one finger on the other hand – this is not a concertina. You hold it up against your teeth like that [demonstrates and "Boings"]. Keep your teeth open enough to keep this part here, which is called the tongue, to go back into your mouth. When that happens, you have two tongues in your mouth at the one time – this tongue here and your own tongue. Now you have to keep your own tongue well away from this tongue or you could end up with no tongue! Then from the top lip to the bridge of your nose you make a sound like "shichocha" [plays the reel "The Shaskeen"].[46]

---

[41] E.P. Shirley, 'Extracts from the Journal of Thomas Dineley, Esquire, Giving Some Account of His Visit to Ireland in the Reign of Charles II (continued)', *Journal of the Kilkenny and South-East of Ireland Archaeological Society*, 4(1) (1863), p. 182.

[42] Wright, interview, 2013.

[43] Both Devaune and Sweeney were recorded in 1966 by John Wright and Catherine Perrier, unpublished.

[44] From CD *Ebb and Flow* with Len Graham.

[45] From CD *Two for the Road* with Len Graham.

[46] From http://www.itma.ie./inishowen (accessed 15 June 2015).

Figure 9.5   John Campbell
Source: Photograph taken from 'Exploring Irish Music and Dance' by Dianna Boullier, by kind permission of Dianna Boullier.

Irish radio uses a recording of a tune composed and played by Máirtín Sheamais Ó Fátharta of Na hAille, Indreabhán, Conamara, recorded at his home, that has become the signature tune 'Raidió na Gaeltachta' for Raidió Teilifís Éireann, opening their broadcasts every morning at 6.30 a.m. The reasons for the choice, his nephew Meaití Jó Shéamais surmised, were:

> 1) The sound was unique, unmistakeable, attractive and a little unusual because the use of the instrument was then starting to decline – it would thus serve well as a signature tune.
>
> 2) The sound and the history of the instrument, which was so common in rural Ireland up until the 1960s/1970s, seemed to reflect the station's target audience. The spirit of the recording seemed to reflect the spirit of the community at that time.
>
> Meaití is proud of the radio's choice, of the impact that it had, and of the part that he and his uncle played in the story.[47]

The Irish had their own slant on songs on the jews-harp. 'Na Trumpal' is part of a tradition of songs bemoaning the loss or theft of a musical instrument. The following is translated from the original Irish:

---

[47] I am grateful to Dr Deirdre Ní Chonghaile, Comhalta Iardhochtúireachta and Chomhairle um Thaighde in Éirinn, for this information.

> Doleful am I in mind,
> Troubled, worried and distracted,
> With no heart for fun or romancing
> Or flirting with the girls;
> Joyless and dispirited,
> Without interest in anything
> Frenzied and tormented night and day,
> Ever sobbing and sighing.
> Whatever robber stole away my Jew's harp,
> Unless he quickly returns with it or duly pays for it,
> I'll read the Cursing Litany on him,
> Which will turn him into a mass of disease,
> And leave him week and helpless,
> Without energy or power in his bones.

The owner goes on to describe the effect it has had on him and ends by explaining the consequences of the theft for his love life:

> Bribes used to be given to me by faultless maidens,
> And though I seem to boast, I had the freedom of the fields;
> Now they don't care about talking to me
> Since I've lost my strength and vigour,
> And that's the reason
> I'm as tearful as I am.[48]

English Players

As with shepherds, jews-harps were small enough to be carried by those on the move. According to Pat Warner, when describing life as a lock-keeper's daughter,

> Some of the boat people were ardent Methodists and Salvationists. Sunday evening services would be held on a boat where three or four families had moored up together. To the strains of an accordion, melodeon, Jew's harp or mouth organ they would put every ounce of feeling into the well-known hymns.[49]

Most performances mentioned in newspapers were by amateur players in small concerts and anniversary dinners. Master Tripes was 'astonishing; more firmness of finger, and delicacy of touch, we never witnessed';[50] Mr Fothergill's 'novelty

---

[48] I am grateful to Grace Toland of the Irish Traditional Music Archive for this song.
[49] Pat Warner, *Lock Keeper's Daughter: A Worcestershire Canal Childhood* (Shepperton: Shepperton Swan Ltd, 1986), p. 72.
[50] *Staffordshire Advertiser*, 19 April 1800, p. 3.

[was] highly appreciated, as the encore testified';[51] Fireman Wadham 'enlivened the proceedings by a clever performance on a much-neglected instrument – the Jew's harp';[52] while Mr. Johnson 'deserves special mention for his unique performance'.[53] A competition was held at Alnwick in 1886, where 'there was again a good attendance of the working classes of Alnwick at the Sociables, in the Town Hall ... Seven competitors entered for the Jew's harp contest, the prizes being won by J. Knox, T. Haley, sen., and C. Baxter respectively'.[54]

Tunes are mentioned occasionally prior to the era of recording. In 1800 Master Tripes accompanied 'For Sol and the Gift of the gab';[55] in 1831, Teddy O'Rourke played 'Off she goes';[56] in 1837, 'The Great Magician, Mr. Sutton, will introduce TWO JEWS' HARPS, And play a Melody Overture, and the Scotch air "Roy's Wife", with variations'.[57] In 1838, young men at a wedding played 'Haste to the Wedding and My love is but a Lassie yet';[58] in 1847, at his trial, John Cassidy was said to have played 'Buffalo Gals'.[59] In 1866, an unnamed player performed 'Johnny comes marching home', while in 1889, Mr E. Wilson played 'The Campbells Are Coming'.[60] Aptommas, the king of the harpists, played 'Songs without words', 'Harmonious Blacksmith' and 'American Airs' in 1890.

Though born in England, the Wright family of John, Michael, David and his daughter, Lucy, have Irish ancestry that influences the music they play. Michael and David Wright were taught the basics of playing by John in 1968, and Lucy continues the tradition. A rare series of recordings of the whole family were made in 2008 and 2009, and many of these can be heard on the accompanying CD.[61]

John Wright recorded on *The Lark in the Clear Air* in 1974, playing solo on 'The Shaskeen Reel', 'Clancy's Fancy', 'Miss McLeod' and 'The Flowers of Edinburgh'; duets with John Doonan on piccolo on 'Gillan's Apples', 'The Prize Jig', 'The Skylark' and 'Tie the Bonnet'; trios with his brothers, Michael and David, on 'Banish Misfortune', 'The Maid Behind the Bar' and 'The Foxhunters' Jig'; and an ensemble piece 'Cherish the Ladies' and 'Father O'Flynn'. John Wright played jews-harp on several tracks on the Topic LP *John Wright Unaccompanied*, released in 1978. Wright also played on the French films *Le Shérif*, directed by Yves Boisset (1977); *Ils sont grands ces petits*, directed by J. Santoni (1979); and the television serial *Mandrin* (1972), as well as playing in a number of theatrical

---

[51] *Exeter and Plymouth Gazette*, 28 December 1885, p. 3.
[52] *Isle of Wight Observer*, 8 March 1890, p. 8.
[53] *Whitstable Times and Herne Bay Herald*, 17 January 1891, p. 8.
[54] *Morpeth Herald*, 4 December 1886, p. 3.
[55] *Staffordshire Advertiser*, 19 April 1800, p. 3.
[56] *Bath Chronicle and Weekly Gazette*, 19 November 1831, p. 4. See Appendix: Notes: Track 4.
[57] *The Morning Post*, London, 1 July 1837, p. 1.
[58] *Yorkshire Gazette*, 9 February 1838, p. 3. See Appendix: Notes: Track 5.
[59] *Freeman's Journal*, 27 November 1847, p. 3. See Appendix: Notes: Track 1.
[60] *Western Daily Press*, Bristol, 16 January 1889, p. 6. See Appendix: Notes: Track 6.
[61] See Appendix: Tradition Bearers: tracks 7 to 17.

performances. Michael Wright played what is thought to be the first performance in Britain of Albrechtsberger's 'Concerto in D', with Lynda Sayce on Mandola and a small Baroque ensemble in 2007.

Other more widely known English traditional players of note include Tommy Hayes, Jonny Handle and Colin Ross, the latter two members of the north-east group, The High Level Ranters. Ross plays 'Meggy's Foot' and 'Mi' Laddie Sits Ower Late Up' on their recording *Northumberland Forever*. Jack Elliott plays 'Broken Tanner', 'Jack's Choice' and 'In the Bar-Room' on the record *Jack Elliott of Birtley: The Songs and Stories of a Durham Miner*.

Figure 9.6   Recording of *The Lark in the Clear Air*, Topic Suite, 1974
Source: Photograph by author.

Figure 9.7   Allan MacDonald, by Sean Purser
Source: By kind permission of Allan MacDonald.

Cinema, Radio and Television

Mass media in Britain have pretty much ignored the jews-harp. Angus Lawrie was a regular artist on the radio in the 1950s and 1960s, while television appearances have occurred in Scotland on a few occasions. Allan McDonald, for instance, played on a number of the BBC TV series *The Highland Sessions* during the 2000s.

The 1939 film *Molly and Me*, staring Gracie Fields, has a dog scratching its neck with a joke 'boing!' accompaniment. The 1973 film, *The Wicker Man* has a brief scene, the Maypole Song, as does the deck-hands' social-evening scene in the 2003 film *Master and Commander: The Far Side of the World*, the jews-harp player being Jim Walker. In both, jews-harps are used to accompany other instruments. In *The Emerald Forest*, released in 1985, there is a very effective use of a breathy jews-harp for two scenes and the beginning of the credits, though the player is not named.

December Bride, set in 1909 Northern Ireland, winning a special jury award at the 1990 European Film Awards, includes a scene with two characters dancing to a third playing the jews-harp over-dubbed by John, Michael and David Wright's recording 'Banish Misfortune' from the *Lark in the Clear Air* recording of 1974.

Michael Wright appeared on *Today with Des and Mel* in 2004, and there may be other such examples, but there is nothing of any great significance featuring British players. Generally radio broadcasts have been restricted to broadcasting Albrechtsberger's concertos on Radio 3. The Wright family, Tran Quang Hai from France and a few others have appeared on *Late Junction*, plus there have been a few one-off interviews on local stations and the BBC World Service.

Stage Acts

Impersonations of jews-harps were popular. Mr Wilmer as 'Mr T. Major', Herr Sangerman, Mr G.A. Foote, Mr Sydney Locklynne and Walter Stanton, the last 'wonderfully clever', all had a stage act that included imitation jews-harps.

Burlesques

Eighteenth-century wit Bonnell Thornton created a series of burlesques performed at 'Mrs Midnight's'. In his 'An Ode on Saint Cecilia's Day', written under the pseudonym Fustian Sackbut, Thornton wrote the following two poems:

> Strike, strike the soft Judaic Harp,
> By teeth coercive in firm durance kept,
> And lightly by the Volant finger swept.
>
> Buzzing twangs the Iron Lyre,
> Shrilling thrilling,
> Trembling, trilling,
> Whizzing with the wavering wire.[62]

Music Hall Songs and Monologues[63]

The music halls inspired five songs and monologues extant that mention jews-harps. 'The Inventor's Wife' by Mrs E.T. Corbet, verse 7, has,

> He invented a Jew's-harp to go by steam
> And a new-fangled powder-horn
> While the children were going barefoot to school
> And the weeds were a-choking our corn!

---

[62] Thornton, 'An Ode', p. 9.
[63] Lyrics in this section may be found at: http://www.monologues.co.uk/.

There is also 'Spank the Grand Piano, Matilda', written and composed by George Dance, performed by J.W. Rowley (1847–1924), verse 3:

> Now Matilda's young man can play the banjo,
> And he comes every night after tea,
> And Harry, the lodger, can play on the flute,
> And a first-class musician is he.
> Then my eldest daughter plays on the guitar,
> As she did at "The Eagle" so grand,
> And then my old woman strums on the jew's harp,
> While I am the gaff of the band.
> [Spoken:]
> Yes! I am the gaff of the band. I give them a sentimental song entitled "Mother, Smack Little Willie's Bottom Lip". Then my old woman gives them a tune on the jew's harp; then Matilda sits down to the piano; then the lodger takes out his flute. I may remark that we are all very fond of the lodger's flute. Then I get up on the table with the poker in my hand and shout to them, "Are you ready? One – two – three –" (Chorus).

'Four Fingers and a Thumb', written and composed by Eldred Powel in 1895, performed by Charles Coborn (1852–1945) has the chorus,

> Build a mighty city, or a Jew's harp strum
> Show your affection for a chum
> Make a fellow talk when he's dumb
> There's nothing in the world so handy
> As four fingers and a thumb.

'Liza Johnson or The Rag-Time Coster', written by Edgar Bateman, composed by George Le Brunn in 1901, was originally sung by Kate Carney, but also by Margaret Lockwood in the 1945 film *I'll be your Sweetheart*:

> Since my bloke went to a panto, all the pretty girls to see,
> He's got mashed upon a Yankee, and her rag-time melody
> Now he's trying to compose one, on a Jew's harp for to play,
> He fairly drives me crazy, for he's singing all the day ... (Chorus).

The comedian and monologue writer Billy Bennett ('Almost a Gentleman'), in 'The Lights of London or Shamms O'Brian, Oy! Oy!' verse 3, has,

> And only his swateheart "Rachael" knew
> That he was the "Minstrel Boy"
> And made 'em all garp when he played the Jew's Harp
> And his favourite song was "OY! OY!" (Muzel toff).

Figure 9.8 Miss Flo Hastings, from a music sheet cover (detail)
Source: Courtesy of Max Tyler.

From 1893, *The Era* advertised, 'Miss Flo Hastings, the London belle, has a low comedy impersonation in which she sings of a serenade on a Jew's harp, and rejoices in considerable popularity'. Her song was 'On his Jew's harp – Coster Characters',[64] though no copy has been found to date.

There are two recordings from around 1933 of 'I took my harp to a Party' that feature jews-harps, one of which, sung by Jenny Howard ('the poor man's Gracie Fields') has the line, 'A North Country person called Sandy MacPherson, is now going to play his jews-harp'. This, along with the other by the Henry Hall Orchestra with Phyllis Robins, also 1933, is one of the earliest recordings of a jews-harp. The playing is basic, but cannot be another instrument.

In the Irish stage song 'The Irish Beauty', verse 3 has,

> She's a nate taper waist like a butt in the middle,
> She plays on the Jew's harp and I on the fiddle,
> And Och! But such music there never was heard …[65]

---

[64] *The Era*, London, 14 January 1893, p. 31.
[65] Gaskel, *Gaskel's Original Comic Songs* (Manchester: Abel Heywood, 1847), p. 51.

The Armed Forces

Soldiers

Some of the more obscure references come from the jews-harp's use by the Armed Forces or in celebration of their achievements. In 1899 troops embarking for South Africa played 'Soldiers of the Queen' on the jews-harp, while on the Relief of Mafeking schoolchildren formed an impromptu band including 'whistles, mouth organs, Jews' harps, and (in the place of kettle-drums) o dlkettles [*sic*], tins'.[66]

Harmonicas are associated with the troops during World War I, but jews-harps were also popular. According to the *Liverpool Echo* the war certainly boosted the jews-harp industry:

> Some of the quaint trades of the Midlands are profiting as a result of the war. The Jews' harp-making industry, which is practically restricted to Birmingham and Cradley, in South Staffordshire, was until recently in a very parlous state; but owing to the immense demand for "music" for the trenches, the supply of mouth-organs, concertinas, and accordions being quite inadequate, the Jews' harp has entered upon a new lease of life.[67]

Gunner H. Carpenter wrote in May 1915: 'The mother superior at the convent sent me a parcel containing biscuits, a mouth organ, and a Jew's harp. Wasn't that kind of her?'[68] The *Western Daily Press*, meanwhile, reported,

> In the course of a cheery letter from France, Private C.W. Brooks, of the 12th Gloucesters ("Bristol's Own"), writes: "Bye the bye, can you persuade any generous-hearted citizen of dear old Bristol to send out a one-string violin and a Jew's harp. We have an expert here on these instruments of 'torture', and he promises us no end of entertainment if only he can obtain the apparatus."[69]

The popularity of the instrument was noted in the *San Diego Union*:

> On the battlefields of Europe, where trench and artillery warfare has exaggerated nervous and mental tension to its highest conceivable development, the furnishing of entertainment is a serious military requirement ... In Greenville Barker's accounts of his visits to the western front he tells pathetic tales about the great comfort which even such a little article of entertainment as a jew's-harp gives to the weary and forlorn battle men.[70]

---

[66] *Northampton Mercury*, 25 May 1900, p. 7.
[67] *Liverpool Echo*, 9 March 1917, p. 4.
[68] *Newcastle Journal*, 5 May 1915, p. 4.
[69] *Western Daily Press*, Bristol, 29 February 1916, p. 5.
[70] *San Diego Union*, 10 January 1918, p. 7.

A song for the Home Front was 'Patsey Cohen's Jews-harp band', sung 'with great success' by Gus Harris:

> When Patsey Cohen introduced his famous Jew's harp band
> The Germans though(t) that we had started shelling "no man's land"
> One German shouted "hoch" it sounds like a bees about to swarm
> So "donner watter" I'm for home it's getting much too warm.
> Oh, Patsey Cohen's Jew's harp band
> It's the finest in the land
> The difference you can't tell
> From the humming of a shell
> You can hear the Germans shout "yoi, yoi" (kamerad kamerad)
> What was it made the Germans run
> A tune of real good Irish brand
> By Killarney's lakes and fells
> On Patsey Cohen's Jew's harp band – oh band.

Sailors

There are surprisingly few references to the use of the jews-harp at sea, even given John Purser's view that the instrument 'fits in the pocket, is durable, and does not require too much breath or activity'.[71] 'Farewell the Tarwathie' was apparently a favourite of whalers,[72] while in 1889 an 'Old Salt' wrote,

> during the dog watch on board fixed between the hours of four and eight in the evening; and the time is sacredly devoted by all honest tars to eating, smoking, and playing the concertina or Jew's harp, or any instrument that may be available.[73]

Recordings

In addition to those mentioned above, the jews-harp has been used on quite a few recordings. Finding recordings relies on luck and having an ear for the distinctive sound of the instrument, while the styles of playing on the recordings studied vary from a simple effects 'boing!' to rhythmic, melodic/rhythmic and melodic playing.

The Irish in America appear to have been the first to record tunes rather than use the jews-harp for effect, and early examples from 1930 are the Flanagan

---

[71] John Purser, *Scotland's Music: A History of the Traditional and Classical Music of Scotland from Earliest Times to the Present Day* (Mainstream Publishing in conjunction with BBC Scotland, Edinburgh, 1992), p. 235.
[72] Purser, *Scotland's Music*.
[73] *Daily Gazette for Middlesbrough*, 23 March 1889, p. 4.

Brothers recordings of 'On the Road to the Fair' and 'Miss McLeod's Reel', with Joe Flanagan on jews-harp playing in a melodic style.

Every now and then a field recording has a jews-harp. Albert Smith was recorded by Keith Summers at his home in 1977 and is on *The Voice of the People Volume 14 – Troubles They Are But Few*, playing 'The Pigeon On The Gate – Stepdance' in a basic but melodic style. In the same series, *Volume 7 – First I'm Going to Tell You a Ditty*, Willie Kemp plays 'Glendarel Highlands', 'Lovat Scouts' and 'Monymusk'.

Archives

Three useful sources are the Tobar an Dualchais website for recordings and interviews of Scottish players; the Irish Traditional Music Archive, Dublin, with early recordings of the Flanagan Brothers and other later players, mainly from commercial sources at the moment; and the Vaughan Williams Memorial Library at Cecil Sharpe House, London, that has the Peter Kennedy BBC recordings of Angus Lawrie in particular.

Popular Music

Most recordings use the jews-harp as a novelty sound or to add rhythm. In 1967 John Lennon produces a single 'boing!' on The Beatles's 'Fool on the Hill' and in 1969 John Peel played a series of sound effect 'boing!'s on Third Ear Band's 'Area Three', while Pete Townshend of The Who plays a fine melodic riff on the 1972 'Join Together with the Band'. The Clash used a sound effect 'boing!' on their 1990 'The Guns of Brixton', Michael Wright (melodic/rhythmic) and Saul Eisenberg (rhythmic) played on 'George Collins' and 'Jew's Garden', and Michael Wright also performed on 'Wild Wood Amber' on Sam Lee's Mercury Prize-nominated *Ground of his Own*. Peter Hope-Evans of the group Medicine Head used the jews-harp consistently throughout the 1970s and continues to do so. In his view:

> A history of the Jews harp in the UK would note the role of the Sonny Terry LP "Sonny Terry's New Sound: the jaw harp in blues and folk music".[74] I and many others in the early 1960's were enthrall'd, enraptur'd, endlessly inspir'd by blues music. Driven to our mouthorgans could not help to discover this Sonny Terry record. The Jews harp then was forever twinned with the mouth organ, both free reed instruments. I sometimes declare that I play a mouth organ like a Jews harp. I play a jews-harp like a mouth organ.[75]

---

[74] *Sonny Terry's New Sound: The Jaw Harp in Blues and Folk Music* (folkways FS 3821, 1961).
[75] Peter Hope Evans, personal correspondence.

180 The Jews-Harp in Britain and Ireland

Figure 9.9 Author and Dogan Mehmet at the Traditional Music Day, Stowmarket, Sussex, UK
Source: Author's collection.

Figure 9.10 'Desoeuvrement-breath mask'
Source: By kind permission of Peter Hope-Evans.

A New Generation of Players

Though lagging behind the exciting developments of European players, there is a resurgence of interest in the jews-harp in the British Isles, partly inspired by the access to performances of Asian players, particularly from the Sakha-Yakutia Russian Republic. Jonathan Cope has been at the forefront of this movement, not only as a player, but as a maker and a supplier of good quality instruments.

> I found the basic techniques used in JH playing very similar to those used for playing didgeridoo, which I have done professionally for many years, and "overtone" or "throat" singing so I was initially self-taught until I met other players. Influences probably need to be put down to everyone I meet who plays and I've been lucky enough to meet some quality players who have been happy to swap / share techniques with me. It never ceases to amaze me how varied the instrument can be in terms of construction and playing style: from the difficult to play Geng-Gong bamboo traction styles from Bali and Papua, the infinitely subtle multi-bladed Khou Xhiang from northern China, to the big metal types like the Yakutian Khomus and Indian Morsing.[76]

Figure 9.11   Jonathan Cope playing jews-harp at the MBS Festival 2013
Source: Photograph by Viktor Klements, © 2014 Jonathan Cope.

---

[76] Jonathan Cope, 'Membership Profile', *Islands of the North Atlantic Jew's Harp Association Newsletter*, 6 (2010), p. 2.

World Wide Web

Workshops have been regularly run at folk festivals and there is a growing interest in learning more about the instrument. The jews-harp has been a regular feature at the Elphinstone Institute 'Button Boxes and Moothies' festival that celebrates free reed instruments held every three years in Aberdeen, but it is the internet that is having the greatest impact on young players. The World Wide Web has provided a considerable boost in interest and any search of YouTube clips reveals many uses, from folk to pop to experimental. There are websites looking at the music, the players and the history of the instrument, along with internationally acclaimed masters in performance, sellers, and how to play. In addition, international or regional societies and social groups give enthusiasts a voice and an opportunity to share our enthusiasm worldwide.

A Future?

Crucially, there is an open-minded attitude of young musicians to the musical possibilities of the jews-harp, rather than any preconceived notion as to what it can do – and that, perhaps, is an optimistic note with which to conclude.

Conclusion

In common with a number of other instruments such as the theremin and the accordion, the jews-harp does not feature as part of the Ark of Civilization. It does not sit within the boundaries of the recognized western art movement of the medieval period or the modern period since the Renaissance. Instead, it transcends established cultural boundaries.[1]

Looking at the history of the jews-harp began with asking what is a seemingly simple question: how is it that a musician in England, Scotland, Ireland or Wales can hold in their hand a musical instrument called a jews-harp? The instrument must have come from somewhere, been made by someone, transported by someone – and have, in fact, a history.

Sitting below the radar, running parallel with more established and acceptable musical instruments, the jews-harp survives ridicule, objections to its name, poor usage and manufacture of poor-quality products. Throughout its history the jews-harp has been used as barter, been part of an international trade, been used to explain acoustics, and been sufficiently recognised as a term to be the subject of myth and humour. Underestimated, unsung and misused, it nevertheless keeps appearing, often in the most unexpected places. A thirteenth-century carving, a fourteenth-century enamel, a witch trial, workers' rights, the purchase of land, burlesque entertainments, royal commands, wars – in just about any aspect of life the jews-harp makes an appearance, quietly and easily missed. It is only when drawing together all the off-hand comments and snippets of information that a picture emerges and the instrument's impact on individuals can be assessed.

What is revealed by looking at seemingly infinitesimally small and irrelevant details, where often there is a single reference hidden within a list or article, is a picture of the social impact of the jews-harp, whose story is no less complex than any other musical instrument. There are literally thousands of references, most of which are, as Busby put it, 'insignificant' in their own right, and though interesting in that the jews-harp is mentioned, of apparently little importance – a lockout of workers protesting about the introduction of new methods of production; a shipment of goods imported into the United States auctioned off in Charleston; one of a list of goods from a Customs Account; a tavern in North London – and so on. Overlay an historical context, however, and these references gain more significance – worker's rights, along with the beginnings of the Trades Union Movement and the impact of the Industrial Revolution; blockade runners

---

[1] Andrew Lamb, Bate Collection of Musical Instruments, personal correspondence.

of the American Civil War; the effect of a Commercial Revolution; a landmark obliterated by the expansion and development of London.

There has been a fascination with the jews-harp's acoustic properties, which when looked at in depth provide a description of the subtle nuance of the sound. The facts of the instrument's origins reveal a transition away from individual blacksmiths working within a community, to a manufacturing and distribution system taking advantage of the beginnings of a commercial revolution that developed in Europe from the thirteenth century – a story that exemplifies the globalization of the music industry in its early phase. Its name, even given the difficulties of a perceived cultural slur, has been adopted worldwide as the default name for the instrument after any local one. Location names are all but lost, yet streets, taverns, woods, paddocks and decorative styles have all borne the name at some point, along with race horses, greyhounds and farm animals.

Tracing the jews-harp's availability reveals a complex story of making and trading that had an impact far beyond the shores of the British Isles. Manufacturing techniques provided shapes of frame from the basic to the bizarre, while still retaining some degree of musicality. Visual representations are not abundant, yet can be traced to carvings dated thirteenth-century, and there are drawings and paintings, many inspired by the genre work of Wilkie, and even cartoons. The instrument's enigmatic musical quality has inspired traditional stories; its musicality has been noted in trials; and songs have been written, most mentioning the jews-harp in passing, but at least one from Ireland was written specifically about the jews-harp.

In the end, however, it is really how the instrument is played and used within any musical context that matters. Like any musical instrument, there are reasons and occasions when its use enhances an arrangement, whether leading, adding rhythm or atmospheric ambiance – though sometimes, perhaps, it is not appropriate at all. It is, after all, just another musical instrument.

Appendix:
Accompanying CD Track Notes

The Jews-Harp in Britain and Ireland Sampler

The examples included are divided into two sections. 'Tunes from Text' refers directly to those tunes mentioned in the text, with notes on the source. The 'Tradition Bearers' tracks are from two sessions recorded by the Wright Family at the School of Oriental and African Studies studio in 2008 and 2009. They represent ways in which the jews-harp can be used: as a group, duet and solo instrument, including various harmonies and base rhythms, plus an example of song accompaniment. The notes explain who is playing what and the various types of tunes – reel, jig, hornpipe and so on. Where known, the maker of the instruments played is mentioned.

Tunes from Text – Michael Wright[1]

1. Buffalo Gals, The Girl I Left Behind Me and The Keel Row (traditional)
2. Kathleen O'More (traditional)
3. Suo Gan (traditional)
4. Off She Goes (traditional)
5. Haste to the Wedding and My love is but a Lassie Yet (traditional)
6. The Campbells Are Coming (traditional)

Tradition Bearers – The Wright Family: John, Michael, David and Lucy Wright[2]

7. My Love is in America and Devanie's Goat (traditional)
8. Donald MacLean's Farewell to Oban (A. MacNeil)
9. Boys of the Blue Hill and Harvest Home (traditional)
10. Hollow Tree (Sherbourne Town) (B. Berry)
11. Lark in the Morning (traditional)
12. Old Toasty (A. Lawrie) and Haughs of Cromdale (traditional)

---

[1] Tracks 1–4, recorded in 2015 by Michael Wright. Recorded at Brigné sur Layon, France.
[2] Tracks 7–9, 11–12, 14–15 and 17 recorded in 2008 by Jeremy Glasgow. Recorded at the School of Oriental and African Studies studio, London. Tracks 10, 13 and 16 recorded in 2009 by Jeremy Glasgow. Recorded at the School of Oriental and African Studies studio, London.

Figure A.1   The Wright Family recording at the SOAS studio, 2008
Source: Photograph by Jeremy Glasgow. By kind permission of Jeremy Glasgow.

13. Kempe's Jig (traditional)
14. Inns of Court Jig, 'Inner Temple Jigg' (traditional)
15. The Maid behind the Bar (traditional)
16. Miss Thompson's Hornpipe (traditional; from an arrangement by Colin Ross)
17. Banish Misfortune (traditional)

Notes

Tunes from Text – Michael Wright

Track 1
Jim Spriggs: 'The Yorkshire Longsword team I belong to helped to provide the entertainment after the service, in our case at St Helen's, Bolton Percy, near York … The tunes used are the usual common folk tunes that go with this type of dancing: "The Girl I Left Behind Me"; "Buffalo Girls"; "the Keel Row"'.[3]

James Cassidy: 'DUBLIN POLICE – Yesterday. Inspector O'Neil charged a "batch" of tipplers, whom he found drinking in an unlicensed house … The inspector said his attention was drawn … by rather unusual sounds, and on

---
[3]   Jim Spriggs, personal correspondence.

approaching "loud resounded mirth and dancing". He stole slyly forward, when he observed a number of persons collected on the centre of the bridge around a gentlemanly-looking person [Cassidy], who was discoursing most eloquent music from two jaw's harps, which he played most scientifically; on closer examination he discovered the tune to be "Buffalo Gals won't you come out tonight?"'[4] Three tunes from America, England and Northumbria played on a Nesland, Norwegian 'D' *munnharpe*.

Track 2
'Mr Eulenstein played a variety of striking and elegant airs, all of which were distinguished in their execution by brilliancy and real pathos. The celebrated "Kathleen O'More" was one of these'.[5] An Irish air played on a Nesland, Norwegian 'E' *munnharpe*.

Track 3
'After settling the candles in their proper places, and attending to the fire, and seeing that everything was in order, the man of the house favoured us with a solo performance on the jew's harp'.[6] A Welsh lullaby played on a Nesland, Norwegian 'E' *munnharpe*.

Track 4
Teddy O'Rourke: 'for there was not another who could touch an instrument, while he had lost a leg in the band of the regiment, while playing "Off she goes", could master every thing, from a church organ to a Jew's harp'.[7] A jig found in the English, Irish and Scottish traditions, played on a Nesland, Norwegian 'G' *munnharpe*.

Track 5
'The happy pair were escorted to and from church by a party of young men bearing a crimson banner, and playing on a gewgaw or jew's harp, the favourite airs of "Haste to the wedding", and "My love is but a lassie yet", &c'.[8] An Irish jig and a Scottish tune associated with a Robert Burns poem, first appearing in Bremner's *Scots Reels of 1757* as 'Miss Farqharson's Reel'.[9] The tune is played on three different jews-harps: Nesland, Norwegian 'G' *munnharpe* (centre); Jofens, Austrian 'G' *maultrommel* (left); Schlütter, German 'G' *maultrommel* (right).

---

[4] *Freeman's Journal*, 27 November 1847, p. 3.
[5] *The Times*, 31 May 1833, p. 5.
[6] Lloyd and Lloyd, 'A Merry Evening at the Hafod', in Lloyd and Lloyd, *A Book of Wales*, pp. 159–60.
[7] *Bath Chronicle and Weekly Gazette*, 19 November 1831, p. 4.
[8] *Yorkshire Gazette*, 9 February 1838, p. 3.
[9] See http://tunearch.org/wiki/Annotation:My_Love_is_but_a_Lassie_Yet_(1) (accessed 19 June 2015).

Track 6
'At the Langton Street Christian and Literary Association Mr E. Wilson delighted the audience by a remarkable performance on the Jew's harp of "The Campbells Are Coming"'.[10] A Scottish march played on a Nesland, Norwegian 'G' *munnharpe*.

Tradition Bearers – The Wright Family

Track 7
'My Love is in America and Devanie's Goat' – The Wright Family. Two Irish reels. [Note: all tunes by the Wright Family played on Nesland, Norwegian *munnharpes* or Lalanne-Cassou, French *guimbardes*.] The tunes are played by Lucy, with all joining in after the first time through.

Track 8
'Donald MacLean's Farewell to Oban' – John and Lucy. A Scottish march played at the slower pace of an air. Solo by John joined by Lucy on repeat.

Track 9
'Boys of the Blue Hill and Harvest Home' – The Wright Family. Two Irish hornpipes. All play the same tunes.

Track 10
'Hollow Tree (Sherbourne Town)' – Michael, David and Lucy. A song tune written by Barbara Berry and adapted by her for a Kirtlington Morris Men stick dance. Michael and Lucy playing tune, changing key from 'D' to 'G', David 'D', 'G' and 'A' bass harps, with Michael singing.

Track 11
'The Lark in the Morning' – The Wright Family. A four-part Irish jig. The tune is repeated three times, the first and second time all together; third, David on simple bass rhythm.

Track 12
'Old Toasty and Haughs of Cromdale' – The Wright Family. A Scottish set-dance and a 6/8 march. 'Old Toasty' was the nickname of Oban piper and jews-harp player Angus Lawrie and the 'Haughs of Cromdale' was recorded by Lawrie on a number of occasions. Michael leads, with all playing the tune; the 6/8 rhythm for 'Cromdale' achieved by striking the lamella two times out of the three parts of the rhythm.

Track 13
'Kempe's Jig' – trio by David, Michael and Lucy. In 1600 the renowned clown from Shakespeare's Globe Theatre, Willie Kempe, danced a 'Nine Days Wonder'

---

[10] *Western Daily Press*, Bristol, 16 January 1889, p. 6.

from Norwich to London, a distance of one hundred miles (about 160 km). David leads, Michael joins on first repeat; David harmony second and third repeat, Lucy joins with bass; Lucy drops out after fourth repeat; sixth repeat, David to fade-out.

Track 14
'Inns of Court Jig, Inner Temple Jigg' – solo by John. Adapted from a seventeenth-century manuscript and an example of John's second 'closed throat' technique. Played through five times, John subtly changing the ornamentation.

Track 15
'The Maid behind the Bar' – trio by John, Michael and David. An Irish reel and one of the first three tunes taught to Michael and David in 1968. All three players play the same tune.

Track 16
'Miss Thompson's Hornpipe' – duet by David and Michael. A Northumbrian hornpipe from *The Northumbrian Pipers' Duet Book*,[11] arranged by Colin Ross. David plays the main tune and Michael the harmony.

Track 17
'Banish Misfortune' – The Wright Family. An Irish jig, and the first tune taught to Michael and David by John in 1968. The tune is repeated six times – the first time all play together; second and third, Michael, high harmony; third, David, low harmony; fourth and fifth, Michael and David counterpointing high and low rhythm; sixth, fade-out to one player, John.

---

[11] *The Northumbrian Pipers' Duet Book* (Newcastle upon Tyne: The Northumbrian Pipers' Society, 2001), p. 16.

Bibliography

Adkins, C.J., 'Investigations of the Sound-Producing Mechanism of the Jew's Harp', *The Journal of the Acoustical Society of America*, 55(3) (1974), pp. 667–70.
Allan's Illustrated Edition of Tyneside Songs (facsimile, Newcastle-upon-Tyne: Frank Graham, 1972).
Atkinson, G., *On Saxon Architecture, and the Early Churches in the Neighbourhood of Grimsby. A Paper Read at the Meeting of the Lincoln Diocesan Architectural Society ...* (Lincoln: W. & B. Brooke, 1859).
Axtell, J., *Beyond 1492: Encounters in Colonial North America* (Oxford and New York: Oxford University Press, 1992).
Bacon, F., *Sylva Sylvarum: or, A Natural History, in Ten Centuries*, tenth edition (London, 1676).
Baines, Anthony, *The Oxford Companion to Musical Instruments* (Oxford: Oxford University Press, 1992).
Berry, W., *Encyclopaedia Heraldica, Complete Dictionary of Heraldry, vol. III* (London: Sherwood, Gilbert and Piper, 1828–1840).
Beskrovny, A., *Jew's Harps in Russian Archaeology (II BC–XIII AD)* (2013). Unpublished research.
Bhraonáin, Donla uí (ed.), *Seanfhocla Chonnacht [Proverbs of Connacht]* (Dublin: Cois Life, in association with Foras na Gaeilge, 2010).
Boswell, J. and Erskine, A., *Letters Between the Honourable Andrew Erskine and James Boswell, Esq.* (London, 1763).
Bottrell, W., *Stories and Traditions of Penwith* (Penzance, 1870).
——— *Stories and Folk-Lore of West Cornwall, Traditions and Hearthside Stories of West Cornwall Third Series* (Penzance, 1880; facsimile reprint 1996 by Llanerch Publishers, Felinfach, 1996).
Brathwaite, R., *Whimzies: or, A New Cast of Characters. [The epistle dedicatory signed Clitus-Alexandrinus. Followed by] A cater-character, throwne out of a boxe* (London, 1631).
——— *Ar't Asleepe Husband?* (1640).
Britnell, R.H., *The Commercialisation of English Society, 1000–1500* (Cambridge: Cambridge University Press, 1996).
Buckley, A., 'Jew's Harps in Irish Archaeology', in *Second Conference of the ICTM Study Group on Music Archaeology* (Stockholm: Royal Swedish Academy of Music, 1986).
Burns, R., *The Heron Ballads, or The Election Ballads no. 2* (1795–1796, British Newspaper Archive, Literature Network).

Busby, T., *A Complete Dictionary of Music* (London, 1801).
Chettle, H., 'Kind-hart's dreame: containing five apparitions with their invectives against abuses reigning', in *Early English Poetry, Ballads, and Popular Literature of the Middle Ages, vol. V* (London, 1841).
Cobb, H.S. (ed.), *The Overseas Trade of London Exchequer Customs Accounts* (London: London Record Society, 1990).
Conan Doyle, A., 'The Adventure of the Empty House', in *The Return of Sherlock Holmes* (London: George Newnes, Ltd., 1905).
Cope, J., 'Membership Profile', *Islands of the North Atlantic Jew's Harp Association Newsletter*, 6 (2010).
Cox, N., *The Complete Tradesman: A Study of Retailing, 1550–1820* (Aldershot and Burlington, VT: Ashgate, 2008).
Crane, F., 'The Jew's Harp as Aerophone', *The Galpin Society Journal*, XXI (1968), pp. 66–9.
―――― *Extant Medieval Musical Instruments: Provisional Catalogue by Types* (Iowa City, IA: University of Iowa Press, 1972).
―――― 'Jew's (Jaw's? Jeu? Jeugd? Gewgaw? Juice?) Harp', *Vierundzwanzigsteljahrsschrift der Internationalen Maultrommelvirtuosengenossenschaft*, 1 (1982), pp. 29–41.
―――― 'Monsieur Le Vaillant Wows the Hottentots', *Vierundzwanzigsteljahrsschrift der Internationalen Maultrommelvirtuosengenossenschaft*, 4 (1994), pp. 38–44.
―――― 'The Trump in British Literature', *Vierundzwanzigsteljahrsschrift der Internationalen Maultrommelvirtuosengenossenschaft*, 5 (1996), pp. 66–92.
―――― 'Trolls and Trumps', *Vierundzwanzigsteljahrsschrift der Internationalen Maultrommelvirtuosengenossenschaft*, 9 (2000), pp. 7–26.
―――― *A History of the Trump in Pictures: Europe and America* (Mount Pleasant, IA: Frederick Crane, 2003).
―――― 'Trolls and Trumps', *Vierundzwanzigsteljahrsschrift der Internationalen Maultrommelvirtuosengenossenschaft*, 11 (2003), pp. 18–21.
―――― 'Catalog of the F. Crane Trump Collection, Part 1 – England', *Journal of the International Jew's Harp Society*, 2 (2004), pp. 63–95.
―――― 'Trumps in American Musical Instrument Trade Catalogs', *Vierundzwanzigsteljahrsschrift der Internationalen Maultrommelvirtuosengenossenschaft*, 11 (2004), pp. 67–116.
Dalyell, Sir John Graham, *Musical Memoirs of Scotland: With Historical Annotations and Numerous Illustrative Plates* (Edinburgh: T.G. Stevenson, 1849).
Dauney, William, *Ancient Scottish Melodies* (Edinburgh, 1838).
Defoe, D., *The Complete English Tradesman, in familiar letters; directing him in all the several parts and progressions of trade ...* (London, 1725).
Douglas, W.S., *In Ayrshire; A Descriptive Picture of the County of Ayr, with relative Notes on Interesting Local Subjexts, chiefly derived during a recent personal tour* (Kilmarnock: McKie & Drennan, 1874).

Dournon-Taurelle, G. and Wright, J., *Les Guimbardes du Musée de l'Homme* (Paris: Institut d'Ethnologie, Musée de l'Homme, 1978).
Drabble, P., *Black Country* (London: Robert Hale Limited, 1952).
The Dublin Almanac and General Register of Ireland (Dublin: Pettigrew and Oulton, 1838).
The Dublin Almanac and General Register of Ireland (Dublin: Pettigrew and Oulton, 1841).
The Dublin Almanac and General Register of Ireland (Dublin: Pettigrew and Oulton, 1845).
Egan, G., *The Medieval Household: Daily Living c.1150–c.1450* (London: The Stationery Office, 1998).
Felton, William, *A Treatise on Carriages* (London, 1794).
Fielding, H., *The History of the Adventures of Joseph Andrews, and of his friend Mr. Abraham Adams* (1742).
Fisher, A., *An accurate new spelling dictionary, and expositor of the English language. Containing a much larger collection of modern words than any book of the kind and price extant: and shewing how the same are to be written correctly, and pronounced properly; with the different meanings or significations of each word. To which is added, an entire new dictionary of all the Heathen Gods and Goddesses: and also of the illustrious heroes treated of by Homer, Virgil, Ovid, and other antient poets: with a summary account of their origin, descent, expolits, &c. To the whole is prefixed, a compendious, practical grammar of the English language. By A. Fisher, author of the practical new English grammar, with exercises of bad English: the new English tutor, calculated for the new method of teaching, &c.* (London, 1773).
Fletcher, J. and Massinger, P., *The Faire Maide of the Inne* (1626).
Flick, A.C. (ed.), *The Papers of Sir William Johnson, vol. VII* (Albany, NY: The University of the State of New York, 1931).
Fontaine, L., *History of Pedlars in Europe*, translated by V. Whittaker (Cambridge: Polity Press, 1996).
Fox, L. (ed.), *The Jew's Harp: A Comprehensive Anthology* (Lewisburg, PA: Bucknell University Press; London: Associated University Presses, Inc., 1988).
Galpin, Francis W., *A Textbook of European Musical Instruments: Their Origin, History and Character* (London: Williams & Norgate, Ltd., 1937).
Gaskel, *Gaskel's Original Comic Songs* (Manchester: Abel Heywood, 1847).
Guthrie, J., *The Ordinary of Newgate his Account, of the Behaviour, Confession, and Last Dying Words of the Malefactors, Who Were Executed at Tyburn, on Monday the 24th of this Instant March, 1729* (London, 1729).
Hakluyt, R., *Voyages and Discoveries: Principal Navigations, Voyages, Traffiques and Discoveries of the English Nation, vol. III* (New York: American Geographical Society, 1928).
Halyburton, A., *The Book of Customs and Valuation of Merchandises in Scotland 1612*, edited by C. Innes (Edinburgh: Her Majesty's General Register House, 1867).

Hornbostel, E.M. von and Sachs, C., 'Classification of Musical Instruments: Translated from the Original German by Anthony Baines and Klaus P. Wachsmann', *The Galpin Society Journal*, XIV (1961), pp. 3–29.

Impey, A., 'Sounding Place in the Western Maputaland Borderlands', *Journal of the Musical Arts in Africa*, 3 (2006), pp. 55–79.

—— 'Songs of Mobility and Belonging', *Interventions: International Journal of Postcolonial Studies*, 15(2) (2013), pp. 255–71.

Jonson, B., *Every Man Out of His Humor* (1599).

—— 'Bartholomew Fair', *The Workes of Benjamin Jonson, the second volume* (1614).

Johnson, S., *A Dictionary of the English Language* (1755).

Jones, E., *Musical and Poetical Relicks of the Welsh Bards* (London, 1794).

Kelly, J.A., *A Complete Collection of Scotish Proverbs Explained and Made Intelligible to the English Reader* (London, 1721).

Kelly's Directory (1889).

Joyce, J., *Ulysses* (London: Egoist Press, 1922).

Kingsley, C., *The Water Babies* (London, 1912).

Kolltveit, G., *Jew's Harp in European Archaeology*, BAR International Series 1500 (Oxford: BAR, 2006).

—— 'The Jew's Harp in Western Europe: Trade, Communication, and Innovation, 1150–1500', *2009 Yearbook for Traditional Music*, 41 (2009), pp. 42–61.

Kooper, E. (ed.), *Sentimental and Humorous Romances* (Kalamazoo, MI: Medieval Institute Publications, 2006).

L.S., *The Porcupine, Alias the Hedge Hog or, The fox turned preacher. Written after the manner of Ignatius Irony, Bartholomew Burlesque, and Samuel Satire* (Boston, MA, 1784).

Lawson, G., 'Musical Relics', in K.L. Mitchel, K.R. Murdock and J.R. Ward (eds), *Fast Castle Excavations 1971–86* (Edinburgh: Edinburgh Archaeological Field Society, 2001).

Legand, O.K., 'On the Acoustics and the Systematic Classification of the Jaw's Harp', *Yearbook of the International Folk Music Council*, 4, 25th Anniversary Issue (1972), pp. 95–103.

Libin, L., *The Grove Dictionary of Musical Instruments*, second edition (New York and Oxford: Oxford University Press, 2014).

The Lives of the Most Remarkable Criminals: Who Have Been Condemn'd and Executed; For Murder, Highway, House Breakers, Street-Robberies, Coining, or Other Offences; From the Year 1720, to the Present Time, vol. III (London, 1735).

Lloyd, D.M. and Lloyd, E.M. (eds), *A Book of Wales* (London and Glasgow: Collins, 1953).

Local Register and Chronological Account of occurrences and facts connected with the town and neighbourhood of Sheffield (Sheffield, 1830).

MacDougall, J., *Folk Tales and Fairy Lore in Gaelic and English* (Edinburgh, 1910).

Macphail, J.R.N. (ed.), *Highland Papers* (Edinburgh: Scottish History Society, 1914–1934).
Mancall, P.C., *Deadly Medicine: Indians and Alcohol in Early America* (Ithaca, NY and London: Cornell University Press, 1996).
Marshall, W.H., *The Rural Economy of Yorkshire, vol. II* (London, 1788).
Martin, M., *A Late Voyage to St. Kilda, the Remotest of All the Hebrides or Western Isles of Scotland &c* (London, 1698).
Masters, J., *Pilgrim Son: A Personal Odyssey* (London: Corgi Books, 1973).
MacGill, P., *Soldier Songs* (London, 1917).
Miège, G., *The Great French Dictionary* (London, 1688).
Mihura, B.L., 'The Jew's Harp in Colonial America', *Vierundzwanzigsteljahrsschrift der Internationalen Maultrommelvirtuosengenossenschaft*, 1 (1982), pp. 62–66.
Montagu, J., 'The Crozier of William of Wykeham', *Early Music* (November 2002), pp. 540–62.
Mount, C.B., *Notes and Queries* (Oxford: Oxford University Press, 1897).
Murray, J.A.H. (ed.), *A New English Dictionary on Historic Principles, vol. V. E–K* (Oxford at the Clarendon Press, 1901).
A new tea-table miscellany or, bagatelles for the Amusement of The Fair Sex. To which are added, A Collection of Conundrums with their solutions (London, 1750).
Newberie, R. and Denham, D., *The Nomenclator, or Rememberbrancer of Adrianus Iunius* (1585).
Newes from Scotland, declaring the damnable life and death of doctor Fian, a notable sorcerer, who was burned at Edenbrough in Ianuary last, 1591 (London, 1591?).
Norman, L. and Roberts, G., *Witchcraft in Early Modern Scotland: James VI's 'Demonology' and the North Berwick Witches* (Exeter: University of Exeter Press, 2000).
The Northumbrian Pipers' Duet Book (Newcastle upon Tyne: The Northumbrian Pipers' Society, 2001).
O'Brian. P., *Far Side of the World* (London: Harper Collins, 1984).
——— *The Reverse of the Medal* (London: Fontana Books, 1986).
——— *Clarissa Oakes* (London: Harper Collins, 1997).
——— *The Nutmeg of Consolation* (London: Harper Collins, 1997).
Oxford English Dictionary, vol. VIII (Oxford: Oxford University Press, 1989).
Onions, C.T. (ed.), *Oxford Dictionary of English Etymology* (Oxford: Clarendon Press, 1978 [1966]).
Palmer, R., *The Folklore of the Black Country* (Almeley: Logaston Press, 2007).
Parsons, H., *The Black Country* (London: Robert Hale Limited, 1997).
Paterson, J., *History of the Counties of Ayr and Wigton, vol. V/II* (Cunninghame, Edinburgh: J. Stillie, 1863–1866).
Pegge, S., *Anonymiana or, Ten Centuries of Observations on Various Authors and Subjects* (London, 1809).

Pennant, T., *A Tour in Scotland; MDCCLXIX* (Warrington, 1774).
Pitcairn, R., *Criminal Trials and Other Proceedings before the High Court of Justiciary, vol. II*, Bannatyne Club Publications 42, Maitland Club Publications 19, 3 vols (Edinburgh: printed for the Maitland Club, 1831–1833).
Plate, R., *Kulturgeschichte der Maultrommel* (Bonn: Verlag für systematische Musikwissenschaft, 1992).
The pleasant companion or, merry & complete favourite jester, containing all the fun, all the humour, all the learning, and all the judgement which so lately flowed from the two universities (London, 1775?).
Purser, P., *Scotland's Music: A History of the Traditional and Classical Music of Scotland from Earliest Times to the Present Day* (Edinburgh: Mainstream Publishing in conjunction with BBC Scotland, 1992).
R.M., *Micrologia: Characters or Essayes, Of Persons, Trades, and Places offered to the City and Country* (London, 1629).
Randolph, T., *Hey for Honesty, Down with Knavery* (1651).
Roderick, J., *The English and Welch dictionary: or, the English before the Welch. = Y geirlyfr Saesneg a Chymraeg; ... Containing all the words that are necessary to understand both languages; but more especially, for the translation of the English into Welch ...* (Salop, 1725).
——— *Y geirlyfr Saesneg a Chymraeg; neu'r Saesneg o flaen y Cymraeg. ... A ddechreuwyd ar y cyntaf gan Sion Rhydderch, ag a ddibenwyd yn awr, ynghyd a chwanegiad o lawer cant o eiriau gan y Parchedig Mr. John Williams ... ac Mr. Lewis Evans ...* (Shrewsbury, 1837).
Rounding, C.M., *Quaint Signs of Olde Inns* (London: Herbert Jenkins, 1926).
Roussignol, S.R., *J.M. Thaurin et Rouen Gallo-Romain, vol. 1* (thesis, U.F.R. Lettres et Sciences Humaines, Institut d'Histoire, University de Rouen, 1991–1992).
Rowlands, M.B., *Masters and Men in the West Midland Metalware Trades before the Industrial Revolution* (Manchester: Manchester University Press, 1975).
Roycroft, T., *Etymoloicon Lingue Anglicanae* (1671).
Sadie, S. (ed.) and Tyrrell, J. (exec. ed.), *The New Grove Dictionary of Music and Musicians* (London: Grove, 2001).
Scholes, P.A., *Oxford Companion to Music* (London: Oxford University Press, 1970).
Scott, Sir W., *Rob Roy, vol. II* (Edinburgh: Archibald Constable and Co.; London: Longman, Hurst, Rees, Orme, and Brown, 1818).
Semmes, R., *Captains and Mariners of Early Maryland* (Baltimore, MD: The John Hopkins Press, 1937).
Shane, S., *A General Theory of Entrepreneurship: The Individual Opportunity* (London: Springer, 2003).
Shaw, G.B., *Man and Superman; A Comedy and a Philosophy* (Westminster: Archibald Constable & Co, Ltd., 1903).
Sherman, J. 'Serving the Natives: Whiteness as a Price of Hospitality in South African Yiddish Literature', *Journal of Southern African Studies*, 26(3) (2000), pp. 505–22.

Sherman, J. (ed.), *From a Land Far Off: A Selection of South African Yiddish Stories* (Cape Town: Jewish Publications, and Joseph Sherman, 2000).
Shesgreen, S. (ed.), *Engravings by Hogarth* (Dover Fine Art, 1973).
Shirley, E.P., 'Extracts from the Journal of Thomas Dineley, Esquire, Giving Some Account of His Visit to Ireland in the Reign of Charles II (continued)', *Journal of the Kilkenny and South-East of Ireland Archaeological Society*, 4(1) (1863), pp. 170–88.
Shurov, V., *Khomus: Jew's Harp Music of Turkic Peoples in the Urals, Siberia, and Central Asia* (Paradox PAN 2032CD, 1995).
Spufford, P., *Power and Profit: The Merchant in Medieval Europe* (London: Thames & Hudson, 2002).
Steel, David, *The Elements and Practice of Rigging and Seamanship* (London, 1794).
Sterne, L., *The Life and Opinions of Tristram Shandy* (Harmondsworth: Penguin Classics, 1985).
Stevenson, W., –1575; John Bridges, –1618, *A Right Pithy, Pleasant, and Merry Comedy, entitled Gammer Gurton's Needle. Played on Stage not long ago in Christ's College in Cambridge. Made by Mr. S., M.A.* (London, [1575]).
Stockman, E., 'The Diffusion of Musical Instruments as an Internal Process of Communication', *Yearbook of the International Folk Music Council*, 3 (1971), pp. 128–37.
Stubbes, P., *Philip Stubbe's Anatomy of the abuses in England in Shakspere's youth, vol. I* (London: Pub. for the New Shakspere Society, by N. Trübner & co.).
SUBSIDY OF POUNDAGE, And Granting A SUBSIDY OF TUNNAGE. And other Sums of Money, UNTO His Royal Majesty, His Heirs and Successors: The same to be paid upon MERCHANDIZES Imposed and Exported into and out of the Kingdom of Ireland, according to a Book of Rates hereunto annexed (1669).
Sullivan, J. (ed.), *The Papers of Sir William Johnson, vol. III* (Albany, NY: The University of the State of New York, 1921).
Tadagawa, L., 'Asian Excavated Jew's Harps: A Checklist', *Journal of the International Jew's Harp Society*, 4 (2007), pp. 5–11.
Thornton, B., *An Ode on Saint Cæcilia's Day* (London, 1749).
Thoroton, R., *Thoroton's History of Nottinghamshire, vol. 1* (London, 1797).
Troman, D.H., *Scattia Pensieri: A History of the Jews Harp and its Manufacture* (unpublished thesis, Birmingham and Midland Institute, 1953).
Vertkov, K., Blagodatov, G. and Yazovitskaya, E., 'The Jew's Harp in the Soviet Union', *Vierundzwanzigsteljahrsschrift der Internationalen Maultrommelvirtuosengenossenschaft*, 3 (1987), pp. 39–59.
Warner, P., *Lock Keeper's Daughter: A Worcestershire Canal Childhood* (Shepperton: Shepperton Swan Ltd., 1986).
[Wedderburn, R.], J. Leyden, *The Complaynt of Scotland written in 1548, with a preliminary dissertation and glossary* (Edinburgh, 1801).
Wilson, W., *The Pitman's Pay, and Other Poems* (Gateshead: William Douglas, 1843).

Wright, J., 'Another Look into the Organology of the Jew's Harp', *Bulletin du Musée Instrumental de Bruxelles*, II (1972), pp. 51–9.

—— 'Jew's Harp: The Classifier's Nightmare – or How I Became Embroiled in All This', *Journal of the International Jew's Harp Society*, 5 (2008), pp. 14–16.

Wright, L., *Travels wi' a Trump*, unpublished film (SOAS MA course, 2008).

Wright, M. 'Trump Manufacture in the West Midlands – Part One: 1800 to 1900', *Journal of the International Jew's Harp Society*, 3 (2003), pp. 4–14.

—— 'Jew's Trumps and their Valuation, 1545–1763', *Journal of the International Jew's Harp Society*, 2 (2004), pp. 41–6.

—— 'Jue harpes, Jue trumpes, 1481', *Journal of the International Jew's Harp Society*, 2 (2004), pp. 7–10.

—— 'The Mystery of St Kilda and the Jew's Harp', *Journal of the International Jew's Harp Society*, 2 (2004), pp. 53–5.

—— 'The Jew's Harp in the Law, 1590–1825', *Folk Music Journal*, 9(3) (2008), pp. 349–71.

—— 'The Jews Harp Trade in Colonial America', *The Galpin Society Journal*, LXIV (2011), pp. 209–18.

—— and Impey, A., 'The Birmingham–KwaZulu-Natal Connection', *Journal of the International Jew's Harp Society*, 4 (2007), pp. 44–8.

Wright, T. (ed.), *The Turnament of Totenham and the Feest. Two Early Ballads* (London, 1836).

Ypey, J., 'Mondharpen', *Antick*, 11(3) (1976), pp. 209–31.

Archives

Irish Traditional Music Archive, 73 Merrion Square, Dublin 2.
London Metropolitan Archives, St Giles, Cripplegate. Composite register, 1634/5–1646, P69/GIS/A/002/MS06419, Item 003.
The National Archives, Kew, Richmond, Surrey, TW9 4DU.P.R.O., E.122/194/25.
National Archives of Scotland, SC40/7/14, fols 239v–241r.
Pitt Rivers Museum, Parks Road, Oxford, OX1 3PW.
St Giles Church Records.

Websites

The British Newspaper Archive, http://www.britishnewspaperarchive.co.uk/, accessed 15 June 2015.
Broadside Ballads Online from the Bodleian Library, Johnson Ballads 370, http://ballads.bodleian.ox.ac.uk, accessed 15 June 2015.
The Census of Ireland for the Year 1851, part VI, General Report. At http://www.histpop.org/ohpr/servlet/AssociatedPageBrowser?path=Browse&active=yes&mno=409&tocstate=expandnew&display=sections&display=tables

&display=pagetitles&pageseq=1&assoctitle=Census%20of%20Ireland,%20 1851&assocpagelabel=, accessed 10 June 2015.

Charles Wheatstone and the Concertina, at http://www.free-reed.co.uk/galpin/ g2.htm, accessed 15 June 2015.

Cox, N. and Dannehi, K., 'Traded Goods & Commodities 1550–1800', *The Dictionary Project* (University of Wolverhampton), at http://www2.wlv.ac.uk/ tradedictionary/, accessed 15 June 2015.

Dekker, D., *If it be not good, the Diuel is in it. A nevv play, as it hath bin lately acted, vvith great applause, by the Queenes Maiesties Seruants: at the Red Bull. Written by Thomas Dekker* (1612), at http://quod.lib.umich.edu/cgi/t/text/ text-idx?c=eebo;idno=A20066, accessed 15 June 2015.

The Genealogy Bank, Newspaper Archives 1690–2010, All 50 States, http://www. genealogybank.com/gbnk/newspapers/, accessed 15 June 2015.

Make 'Em Laugh! Monologues and Music Hall Lyrics, http://www.monologues. co.uk/, accessed 27 August 2015.

'Parishes: Stoke by Newark', *Thoroton's History of Nottinghamshire, vol. 1: Republished with large additions by John Throsby* (1790), pp. 345–51, at http://www.british-history.ac.uk/report.aspx?compid=76007, accessed 15 June 2015.

Proceedings of the Old Bailey, www.oldbaileyonline.org, version 7.0, accessed 24 September 2013.

Tobar an Dualchais/Kist o Riches, http://www.tobarandualchais.co.uk/, accessed 15 June 2015.

Trove, Digitised Newspapers, https://trove.nla.gov.au/newspaper, accessed 15 June 2015.

Whitehouse, J., *Lewis–Clark Expedition, 1804*, http://www.lewis-clark.org, accessed 15 June 2015.

Newspapers

Aberdeen Journal
Aldershot Military Gazette
Baltimore Patriot
Bath Chronicle and Weekly Gazette
Belfast Morning News
Belfast News-Letter
Berkshire Chronicle
Berwickshire News and General Advertiser
Birmingham Daily Post
Birmingham Evening Mail
Birmingham Gazette
Bismarck Daily Tribune
Boston Evening Post

Boston Gazette
The Braidwood Dispatch and Mining Journal
Burnley Express
Bury and Norwich Post, Suffolk
Cambridge Chronicle and Journal
Cardiff Directory
Charleston Mercury
Cheltenham Looker-On
Coventry Evening Telegraph
Daily Gazette for Middlesborough
Derbyshire Times and Chesterfield Herald
Dudley Herald
Dudley Official Guide, 1968 and 1970
Dundee Courier
Dunfermline Saturday Press
The Era, London
Evening Angus, Angus
Evening Telegraph, Angus
Exeter and Plymouth Gazette
Exeter Flying Post
Falkirk Herald, Stirlingshire
Freeman's Journal
Glasgow Herald
The Graphic, London
Greensboro Daily News
Greensboro Record
Hampshire Telegraph
Hereford Times
Hobart Town Gazette and Van Diemen's Land Advertiser
Hull Daily Mail
Hull Packet
Isle of Wight Observer
Kentish Gazette
Leamington Spa Courier
The Leeds Times
Literature and Language (Charlestown [S.C.], 1774)
Literature and Language, vol. 2 (London, 1764)
Liverpool Echo
Liverpool Mercury
London Evening Post
London Standard
Manchester Courier and Lancashire General Advertiser
Manchester Evening News
The Morning Post, London

Morpeth Herald
New York Gazette
New York Mercury
Newark Directory
Newcastle Journal
North Devon Journal
Northampton Mercury
Nottingham Evening Post
Pennsylvania Packet
Picture Post
Public Advertiser
Riverside Daily Press
San Diego Union
Sheffield Daily Telegraph
Sheffield Independent
Sherborne Mercury, Dorset
Shields Daily Gazette
Staffordshire Advertiser
Stamford Advocate
Stirling Observer
The Sydney Morning Herald
Tamworth Herald
The Times
The Times Literary Supplement, London
Tomahawk Or Censor General
Western Daily Press, Bristol
Western Mail, South Glamorgan
Western Morning News, Devon
Western Times, Devon
Whitstable Times and Herne Bay Herald
Worcestershire Chronicle
Wrexham Advertiser
Yorkshire Evening Post
Yorkshire Gazette

Index

Aberdeen, 72, 164
Aberdeen pattern, 69, 83
accordions, 3
An Accurate New Spelling Dictionary (Fisher), 46
acoustics, 17
Acoustics Lab (Faculté des Sciences de Jussieu, Paris), 18
Addams, Mr, 17
Aeneid (Virgil), 148
agach-kumyz, 5
Alexeyev, Ivan, 28
Alford, Clara Ellen, 140
alien traders, 32, 62–3
Allan's Illustrated Edition of Tyneside Songs, 46
alphabet rhymes, 147–8
American Civil War, 114
'An Ode on Saint Cecilia's Day' (Thornton), 174
Ancient Scottish Melodies (Dauney), 14–15
Andrews, David, 91, 95
Andrews, Joseph, 92
Andrews, Peter, 92
Andrews family, 91–2
animals with names of jews-harp, 47
Annesley, Dr, 128
Anonymiana or, Ten Centuries of Observations on Various Authors and Subjects (Pegge), 13–14
'Another Look at the Organology of the Jew's Harp' (Wright), 19
anti-Semitism, xiv, 37, 42, 138
Antwerp, 62
archaeological finds of jews-harps
   in Asia, 23, 24, **25**, 26
   in Britain
      dating of, 59, 61
      find locations, **58**, **60**
      types of, **59**
   in Eastern Europe, 24, **25**, 26
   in Europe, 26, 30, **31**, 32, 65, **65**
   in Ireland
      dating of, 59
      find locations, **58**, **60**
      types of, **59**, 64
   research on, 19
   in Scotland, 64
   in Sweden, 65
   in USA, 107, **108**, 112
   in Wales, 64
   in Yorkshire, 80
   views on
      of Beskrovny, Aksenty, 24
      of Kolltveit, Gjermund, 19, 23, 24, 30, 33
archives, 179
'Area Three' (Third Ear Band), 179
Arnemuiden, 62
art depicting jews-harps
   coats of arms, 125, **126**
   enamels, 35, 126
   engravings, 126, **127**, 128, 129, **129**
   miniatures, 126
   paintings/drawings etc.
      contemporary, 130, **131**, **132**, **133**, **134**, **135**
      older, 126–30, **127**, **129**
   seals, 124
   stonework, 35, **123**, 124–5, **125**
Ar't Asleepe Husband (Brathwaite), 67
Asia, jews-harps in
   archaeological finds of, 23, 24, **25**, 26
   place in society, 28
Atkinson, George, 124–5
Aubrey–Maturin series, 143–4
Australia, jews-harps in, 57, 114–15
Austria, jews-harps in, 64, 69, 75, 76
Axtell, James, 106

Bacon, Francis, 16, 40–41
Bailey, John, 161
Bailey, Nathan, 13
bambaro, 116
Bamis Mart (Antwerp), 62
'Banish Misfortune', 171, 174, 186, 189
Barnsley, Alfred, 84
Barnsley, Benjamin, 83
Barnsley, Ernest, 84
Barnsley, John, 69, 71, 82, 83
Barnsley, John W., 84
Barnsley, Robert, 84
Barnsley, Rowland Glegg, 84
Barnsley family
    collaboration with Troman family, 88–9
    family background, 82–4
Barnsley works
    employees of, 96
    jews-harps of, **71**, 83, **84**
        export to South Africa, 118
        maker identification on, 102
        prices of, **70**
        types of, 69, **71**, 83
    map showing site of, **82**
Bartholomew Fair (Jonson), 67
Bate Collection of Musical Instruments, 3, 22, 40
Bateman, Edgar, 175
Baxter, C., 171
The Beatles, 179
The Beggar's Opera Burlesqued (Hogarth), 126–7
Belfast, 69, 91–2
Bellamy, Alfred, 96
Bennett, Billy, 175
Bennett, Elizabeth, 89
Bentley, Richard, 106
Bergen-op-Zoom, 62
Berkshire Chronicle, 161
Beskrovny, Aksenty, 24, 26
Billings, William, 41
Billingsgate types, 33
Birmingham, 71, 96, 112, 113, 118, 177
Birmingham Art School, 87
Birmingham Evening Mail, 82
Birmingham Gazette, 73, 96
Bismarck Daily Tribune, 94

biwba, 37
biwbo, 37
Black, Don, 164
blacksmiths, 28, 32, 33, 78, 184
Blair, W., 166
Blake, William, 51, 143
Blues Jaw Harp, 38, 47
Boccorio, 64
Boer War, 177
Boisset, Yves, 171
Boston, 109
Boswell, James, 150
Boy Playing a Jew's Harp (Lely), 126
boys and jews-harps, 161–2
'A Boy's Pockets - What they contain (sometimes)', 161
Brabant Fairs, 62
brass harps, 5, 15, 17, 69, 83, 110
Brathwaite, Richard, 67
Breadin, Sean, 162
The Bride of Lammermoor (Scott), 139
Bridges, Thomas, 148
Bristol, 71, 112
Britain
    jews-harps in
        archaeological finds of
            dating of, 59, 61
            find locations, **58**, **60**
            types of, **59**
        buying of, 75
        manufacturing/makers of, early, 77–80, **79**
        sale of
            by chapmen, 68, 72
            at fairs, 62, 66, 67, 71–2
            by pedlars, 32, 42, 62, 72
        trading/traders in
            distribution by, 66–8
            exports by, 106–10, 112–16, 118
            imports by, 32–3, 57, 62–4, 81
            Industrial Revolution's impact on, 113–14
            locations of, **66**
        types of, 33, **34**, **35**
        transportation in, 71
        see also England; Scotland; Wales
Brookes, John, 96

Brooks, C.W., 177
Bruce Harp, xiii, xiv, 37, 38, 47
Bruck types, 107
Buckley, Anne, 19
Bucolics and Georgics of Virgil, 126
'Buffalo Girls', 156, 171, 185–7
buildings, 48
burlesques, 41, 45–6, 126–7, 148, 174
Burnett, John, 128
Burns, Robert, 137, 139
Busby, Thomas, xiii, 14
'Button Boxes and Moothies' festival, 182
Byron, Lord, 143

Camand, John, 168
Campbell, Calum, 164
Campbell, John, 168, **169**
'The Campbell's are Coming', 171, 185, 188
'Can You Tell – ?' (game), 153
canals, 71
Cantiteau, Denis, **ii**, 130
Carney, Kate, 175
Carpenter, H., 177
Carrol, Richard, 53
Cassidy, John, 171
Castellengo, Michèle, 18
casting, *see* frames of jews-harps
The Census of Ireland, 92
Ceredigion (Wales), 137
Chalmers, George Paul, 128
Chalmers, Norman, 164
Chapel of New College (Oxford), 35, 126, 157
chapmen, 67, 68, 71–2
Chapter House (York Minster), 35, **123**, 124, 157
Charleston, 114
Charlie Brown, 47
Chettle, Henry, 45, 141
churches, 124–5
C.J. Whitney & Co., 113
Clark, Bob, 156–7
Clark, Jonty, 130, **135**
The Clash, 179
Coast/Bruno, 47
coats of arms, 125, **126**
Coborn, Charles, 175

Codde, William, 32–3, 44, 62
Cold Mart (Bergen-op-Zoom), 62
Commercial Revolution, 30
competitions in jews-harp playing, 165–6, **165**, 171
The Complaynt of Scotland, 157
A complete collection of Scottish proverbs explained and made intelligible to the English reader (Kelly), 139
Complete Dictionary of Music (Busby), xiii, 14
Concannon, Mairéad (née Flynn), 75–6
'Concerto in D' (Albrechtsberger), 172
'concession stores', 117
connected jews-harps, 7–8, **8**
Conquer Pudden, 91
Cooper, Ward, 156
Cope, Jonathon, 103, 130, **132**, 181, **181**
A copious Englisg and Nederduytch dictionarie (Hexham), 13
Corbet, E.T., 174
Cork, 92
Cornwall, 140, 144
Cox, William, 96
Cradley, 88, 101, 177
Crane, Frederick, **21**
    importance of, 21–2
    and maker identification, 101–2
    views on jews-harps
        as aerophones, 4
        dating of, 59
        in literature, 140
        naming of, 38–9
crembalum (crembala), 4, 37, **38**, 152
Currey, Fanny W., 146
Curtenius, Peter T., 110
Cybernetic Model, 29

Dalyell, John Graham, 15
dan moi, 5, 76
Dance, George, 175
Dauney, William, 14–15
David, John, 124
December Bride (O'Sullivan), 174
Deerfield, **111**, 112
Defoe, Daniel, 68
Dekker, Thomas, 141
Denizen traders, 62

Devaune, Patrick, 168
Dictionarium Britanicum (Bailey), 13
A Dictionary in Spanish and English
 (Minshoe), 12–13
A Dictionary of the English Language
 (Johnson), 13
didgeridoo, 181
Dineley, Thomas, 168
*A Dissertation on the Musical Instruments
 of the Welsh* (Roderick), 45
Dix, Katherine, 164
Donegal, 92
Doonan, John, 171
Dournon-Taurelle, Geneviève, 18
Doyle, Arthur Conan, 143
Drabble, Phil, 91
drawings/paintings, 126–30, **127**, **129**, **131**,
 132, **133**, **134**, **135**, **139**
drumla, 39
Dublin, 69, 91–2
The Dublin Almanac and General Register,
 91
Dudley, Robert, 1st Earl of Leicester,
 105–6
Dudley Herald, 69, 82–3
Dudley Wood, 82
Duncan, Geillis, 44, 158–9
Dundee Courier, 71
Dunns Bank, 91
Durban, 117
Dutch, *see* the Netherlands, Dutch

East London Observer, 73
Eastern Europe, 24, **25**, 26
Eisenberg, Saul, 179
Ekeberg types, 107
*The Elements and Practice of Rigging and
 Seamanship* (Steel), **48**
Elliott, Jack, 172
Elphinstone Institute (Aberdeen), 182
The Emerald Forest (Boorman), 173
enamels, 35, 126
England
 jews-harps in
  manufacturing/makers of
   Barnsley family, 69, **70**, **71**,
    82–4, **82**, **84**, 88–9, 118
   Boer War's impact on, 177
   Conquer Pudden, 91
   Cope, Jonathan, 103
   early, 77–80, **79**
   equipment of, 101
   identification markers of,
    101–2, **102**
   Industrial Revolution's impact
    on, 69
   Jones family, 84
   Philip-Crawshaw, 83, 91,
    97–101
   quality control by, 101
   Sidaway family, 80–81, **81**
   stump, stool and stake of, **100**
   transportation's impact on, 71
   Troman family, 84, **85**, 86–91,
    86, **87**, **88**, 118
   Watts family, 84, 118
   work process of, 97–101
   workers employed by, 96
   working relations in, 96–7
   workshops of, **87**, **89**
 players of
  amateur, 170–71
  Campbell, John, 168, **169**
  Cooper, Ward, 156
  Cope, Jonathan, 181, **181**
  Duncan, Geillis, 158–9
  Elliott, Jack, 172
  Eulenstein, Karl, 15, 163–4,
   187
  film performances by, 171,
   173–4
  Handle, Johnny, 156–7
  Hope-Evans, Peter, 179
  Kelly, Peter, 160
  McManus, Thomas, **167**, 168
  new generation of, 181
  radio broadcasts of, 174
  recordings of, 171–2, **172**, 179
  Ross, Colin, 172
  shepherds, 40, 157
  Spriggs, Jim, 155–6
  Warren, Mr, 163–4
  Wright, David, 130, 171, 174,
   185, 188–9
  Wright, John, *see* Wright, John
  Wright, Lucy, 171, 185, 188–9

Wright, Michael, 117, 130, **135**, 171, 172, 174, 179, **180**, 185–6, 188–9
Wright family, 171–2, 174
 and popular music, 179
 references to, *see* references to jews-harps
 trading/traders in, *see* trading/traders
 strike of school children in, 162
 trading system of, 68
 see also Britain; Scotland; Wales
English and Welch Dictionary (Roderick), 45
The English Irish National Dictionary, 13, 44
engravings, 126, **127**, 128, 129
Epping, Rick, 168
equipment in jews-harp manufacturing, 101
The Era, 176
Erskine, Andrew, 150
Eulenstein, Karl, 15, 163–4, 187
Europe, jews-harps in
 archaeological finds of, 26, 30, **31**, 32, 65, **65**
 establishment of, 30
 manufacturing of, 32, 64
 popularity of, 32
 types of, 33, **34**
 see also Britain; Ireland
Evans, Platt, 137
Evolution Theory (Darwin), 142
Exeter Cathedral, 124
exports of jews-harps from Britain
 to Australia and New Zealand, 114–15
 to South Africa, 116–18
 to USA, 106–10, 112–14

Fagg, Bernard, 18
Fair o' Dunblane, 72
The Faire Maide of the Inne (Fletcher and Massinger), 141
'The Fairies of Eastern Green', 144
fairs, as point of sale for jews-harps, 62, 66, 67, 71–2, 73
Faraday, James, 17
Fast Castle, 19

Fian, John, 158–9
field recordings, 179
Fields, Gracie, 173
film music, jews-harps in, 171, 173–4
film performances of jews-harp players, 144, 171, 173–4
Finch, Augustus, 161
Finland, 33
'Fireside Questions for the Family' (game), 152
Flanagan Brothers, 178–9
Fleet, Captain, 106
Flemish, *see* the Netherlands, Flemish
Fletcher, J., 141
Folk Lore Congress (1891), 17
folklore, jews-harps in, 144–6, **145**
'Fool on the Hill' (The Beatles), 179
Foote, G.A., 174
Forfar Ploughing Association's diddling competition, **165**, 166
forging, *see* frames of jews-harps
Fort Edwards, 112
Fort Michilimackinac, 107
Fort Pontchartrain, 112
Fothergill, Mr, 170–71
Fothergill, Norah E., 96
'Four Fingers and a Thumb' (Powel), 175
'The Four Hunters and the Four Glastigs', 146
Fox, Leonard, 3, 19
frames of jews-harps
 casting of, 16, 32, 33, 64, **65**, 97–8, 102
 forging of, 28, 33, 64, 103
 plating of, 98, **98**
Frangs, Alec, 117
Freeman's Journal, 94
fur trade, 106–8

Galpin, Francis W., 4
Gammer Gurtons Nedle (anon.), 140–41
Gardner, Paul, 130, **134**
Garnerin, André-Jacques, 49
geographical features named after jews-harps, 48
'George Collins', 179
George IV, King of the United Kingdom, 163

Germany, 32, 35
gewgaw, 37, 38, 46
'The Giant of Towednack', 144, **145**
'The Girl I left Behind Me', 156, 185, 186
Girl with Jews Harp (Jopham), **129**
Gironville types, 64
giwga, 37
giwgan, 37
Glasgow, 94, 112
Glasgow pattern, 69, 83
'Glasynys', 166
'Glenfinlas; or Lord Ronald's Coronach', 146
Gloucester types, 33, 64, 107, **112**
Goelet, Peter, 110
Gould, Dave, 164
The Graphic, London, 162
The Great French Dictionary, 41
Great War, 177–8
Greensboro Record, 23
Greifswald types, 33, 35, **36**, 65, **65**
Groom, William, 161
Grossman of Cleveland, 47, 103, 113–14
Ground of his Own (Lee), 179
guimbardes, 3, 4, 17, 152
Les Guimbardes du Musée de l'Homme (Dournon-Taurelle and Wright), 18
'The Guns of Brixton' (The Clash), 179

Haley, Johnny, 168
Haley, T., sr, 171
Hammond, Blanche, 96
Handle, Johnny, 156–7, 172
Hanse traders, 62–3
Hanseatic League, 30, 62–3, 65
Harmonicas (mouth organ), 47, 87, 177, 179
Harris, Gus, 178
Harvey, Gabriel, 45
'Haste to the Wedding', 171, 185, 187
Hastings, Flo, 176, **176**
Hawthorne, Nathaniel, 143
Hayes, Tommy, 172
Heemskerck, Egbert van, II, 126
Henry Hall Orchestra, 176
heteroglot/inward-orientated jews-harps, 4, **6**, 26

Hewes, Robert, 80
Hexham, Henry, 13
Hey for Honesty, Down with Knavery (Randolph), 141
The High Level Ranters, 172
The Highland Sessions (BBC Scotland), 173
Hodgson, William, 96
Hogarth, William, 126–7
Hohner South Africa, 117
'Hollow Tree (Sherbourne Town)', 185, 188
Holme, Randle, III, 126
Holmes, Sherlock, 143
Hope-Evans, Peter, 179
Hopewell, Thomas, 96
Hornbostel-Sachs classification system, 3, 4, 18
Horniman Museum (London), 22, 53
The House of the Seven Gables (Hawthorne), 143
Howard, Jenny, 176
Howard, Philip, 152
Hull Packet, 163

'I took my harp to a Party' (Gay and Carter), 176
idioglot/outward-orientated string-pull jews-harps, 4, **5**, 26
Iliad (Homer), 148
I'll Be Your Sweetheart (Quest), 175
Ils sont grands ces petits (Santoni), 171
Impey, Angela, 116–18, 119–20
imports of jews-harps
  in Britain, 32–3, 57, 62–4, 81
  in Ireland, 57
  in Scotland, 64
Industrial Revolution, 69, 78, 113–14
Ingley, Ebenezer, 96
inns, 48–9
International Centre for Khomus Music (Yakutsk), 28
Internet, jews-harps and the, 76, 182
'The Inventor's Wife' (Corbet), 174
Ireland, jews-harps in
  archaeological finds of
    dating of, 59, 61
    find locations, **58**, **60**

types of, **59**, 64
buying of, 75–6
in folklore, 146
import of, 64
manufacturing/makers of
    Andrews family, 91–2, 95
    early, **79**
    Industrial Revolution's impact on, 69
    local blacksmiths, 78
    Neade, Patrick, 91
    Sharkey family, 92, **92**, **93**, 94
naming of, **38**, 44
newspaper adverts for, 75
players of, 168–70
sayings and proverbs about, 140
trading/traders in, 57, 75–6
types of, 33, **34**
'The Irish Beauty', 176
Irish pattern, 69, 83
Irish radio, 169
Irish Traditional Music Archive, 168, 179
iron harps, 69, 83
isitolotolo, 119–20
is'tweletwele, 118, 119–20

Jack Elliott of Birtley: The Songs and Stories of a Durham Miner (Folkways Records), 172
Jackson Bros., 117
James IV, King of Scots, 158–9
jaws-harps, 41, 46, 47, 53, 110
Jerusalem: The Emanation of the Giant Albion (Blake), 51
jeugdtromp, 41
jeu-trump, 14, 40–41
Jewishness, 41–2, **43**
'Jew's Garden', 179
Jew's Harp: A Comprehensive Anthology (Fox), 3
'The Jew's Harp among the Peoples of the Soviet Union' (Vertkov, Blagodatov and Yazovitskaya), 24
Jew's Harp Court, 53
Jew's Harp Pattern, 124–5
The Jews Harp (poem), 128
Jew's Harp Tavern and Tea-House
    fields next to, 51
    importance of, 50–51
    locations of, **50**, 51–2
    mentions in trials, 52–3
    reputation of, 49
The Jew's Harp (Wilkie), **127**, 128
'Jew's Harps in Irish Archaeology' (Buckley), 19
Jews-harp in the forge (Cope), **132**
jews-harps
    adverts of, 73–5
    animals named after, 47
    archaeological finds of, *see* archaeological finds of jews-harps
    art, *see* art depicting jews-harps
    on auction, 73
    in Britain, *see* Britain
    buying of, 75–6
    casting of, *see* frames of jews-harps
    classification of, 3–5, 18–19, 33
    connected, 8, **8**
    descriptions of, 13–15
    dispersal of, 26–36, **27**
        along trade routes, 28, 30
        and mass production of, 26, 32, 78
        through social interaction, 29–30
        and trading of, 32–3, 36
    in Europe, *see* Europe
    in folklore, 144–6, **145**
    forging of, *see* frames of jews-harps
    future of, 182
    geographical features named after, 48
    imitations of, 174
    Industrial Revolution's impact on, 69, 78, 113–14
    internet and, 76, 182
    and Jewishness, 41–2, **43**
    keys in, 7–8, 11–12
    lamellas of, *see* lamellas/tongues of jews-harps
    makers of, *see* manufacturing/makers of jews-harps
    mass production of, 26, 32, 78
    materials used for, 5
    museum collections of, 22
    names for, *see* names for jews-harp
    objects named after, 47–8, **47**, **48**
    origins of, *see* origins of jews-harps
    players, *see* players of jews-harps

playing of, *see* playing of jews-harps
popularity, *see* popularity
prices of, 63, 67–8, **70**, 74, 75, 83, 107, **111**, 113–14, 115
quality/quality control of, 7, 77, 90, 101, 108–9
references to, *see* references to jews-harps
representing Jewishness, **43**
sales of, 62, 66, 67, 68, 71–2, 73, 74–5, 76
in shamanistic practices, 28
taverns and inns named after, 48–9, **50**, 50–52
thefts of, 73
trading/traders, *see* trading/traders
types of, *see* types of jews-harps
use of
    in art, *see* art depicting jews-harps
    in burlesques, 41, 45–6, 126–7, 148, 174
    in crossword puzzles and games, 151–3
    in experiments and lectures, 16–17
    in film music, 144, 171, 173–4
    in folklore, 144–6, **145**
    in literature, 142–4, 166–7
    in music hall songs and monologues, 174–6
    in plays, 140–42
    in popular music, 179
    as prizes, 72–3
    in rhymes and poems, 147–8, 150–51
    in sayings and proverbs, 139–40
    in St Kilda, 14–15
    in stage acts, 174–6
    in stories, 137–9
views on, 3–6, 16, 19
see also under specific countries
jews-trumps, 12–14, 37, **38**, 44, 45
Johannesburg, 117
John Barnsley and Sons, 82, 84
John Wright Unaccompanied (Topic Records), 171
Johnson, Mr, 171
Johnson, Samuel, 13
Johnson, William, 107

Johnson Smith and Company, 47
'Join Together with the Band' (The Who), 179
Jones, Edwin, 96
Jones, Owen Wynne, 166
Jones, Philemon, 113
Jones family, 84
Jonson, Ben, 45, 67, 141
Jopham, F.W., 128, **129**
Journal of the International Jew's Harp Society, 19, 21
Joyce, James, 143
Judah, Moses, 110
Juice harp, 38, 41
J.W. Jenkins Sons, 114

Kalamazoo Gazette, 113
Kansas City, 114
'Kathleen O'More', 163, 185, 187
'The Keel Row', 156, 185, 186
Kelly, James A., 139
Kelly, Peter, 160
Kelly's Directory, 125
Kemp, Willie, 164, 179
Kennedy, Peter, 179
Keyes, Sidney, 151
khomus, 28–9
Kidd, W., 166
Kind-Hart's Dreame (Chettle), 141
Kingsley, Charles, 142
Knox, J., 171
Kolltveit, Gjermund, **20**
    research on archaeological finds of jews-harps, 57, **58**
    views on jews-harps
        casting, 32
        chronology cast types, 65, **65**
        classification, 19, 33, **34**
        origin, 23
        spread, 24, 30
Kooper, Erik, 40
Kransen types, 64
kubing, 5
Kuusito types, 33, **35**
KwaZulu-Natal, 116–17

La Rue, Hélène, 6, 124
Lamb, Andrew, 3, 4–5, 183

lamellas/tongues of jews-harps
  alignment of, 7, **7**
  attachment of, to frame of, 4, 5, 77, 100–101
  breaking of, 77
  descriptions of, 13, 15, 17
  making of, 98–9, **99**
  materials used for, 77
  munnharpe, **8**
  triggering of, 5, 9, **9**, **10**
The Lark in the Clear Air (Topic Records), 171, **172**, 174
Late Junction (BBC Radio), 174
A Late Voyage to St. Kilda, the Remotest of All the Hebrides or Western Isles of Scotland &c (Martin), 14
Lawrie, Angus, 164, 173, 179, 188
Lawson, Graham, 19
Le Brunn, George, 175
Lee, Sam, 179
The Leeds Times, 153
Legand, Ola Kai, 4
Legg, Viv, 140
Leipp, Emile, 18
Lely, Peter, 126
Lennon, John, 179
Leo, Tadagawa, 24
LeVaillant, François, 116
Levenson-Gower, Hector Rayner Sutherland, 72
Lewis, Alun, 151
Lewis and Clark expedition, 109
The Life and Opinions of Tristram Shandy, Gentleman (Sterne), 142
'The Lights of London or Shamms O'Brian, Oy! Oy!' (Bennett), 175
Limerick, 92
Lindsay Porteous (Porteous, Nora), **131**
Liverpool, 112
Liverpool Echo, 177
Liverpool Mercury, 71, 73
'Liza Johnson or The Rag-Time Coster' (Bateman), 175
Locklynne, Sydney, 174
Lockwood, Margaret, 175
Logane, Johana, 78
London, 48, 49, 62, 67, 80, 112–13
London Standard, 146, 162

Louisburg, 107
Low Countries, *see* the Netherlands
Lowe, Benjamin, 83
Lowe, Thomas, 83
Lumphead, Frederick Jimmy, 46
Lyly, John, 45

MacDonald, Allan, 164, 173, **173**
MacDonald, Emily, 164
MacDonald, Kenny Dan, 164
MacGill, Patrick, 151
Mackay, Callum, 75, 164–5
Mackay, 'Curly', 164
MacLeod, Peter, 164
Maclise, Daniel, 129
MacPherson, Ewan, 164
Mainistir, 78
makers of jews-harps, *see* manufacturing/makers of jews-harps
Manchester Evening News, 161
Mandrin (television serial), 171–2
manufacturing/makers of jews-harps
  in Austria, 64, 69, 75, 76
  blacksmiths, 28, 32, 33, 78, 184
  in Britain, early, 78–9, **79**
  end of, 102–3
  in England
    Barnsley family, 69, **70**, **71**, 82–4, **82**, **84**, 88–9, 118
    Boer War's impact on, 177
    Conquer Pudden, 91
    Cope, Jonathan, 103
    early, 77–80, **79**
    equipment of, 101
    identification markers of, 101–2, **102**
    Industrial Revolution's impact on, 69
    Jones family, 84
    Philip-Crawshaw, 83, 91, 97–101
    quality control by, 101
    Sidaway family, 80–81, **81**
    stump, stool and stake of, **100**
    transportation's impact on, 71
    Troman family, 84, **85**, 86–91, **86**, **87**, **88**, 118
    Watts family, 84, 118
    work process of, 97–101

workers employed by, 96
working relations in, 96–7
workshops of, **87**, **89**
in Europe, 26, 32–3, 64–5
frames, *see* frames of jews-harps
Industrial Revolution's impact on, 69, 78, 113–14
interview with unnamed maker, 94–5
in Ireland
    Andrews family, 91–2, 95
    early, **79**
    Industrial Revolution's impact on, 69
    local blacksmiths, 78
    Neade, Patrick, 91
    Sharkey family, 92, **92**, **93**, 94
lamellas/tongues, *see* lamellas/tongues of jews-harps
in Scotland, 78, 94
in United States
    Andrews, David, 95
    interview with unknown maker, 94–5
    Pascall, Thomas P., 95, 113
    Smith family, 95–6, **95**, 113
Maoris, 115
Marburg, 65
Marianne Hill Monastery Archives, 116
Martin, Martin, 14
Mashantucket Pequot Museum and Research Center, 107
mass production, 26, 32, 78
Massinger, P., 141
Master and Commander: The Far Side of the World (Weir), 144, 173
McBride, Kevin, 107
McDonald, Allan, 164, 173, **173**
McIlmichall, Donald, 159
McKenzie, Allan, 164
McKenzie, Gordon, 164
McKenzie, Willie, 164
McManus, Thomas, **167**, 168
Medicine Head, 179
Mehmet, Dogan, **180**
Mercer, Robert, 130
Micrologia: Characters or Essayes, of Persons, Trades, and Places Offered to the City and Country (R.M.), 142

Middleton, Arthur, 164
Miège, Guy, 13
migration, 29–30
Miller, W., 166
miniatures, 126
Minsheu, John, 12–13
minsters, 35, **123**, 124, 125, **125**, 157
'Miss McLeod's Reel', 165, 179
Moffat, Duncan, 108–9
Molln, 64, 117
Molly and Me (Seiler), 173
The Monastery (Scott), 139
monologues, *see* songs, tunes and monologues
Montagu, Jeremy, 40, 124
Montreal, 108
Moore, Mary A., 96
Moore, Patrick, 151
morchanga, 5
The Morning Post, 163–4
Morpeth Herald, 71
Mount, C.B., 42
mouth cavity, in playing of jews-harps, 5, 9, **9**, 10
mouth-harps, 47, 53
Mr. S. Mr. of Art, 140–41
mukkuri, 5
munngiga, 46
munnharpe, **8**, 53
Murray, James A.H., 15
music hall songs and monologues, 174–6
Musical Association, 17
musical instruments, jews-harps accompanying, 7
Musical Instruments Trades Protection Association, 97
Musical Memoirs of Scotland (Dalyell), 15
'My love is but a Lassie yet', 171, 185, 187

'Na Trumpal', 169–70
names for jews-harp
    before eighteenth century, 44–5
    analysis of common, **39**
    chronology of development, **38**
    commercial, 46–7
    in dictionaries, 13–16, 44–5
    in early literature, 45
    etymological theories, 38–41

jewish connection, 41–3
in mid-eighteenth century, 45–6
overview of, 37–8
today, 53
views on, xiv–xv, 13–14, 40–42
see also under specific names
Napier, Barbara, 159
Native Americans, 106–9
Neade, Patrick, 91
the Netherlands (Low Countries), 32, 41, 46, 62
  Dutch, 14, 40, 41, 107
  Flemish, 41, 66
Netherton, 69, 71, 82, 83, **83**
Nettleton, 125
A New DICTIONARY French and English With Another English and French (Miège), 13
New Ducie Harp, xiv, 37, 38, 47
New England, 109–12, **111**
A New English Dictionary on Historic Principles (Murray), 15
The New Grove Dictionary of Musical Instruments, 16
new Scotch pattern, 69, 83
New York, 95, 109, 113
New York Gazette, 46
New York Mail and Express, 94
New York Mercury, 46
New Zealand, jews-harps in, 114–15
New Zealand Company, 114–15
Newes from Scotland, 44, 159
newspapers
  adverts of jews-harps, 73–5
  references to jews-harp competitions, 165–6, **165**, 171
Ngomonde, Mampolwane, **118**
Nguni people, 116, 117, 119–20
Nigeria, jews-harps in, 116
Nijmegen types, 65, **65**
North Berwick Kirk, 158–9, **158**
North Devon Journal, 140
Northampton (UK), 124
Northampton Mercury, 89
Northern Anaconda Plan, 114
Northumberland, 156–7
Northumberland Forever, 172
Norway, jews-harps in, 53, 144

Notes and Queries (Rimbault), 40–41
'Now the Tyrant has Stole my Dearest away', 158
Nuremberg, 65

Ó Conghaile, Mícheál Tom Burke, 78
Ó Fátharta, Máirtín Sheamais, 168, 169
O'Brian, Patrick, 143–4
'An Ode on Saint Cecilia's Day' (Thornton), 41–2, 174
'ODE upon a JEW's HARP' (Erskine), 150
Odiham types, 33, 64, 65, **65**
'Off she goes', 171, 185, 187
Omiya (Japan), 26
'On his Jew's harp – Coster Characters', 176
Onslow, Arthur, 50
origins of jews-harps
  and archaeological finds, 24, **25**, 26
  overview, 23–4
  views on
    of Kolltveit, Gjermund, 23
    in newspapers, 23
O'Rourke, Teddy, 171
The Overseas Trade of London: Exchequer Customs Accounts 1480–1, 33, 62
The Oxford Companion to Musical Instruments, 15–16
Oxford Dictionary of English Etymology, 40
Oxford English Dictionary, 42

'Paddy on the Railways', 156
paintings/drawings/artwork, jews-harps in, 126–30, **127**, **129**, **131**, **132**, **133**, **134**, **135**, **139**
Paris (France), 137
Parliamentary Oaths Bill, 42
Parson, Harold, 101
Pascall, Thomas P., 95, 113
Pask or Easter Mart (Bergen-op-Zoom), 62
'Patsey Cohen's Jews-harp band' (Stafford, Edgar and Harris), 178
pedlar supplies, 62
pedlars/travelling salesmen, 32, 42, 62, 72
'The Pedler opening of his Packe, To know of Maydes what tis the lack – The second part', 68–9
Peel, John, 179

Pegge, Samuel, 13–14, 40
Pembrokeshire tradition, 166
Pennant, Thomas, 41
Pennsylvania Packet, 108
The Performer (Porteous, Nigel), **147**
Perm Krai, 26
Perry, Samuel, 96
Petty Customs books, 33, **38**, 44, 63, 64, 81
Philadelphia, 109–10
Philip, Sid, 91, 97, 100, 101, **99**
Philip-Crawshaw, 83, 91, 102, 114
Picture Post, 151
Piper Haugh, 78
Pitlessie Fair (Wilkie), 128
The Pitman's Pay, and Other Poems (Wilson), 46
Pitt Rivers Museum (Oxford), 17–18, 22
players of jews-harps
    in Asia, 181
    earliest, 157–8
    in England
        amateur, 170–71
        Campbell, John, 168, **169**
        Cooper, Ward, 156
        Cope, Jonathan, 181, **181**
        Duncan, Geillis, 158–9
        Elliott, Jack, 172
        Eulenstein, Karl, 15, 163–4, 187
        film performances by, 171, 173–4
        Handle, Johnny, 156–7
        Hope-Evans, Peter, 179
        Kelly, Peter, 160
        McManus, Thomas, **167**, 168
        new generation of, 181
        radio broadcasts of, 174
        recordings of, 171–2, **172**, 179
        Ross, Colin, 172
        shepherds, 40, 157
        Spriggs, Jim, 155–6
        Warren, Mr, 163–4
        Wright, David, 130, 171, 174, 185, 188–9
        Walker, Jim, 173
        Wright, John, *see* Wright, John
        Wright, Lucy, 171, 185, 188–9
        Wright, Michael, 117, 130, **135**, 171, 172, 174, 179, **180**, 185–6, 188–9
    Wright family, 171–2, 174
    in Ireland, 168–70
    in Scotland
        early, 157
        Lawrie, Angus, 164, 173, 179, 188
        MacDonald, Allan, 169, 173, **173**
        Mackay, Callum, 164–5
        McIlmichall, Donald, 159
        overview, 164
        television broadcasts of, 173
    in USA
        Flanagan Brothers, 178–9
    see also playing of jews-harps
playing of jews-harps
    basics of, 9, **9**, **10**
    in competitions, 165–6, **165**, 171
    life-long learning to, 12
    mouth cavity as soundbox in, 6, 9, **9**, 10
    player's voice in, 6
    reminiscences about, 155–7, 162, 168, 170, 179, 181
    in Scotland
        competitions, 165–6, **165**
    sound control in, 10–11
    sound production in, 7
    techniques used in, 12, 181
    teeth in, 5, 9, **10**
    tongue in, 10, 168
    views of Campbell, John, 168
    in Wales, 166–7
    workshops in, 182
    see also players of jews-harps
Plough Sunday, 155–6, **155**
poetry, jews-harps in, 147–8, 150–51
'Poets in the Storm' (Keyes, Douglas and Lewis), 151
popular music, 179
popularity
    of harmonicas with soldiers, 177
    of jews-harps
        with boys, 161–2
        in Europe, 32
        with soldiers, 177–8
        in South Africa, 116
        in USA, 105, 107, 114
The Porcupine, Alias the Hedge Hog (Billings), 41

Port Elizabeth, 117
Portable Antiquities Scheme, 57, **58**
Porteous, Lindsay, 130, **131**, 164, 166
Porteous, Nigel, 130, **139**, **147**, **149**
Porteous, Nora, 130, **131**
Portsmouth (USA), 109
Powel, Eldred, 175
Power, Brendan, 164
prices of jews-harps
    of Barnsley works, **70**, 83
    in *Rates of Merchandizes* books, 63
    in traders records, 67–8
'Prince Ritto; or, the Four-Leaved Shamrock' (Currey), 146
Proceedings of the Old Bailey, 52–3, 158–61
proverbs about jews-harps, 139–40
Punch (magazine), 42, **43**
Purser, John, 178

quality/quality control of jews-harps, 7, 77, 90, 101, 108–9
'The Queen who could not bake gingerbread nuts and the King who could not play the Jew's harp', 144

racehorses with names of jews-harp, 47
radio broadcasts of jews-harp players, 173–4
'Raidió na Gaeltachta', 169
Raidió Teilifís éireann, 169
Railway and Canal Traffic Act (1988), 71
railways, 71
Raleigh, Walter, 44, 105
Randolph, Thomas, 141
Rates of Merchandizes, 33, **38**, 44, 63, 64, 81
recordings
    Campbell, John, 168
    Devaune, Patrick, 168
    Elliot, Jack, 172
    Flanagan Brothers, 178–9
    Henry Hall Orchestra, 176
    Kemp, Willie, 179
    music hall songs, 176
    Ross, Colin, 172
    Smith, Albert, 179
    Sweeney, 168

Wright Family, 171–2, **172**, 174, 185, 188–9
Wright, John, 171, **172**, 185, 188–9
Redgauntlet (Scott), 139
references to jews-harps
    abundance of, 183
    in analytical works, 16–19
    in burlesques, 41, 45–6, 126–7, 148, 174
    competions, in newspapers, 165–6, **165**, 171
    in crossword puzzles and games, 151–3
    in dictionaries, 13–16, 44–5
    early, 12–13
    in folklore, 144–6, **145**
    in literature, 51, 67, 139, 142–4, 166–7
    in music hall songs, 174–6
    players
        in newspapers, 166, 170–71
        from Scotland, 157
        in songs, 158, 175
        in trials, 158–61
    in plays, 140–42
    in rhymes and poetry, 147–8, 150–51
    in sayings and proverbs, 139–40
    from Scotland, 68
    in songs, 68–9, 158, 175, 176
    in traders records, 67–8, **111**
    in trials, 52–3, 158–61
Remsen, Peter, 110
resonance, 16–17
The Return of Sherlock Holmes (Doyle), 143
rhymes, jews-harps in, 147–8, 150–51
Rimbault, Dr, 40–41
Ritichie, Leith, 129–30
Rob Roy (Scott), 139
Robins, Phyllis, 176
Rochester types, 33, 61, **61**, 107
Roderick, John, 45
Ross, Colin, 172
Rothchild, Lionel, 42
Rowley, J.W., 175
Rowley Regis, 81, 83, 86, 89, 91, 98
Royal Institution, 17
Roycroft, T., 42
The Rural Economy of Yorkshire (Marshall), 46

Sackbut, Fustian, 41–2, 174
Sakha-Yakutia Russian Republic,
    jews-harps in, 28, 181
sale of jews-harps
    by chapmen, 67, 68, 71–2
    on fairs, 62, 66, 67, 71–2, 73
    internet's impact on, 76
    in late twentieth century, 76
    by pedlars, 32, 42, 62, 72
Sampson, Agnes, 44, 158–9
San Diego Union, 177
Sangerman. Mr, 174
Santoni, J., 171
Savannah, 109
Sayce, Lynda, 172
sayings about jews-harps, 139–40
school children, strike of, 162
Schumpeter, Joseph, 32
Schwartz company, 117
Scopham family, 125, **126**
Scotland
    jews-harps in
        archaeological finds of, 59, 64
        buying of, 75
        dating of, 59
        in folklore, 146
        import of, 64
        manufacturing/makers of, 78, 94
        naming of, 37, 44, 165
        newspaper adverts for, 74
        players of
            early, 157
            Lawrie, Angus, 164, 173, 179, 188
            MacDonald, Allan, 164, 173, **173**
            Mackay, Callum, 164–5
            McIlmichall, Donald, 159
            overview, 164
            radio broadcasts of, 173
            television broadcasts of, 173
            playing of, in competitions, 165–6, **165**
        sayings and proverbs about, 139
        traders/trading in, 68
        strike of school children in, 162
Scots Trump Player (Porteous, Nigel), **149**

Scott, Walter, 139
seals, 124
Second Conference of the ICTM Study Group on Music Archaeology, 19
Self-portrait with harps (Gardner), **134**
Seneca Indian, 107
shackles, 47, **48**
shamanistic practices, jews-harps in, 28
Shane, S., 32
Sharkey, James (soldier), 94
Sharkey, James (the elder), 94
Sharkey, James (the younger), **93**, 94
Sharkey, Patrick, 92
Sharkey family, 92–4, **92**, **93**
Shaw, George, 96
Shaw, George Bernard, 143
Sheffield, 79–80
Sheffield Independent, 73, 80
Shémais, Meaití Jó, 169
'The Shepherds Delight / Both by Day and by Night', 158
Short, Thomas, 90
Shurov, Vyacheslov, 28
Sidaway, I./Sidaway 'Stafford' type, 80, **81**, 107, 112
Sidaway, James, 81, **83**
Sidaway, John, 81
Sidaway family, 80
Siddaway, Ann, 80
Siddaway, William, 81
Silk Road, 28
Sinxten or Whitsun Mart (Antwerp), 62
Smart, George, 166
Smart, J., 166
Smith, Albert, 179
Smith, George, 83
Smith, Ivor, 156–7
Smith, John (Jr), 96
Smith, John R. (Sr), 95, 113
Smith, William, 96
Snoopy's Harp, xiv, 37, 38, 47
social interaction, jews-harps' spread through, 29–30
Society of Arts, 17
Soldiers Songs (Moore), 151
Solomon, Goodman, 161
Some of the Principal Inhabitants of ye Moon (Hogarth), 127

songs, tunes and monologues
    'Area Three', 179
    'Banish Misfortune', 171, 174, 186, 189
    'Buffalo Girls', 156, 171, 185–7
    'The Campbells Are Coming', 171, 185, 188
    'Concerto in D' (Albrechtsberger), 172
    'Fool on the Hill', 179
    'Four Fingers and a Thumb', 175
    'George Collins', 179
    'The Girl I left Behind Me', 156, 185, 186
    'The Guns of Brixton', 179
    'Haste to the Wedding', 171, 185, 187
    'Hollow Tree', 185, 188
    'I took my Harp to a Party' (Gay and Carter), 176
    'The Inventor's Wife', 174
    'The Irish Beauty', 176
    'Jew's Garden', 179
    'Join Together with the Band', 179
    'Kathleen O'More', 163, 185, 187
    'The Keel Row', 156, 185, 186
    'The Lights of London or Shamms O'Brian, Oy! Oy!', 175
    'Liza Johnson or The Rag-Time Coster', 175
    'Miss McLeod's Reel', 165, 179
    'My love is but a Lassie yet', 171, 185, 187
    'Na Trumpal', 169–70
    'Now the Tyrant has Stole my Dearest away', 158, 172
    'Off she goes', 171, 185, 187
    'On his Jew's harp – Coster Characters', 176
    'Paddy on the Railways', 156
    'Patsey Cohen's Jews-harp band', 178
    'The Pedler opening of his Packe, To know of Maydes what tis the lack – The second part', 68–9
    'The Shepherds Delight / Both by Day and by Night', 158
    'Spank the Grand Piano, Matilda', 175
    'Suo Gan', 185
    'Wild Wood Amber', 179
    'Yankee Doodle', 108
Sonny Terry, 179
sonograms of jews-harps from the playing of Wright, 18
South Africa
    Jewish immigrants from Lithuania in, 117
    jews-harps in
        as part of local musical culture, 115–18, 119–20
        trading/traders in, 117, 118–19
South America, jews-harps in, 105
'Spank the Grand Piano, Matilda' (Dance), 175
St. Kilda, use of jews-harps in, 14–15
St Sepulchre Church, 124
Stafford types, 33, 36, 59, 61, **61**, 64, 65, **65**, 78, 80, 81, **81**, 107, 112, **112**
Stamford Advocate, 95
Stanton, Walter, 174
staples, 47, **47**
Stark, A., 166
Sterne, Laurence, 142
Stevenson, William, 45
Stevenston, 78
Stockmann, Erich, 29
Stokes, George, 96
stonework, 35, **123**, 124–5, **125**
stony batter Jews harps, 109
Stoppard, Tom, 143
stories about jews-harps, 137–9
Stow Minster, 125, **125**
Stratton, John F., 113
streets, 48
Summers, Keith, 179
'Suo Gan', 185
Suttie, Charles, 166
Sutton, Mr, 171
Sweden, jews-harps in, 33, 35, 46, 65
Sweeney (no pre-name), 168
Sweetland, Josh, 96
Switzerland, 32, 124
Sydney, 115
Sylva Sylvarum: or A Natural History, in Ten Centuries (Bacon), 16, 40–41
Syrian styles, 113

Tamworth Herald, 162
taverns, 48–9, **50**, 51–2

Taylor, Joshua, 80
Taylor family, 80
teeth and playing of jews-harps, 5, 9, **10**
television performances of jews-harp players, 171–2, 173
A Textbook of European Musical Instruments: Their Origin, History and Character (Galpin), 4
Thaurin, J.M., 30
Thelwall, John, 51
theremins, 3
Thornton, Bonnell, 41–2, 45–6, 174
thumb piano, 3
Thuringia, 65
The Times, 152
'Times Two' (crossword), 152
tin'd harps, 69, 83
Tipperary, 92
Tobar an Dualchais project, 164, 179
Today with Des and Mel (television chat show), 174
Toms, William Henry, 126
tongue, human, in playing of jews-harps, 10, 168
tongues, *see* lamellas/tongues of jews-harps
Torriano, Giovanni, 13
A Tour in Scotland (Pennant), 41
Townshend, Pete, 179
trade routes, jews-harps' spread along, 28, 30
trading/traders
   of furs, 106–7
   of jews-harps
      as barter goods, 105–8, 114–15, 116
      in Britain
         distribution by, 66–8
         exports by, 106–10, 112–16, 118
         imports by, 32–3, 57, 62–4, 81
         Industrial Revolution's impact on, 113–14
         locations of, **66**
      in England, 36, 72, 115
      in Europe, 32
      in USA, 106–10, **110**, **111**, 112
travelling salesmen/pedlars, 32, 42, 62, 72

A Treatise on Carriages (Felton), 47, **47**
trials
   mentioning of jews-harp players in, 158–61
   mentioning of jews-harps in, 52–3
Tripes, Master, 170, 171
Troman, Benjamin, 88–9
Troman, Charles, 86
Troman, Charlotte, 96
Troman, David, 87, 89, 90, 103
Troman, Derek, **86**
   thesis of, 87, 90, 97–9, 100–101, **100**, 103
Troman, John, 83, 86, 89
Troman, Joseph, 83, 86, 89
Troman, Millicent, 90
Troman, Nealy, 89, 96
Troman, Samuel, 80, 86
Troman, William, 96
Troman family, 84–91
   background, 87–8
   business card of, **119**
   collaboration with Barnsley family, 88–9
   family tree of, **85**
   generations of, 86
   resilience of, 84
Troman works, **87**, **89**
   employees of, 96
   jews-harps of, 69, **88**, 113, 116
   export to South Africa, 118
   maker identification on, 102, **102**
Tromans, Benjamin, 96
trombes, 105
trompadh, 37, 38, 44
trompe, 39
troub, 37, 165
Troy, 95, 113
Trumpel, 39
trumps, 12–13, 14–15, 37, 38–40, **39**, 45, 53, 80
tunes, *see* songs, tunes and monologues
Turnament of Totenham, 39
Tyddall, Professor, 17
types of jews-harps
   in Britain, 33, **34**, **35**, **59**
   cast, 33, 35, 65, **65**
   European, 33, **34**
   examples of, **29**

forged, 33
see also under specific types

Ulysses (Joyce), 143
United Kingdom, *see* Britain
United States
    Civil War in, 114
    fur trade, 106–7
    jews-harps in
        archaeological finds of, 107, **108**, **112**
        manufacturing/makers of
            Andrews, David, 95
            interview with unknown maker, 94–5
            Pascall, Thomas P., 95, 113
            Smith family, 95–6, **95**, 113
        popularity of, 105, 114
        trading/traders in
            as barter goods, 105–8
            Grossman of Cleveland, 47, 103, 113–14
            imports from Britain, 106–10, 112–14
            ports of origin of, 112–13
            trader locations, 109–10, **110**, 112
Universal Etymological English Dictionary (Bailey), 13

Vaughan Williams Memorial Library, 164, 179
Vibert, Lambert, 68
Vierundzwanzigsteljahrschrift der Internationalen Maultrommelvirtuosengenossenschaft (*VIM*, journal), 21
Vietnam, jews-harps in, 76
Vocabbulario Italiano & Inglese, A Dictionary Italian & English (Torriano), 13
voice, jews-harps accompanying, 7
The Voice of the People Volume 7 – First I'm Going to Tell You a Ditty, 179
The Voice of the People Volume 14 – Troubles They Are But Few, 179

Wadham (fireman), 171
Wakeman, John, 83

Wales, jews-harps in, 37, 45, 64, 75, 166–7
Walker, Jim, 173
Walpole, Horace, 106
Ware, Mark, 130, **133**
Warner, Pat, 170
Warren, Mr, 163–4
The Water Babies (Kingsley), 142
Watt, John, 166
Watts family, 84, 118
West Midlands, *see* England
Western Daily Press, 90, 115–16, 177
Western Morning News, 152
Westminster Fairs, 66
Westwood, J., 91
Wheatstone, Charles, 16–17
Whimzies; or, A New Cast of Characters (Brathwaite), 67
The Who, 179
The Wicker Man (Hardy), 173
'Wild Wood Amber', 179
Wilkie, David, **127**, 128
William IV, King of the United Kingdom, 163–4
William of Wykeham, 35, 126, 157
Williams, Elijah, **111**
Williamson, Duncan, 164
Wilmer, Mr, 174
Wilson, E., 171
Wootton, Elizabeth, 96
'Word-Watching' (*The Times*), 152
workshops
    about jews-harp playing, 182
    of jews-harp maker, **87**, **89**
World War I, 151, 177–8
World's largest mouth-harp (Porteous, Nigel), **139**
Wright, David, 130, 171, 174, 185, 188–9
Wright, John, **18**
    on buying jews-harps, 75
    drawings of, **ii**, 130
    playing of
        recordings of, 171, **172**, 185, 188–9
        sonograms of, 18
        techniques used in, **11**
    publications of
        'Another Look at the Organology of the Jew's Harp', 19

Les Guimbardes du Musée de l'Homme, 18
in *The News Grove Dictionary of Musical Instruments*, 16
views on
classification of jews-harps, 4, 18–19
decline in quality of jews-harps, 90
Sid Philip's work process, 97–8, 100
Wright, Lucy, 171, 185, 188–9
Wright, Michael, 117, 130, **135**, 171, 172, 174, 179, **180**, 185–6, 188–9
Wright family, recordings of, 171–2, 174, 185–6, **186**, 188–9

Xiajiadian, 24
Xiongnu, 24

'Yankee Doodle', 109
Yankton Sioux, 109
York Minster Chapter House, 35, **123**, 124, 157
Yorkshire, 46, 80, 155–6
ysturmant, 37, 38, 45

Zulu people, 116, 117
Zululand Times, 117